International Society

THE ETHIKON SERIES IN COMPARATIVE ETHICS

The Ethikon Series publishes comparative studies on ethical issues of current importance. By bringing scholars representing a diversity of moral viewpoints into structured dialogue with one another, the series aims to broaden the scope of ethical debate.

THE ETHIKON INSTITUTE

The Ethikon Institute is concerned with the social and political implications of ethical pluralism. Its programs in intersocietal relations, civil society, bio-environmental ethics, and family life are designed to explore a diversity of moral outlooks, secular and religious, and to identify commonalities and differences between them. By encouraging a systematic exchange of ideas, the Institute aims to advance the prospects for agreement and to facilitate the accommodation of irreducible differences. The Ethikon Institute takes no position on the issues that divide its participants. It serves not as an arbiter but as a forum for the cooperative exploration of diverse and sometimes opposing views.

TITLES IN THE SERIES

Terry Nardin, ed., *The Ethics of War and Peace:*
Religious and Secular Perspectives

David R. Mapel and Terry Nardin, eds.,
International Society: Diverse Ethical Perspectives

International Society

DIVERSE ETHICAL PERSPECTIVES

EDITED BY
DAVID R. MAPEL AND TERRY NARDIN

PRINCETON UNIVERSITY PRESS

PRINCETON, NEW JERSEY

Second printing, and first paperback printing, 1999
Paperback ISBN 0-691-04972-6

The Library of Congress has cataloged the cloth edition of this book as follows

International society : diverse ethical perspectives / edited by David R. Mapel and Terry Nardin
p. cm. — (The Ethikon series in comparative ethics)
Includes index.
ISBN 0-691-05771-0 (alk.paper)
1. International relations—Moral and ethical aspects. I. Mapel, David, 1952– .
II. Nardin, Terry, 1942– . III. Series.
JZ1306.I58 1998   97-19756   172'.4—dc21

This book has been composed in Janson

The paper used in this publication meets the minimum requirements of
ANSI/NISO Z39.48-1992 (R1997) (*Permanence of Paper*)

http://pup.princeton.edu

Printed in the United States of America

10 9 8 7 6 5 4 3 2

CONTENTS

PREFACE

THIS BOOK is the outcome of an Ethikon Institute project undertaken in cooperation with the Center for International Studies at the University of Wisconsin-Milwaukee, with support from The Pew Charitable Trusts. Like other Ethikon Institute projects, ours brings knowledgeable representatives of different ethical perspectives into a structured dialogue with one another. A dialogue, as Ethikon understands it, is an exchange of information in which each participant listens to others articulate their understanding of a given topic. It is a conversational inquiry aimed at the discovery of common ground, not its creation through persuasion.

To generate the information needed for understanding and comparison, we have focused on five historically important philosophical interpretations of the ethical character of international society: legal positivism, natural law, Kantian ethics, contractarianism, and cosmopolitanism. There are two chapters on each philosophical perspective, the first a presentation of how the perspective understands the idea of international society, the second a response to that presentation by a scholar who also knows the perspective well and whose aim is to provide an alternative interpretation of controverted issues. This pairing of chapters is designed to highlight differences within as well as between the perspectives.

Religious communities are important in creating and transmitting ethical ideas, and religious voices continue to influence the discussion of public affairs. The book therefore includes chapters in which experts on the moral theology of Judaism, Christianity, and Islam comment on the themes addressed in the philosophical chapters. All the perspectives are then reviewed in a final chapter designed to identify significant commonalities and differences in how they understand the moral aspects of world order.

The editors join with the Ethikon board in thanking all who contributed to this project, which could not have been completed without the cooperation of many persons in addition to the authors represented here. Among them are the other dialogue participants, whose ideas have often found their way into this book: Nikki Keddie, Lea Ann King, Ryszard Legutko, Onora O'Neill, Ulrich Preuss, Alan Ryan, Henry Shue, Tracy Strong, and Georgia Warnke. Also helpful in advancing the project were the members of the Institute's Committee on Intersocietal Relations, which includes Ruben Apresyan, Joseph Boyle, John Finnis, J. Bryan Hehir, Mark Juergensmeyer, Ted Koontz, Anne Phillips, Zarko Puhovsky, AntonGiulio de'Robertis, Janna Thompson, Bassam Tibi, and Noam Zohar. Michael Walzer provided good advice at the beginning of the project and David Miller contributed a needed chapter as we brought it to conclusion.

David Mapel wishes to thank the University of Utah Humanities Center, and especially its director, Lowell Durham, for providing the time to do much of the editing. We also thank Ann Himmelberger Wald of Princeton University Press for her continuing support.

All royalties earned by this book go to the Ethikon Institute for its programs on intersocietal relations, civil society, bio-environmental ethics, and family life.

CONTRIBUTORS

BRIAN BARRY is Professor of Political Science at the London School of Economics and a former editor of *Ethics* and the *British Journal of Political Science*. He is a fellow of the British Academy and of the American Academy of Arts and Sciences. His books include *Political Argument, The Liberal Theory of Justice, Theories of Justice*, and *Justice as Impartiality*.

CHRIS BROWN is Professor of Politics at the University of Southampton. He is the author of *International Relations Theory: New Normative Approaches* and many articles on international relations and political theory, and editor of *Political Restructuring in Europe: Ethical Perspectives*.

JOHN CHARVET is Present Reader in Political Science at the London School of Economics and a former assistant principal at the Board of Trade. He is the author of *The Social Problem in the Philosophy of Rousseau, A Critique of Freedom and Equality*, and *Feminism*, among other works.

RICHARD B. FRIEDMAN is Associate Professor of Political Science at the State University of New York at Buffalo. He is the author of articles on authority and law and is completing a book on the origins of natural law.

ROBERT P. GEORGE is Associate Professor of Politics at Princeton University and a presidential appointee to the United States Commission on Civil Rights. He is the author of *Making Men Moral: Civil Liberties and Public Morality* and editor of *Natural Law Theory: Contemporary Essays* and *The Autonomy of Law: Essays on Legal Positivism*.

SOHAIL H. HASHMI is Assistant Professor of International Relations at Mount Holyoke College. His interests include comparative international ethics and Middle Eastern and South Asian history and politics. He is currently writing a book on the contemporary Islamic discourse on international ethics.

PIERRE LABERGE is Professor of Philosophy at the University of Ottawa and a former president of the Canadian Philosophical Association. He is the author of *La théologie Kantienne précritique* as well as articles on Kant's practical philosophy and on international ethics.

DAVID R. MAPEL is Associate Professor of Political Science at the University of Colorado at Boulder. He is the author of *Social Justice Reconsidered* and coeditor (with Terry Nardin) of *Traditions of International Ethics*. He is currently writing a book on the ethics of political realism.

DAVID MILLER is Official Fellow in Social and Political Theory at Nuffield College, Oxford. Among his recent books are *Market, State and Community, On Nationality*, and *Pluralism, Justice and Equality* (coedited with Michael Walzer).

TERRY NARDIN is Professor of Political Science at the University of Wisconsin–Milwaukee. He is the author of *Law, Morality, and the Relations of States*, editor of *The Ethics of War and Peace: Religious and Secular Perspectives*, and coeditor (with David R. Mapel) of *Traditions of International Ethics*.

DAVID NOVAK is the Edgar M. Bronfman Professor of Modern Judaic Studies at the University of Virginia in Charlottesville. He is a founder of the Union for Traditional Judaism, vice president of the Institute on Religion and Public Life, and a fellow of the Academy for Jewish Philosophy. His books include *The Theology of Nahmanides*, *Jewish-Christian Dialogue*, and *Jewish Social Ethics*.

MAX L. STACKHOUSE is the Stephen Colwell Professor of Christian Ethics at the Princeton Theological Seminary. He is the author of *Creeds, Society, and Human Rights*, *Public Theology and Political Economy*, and *Apologia: Contextualization, Globalization, and Mission in Theological Education*.

FERNANDO R. TESÓN is Professor of Law at Arizona State University and a former diplomat in the Argentine Foreign Service. His books include *Humanitarian Intervention: An Inquiry into Law and Morality* and *The Philosophy of International Law*.

FREDERICK G. WHELAN is Professor of Political Science at the University of Pittsburgh. He is the author of *Order and Artifice in Hume's Political Philosophy* and *Edmund Burke and India*.

International Society

INTRODUCTION

DAVID R. MAPEL AND TERRY NARDIN

THE MODERN system of independent territorial states emerged in Europe several hundred years ago and today encompasses the world. Despite continuing technological and economic change, the persistence or deliberate revival of ancient ethnic and religious identities, and revolutionary efforts to replace the states system with new forms of community, the territorial state has not disappeared. Our international society remains a society of states. This book is about the basic principles governing this international society—principles that are implicit both in the actual arrangements of international relations and in the criticism of these arrangements from a variety of ethical perspectives.

Because our topic is such a large one, we have approached it by asking the contributors to this volume to consider three related questions. What is the proper structure or "constitution" of international society? On what is the authority of its laws and institutions based? And how adequately do these laws and institutions reflect a concern for justice in a world divided into distinct cultural communities and marked by vast disparities of wealth and opportunity? These questions suggest many others, so let us take a closer look at each.

First, concerning the idea of international society: What kind of relationship is implied by the words "international society"? Is this society best understood as a contractual association for certain purposes, or as an association based on acknowledging the authority of common rules? Should it retain its shape as a loose system of independent states or transform itself into an inclusive confederation or world state? What principles should be used to decide the matter?

Second, concerning the idea of international law: What is the basis of the authority of international law and of the international institutions it establishes? Can the authority of international law be distinguished from its justice or rightness? What does the rule of law in international society entail? Can international law be said to have a moral foundation, and if so, what is it?

Third, concerning the idea of international justice: By what criterion is the justice of international laws and institutions determined? How should tensions between the demands of justice and international law be reconciled? In what ways and to what extent should international law prescribe respect for ethnic, religious, and other cultural differences within and between states?

While these questions should help to clarify the scope of our inquiry, "international society" is still an abstraction that lies at some distance from the gritty particulars of international history and current worries about the prospects for peace, justice, and the rule of law in a world divided not only into states but also by economic and cultural differences. This distance is, in part, intentional: no amount of attention to particular international events, crises, or policy debates can substitute for a moral and philosophical reexamination of the inherited principles in terms of which the issues of the day are debated. We can, however, make our topic more concrete by sketching how the contributors to this volume have handled some of the questions that are implicit in these debates—questions that expose our deepest assumptions about the character and moral significance of the international order.

Because these questions call forth many different responses, we have chosen to highlight the differences by organizing this book as a dialogue among spokespersons for alternative points of view. In Part One, we offer presentations and critiques of five distinct philosophical perspectives on international society. In Part Two we relate these academic understandings to beliefs about world order held by large numbers of people by considering how the issues framed in the philosophical dialogue appear from the perspective of three of the world's great religious traditions. And in Part Three we identify commonalities and differences among the various perspectives with respect to how they respond to the three sets of questions mentioned above. In keeping with the aims of the Ethikon Institute, this way of organizing the book is not designed to yield conclusions about the relative merits of the perspectives discussed. It is, rather, intended to reveal unsuspected areas of agreement and to clarify what really separates the different views.

Terry Nardin's chapter launches the dialogue by considering the idea, important in the tradition of legal positivism, that international society is constituted by international law. After examining several versions of legal positivism, Nardin argues that the theory he calls "rule of law positivism" offers a particularly cogent way of understanding international society.

The fundamental tenet of legal positivism is that law is an autonomous social practice, distinct from morality and religion. Because the relations of states are regulated by law, an international society does exist, however limited in scope or ineffective in execution the norms of that society may sometimes be. International law exists in customs and agreements whose authority is explicitly or implicitly acknowledged by states, and in the activities of lawyers, jurists, diplomats, and administrators who interpret and apply these customs and agreements.

Furthermore, because both the authority of states to make treaties and the validity of these treaties is determined by customary practice, rule of law positivism holds that the constitutive principles of international society are to be found in customary international law, not treaties (even constitutional treaties like the UN Charter). Even though the centralized institutions for declaring and applying international law are few and weak, it is a mistake to conclude that an international society regulated by international law does not exist. To do this would be to confuse the criteria of law with conditions for its effectiveness. A global legal order possessing centralized legislative, judicial, or administrative institutions might or might not be desirable, but such institutions are not necessary to the existence of international law, and rule of law positivism neither recommends nor discourages their development.

While all forms of legal positivism reject moral principles as criteria of legal validity, rule of law positivism also maintains that a particular kind of justice is part of the very definition of "law." Part of this justice lies in what is sometimes called the "inner morality" of the law—principles such as that rules must be general, noncontradictory, and stable, or that there should be no retrospective or private laws. But rule of law positivism holds that these are principles inherent in the idea of legality itself, not moral principles that are external to the rule of law. Rule of law positivism also holds that "law" is noninstrumental or anticonsequentialist in character. Strictly speaking, the rule of law in international society is not concerned with the efficient generation or fair distribution of benefits or outcomes, but exclusively with constraints on the rightness of state conduct represented by diplomatic procedures, the law of treaties, the laws of war, and other parts of customary international law. In rejecting the idea of distributive justice between states, rule of law positivism differs dramatically from most of the other perspectives presented in this book (although not, interestingly, from the positions defended by Kant or Rawls). Even more important for our purposes, however, is the claim that this noninstrumental society is the form of international association most compatible with the freedom of its member communities to be different. According to rule of law positivism, this way of constituting international society encourages international ethnic, religious, and ideological diversity and peaceful coexistence.

In his response to Nardin, Frederick Whelan challenges an idea central to rule of law positivism (and to the internationalist or Grotian tradition). According to Whelan, if by a "society" we mean a collection of individuals or states having something in common beyond a mere selfish desire not to be preyed upon by one another, society can exist on the basis of custom or morality and therefore without law. Law therefore does not necessarily constitute international society, nor does it furnish conclusive empirical evidence that such a society exists. Furthermore, Whelan argues, customary law is only self-validating or authoritative for those who do not explicitly reject it and international legal society must therefore be understood as a voluntary association of those who accept its rules.

With respect to issues of justice and diversity, Whelan agrees that there is a kind of legal or procedural justice inherent in the idea of law. Nevertheless, he thinks that the positivist view of law limits ideological diversity in two distinct ways. First, and most importantly, the central positivist claim that law can be understood as an autonomous social practice represents a radical rejection of many moral and religious views of the nature of law (a contention also put forward in other chapters of this book). Second, Whelan argues that neither a noninstrumental character nor a concern with diversity is analytically part of the idea of law, but that both represent distinct moral commitments. In its emphasis on the inherently moral character of the rule of law, rule of law positivism therefore more closely resembles natural law theory than it does legal positivism, as the latter has historically been understood. Finally, Whelan argues that implicit in the positivist project of distinguishing law from morality and from religion is the idea that the rule of law requires well-defined procedures of legislation, adjudication, and enforcement. He suggests that the historical tendency of positivism has been to favor developed legal institutions in international as well as in domestic society. Whelan's understanding of positivism therefore points away from a decentralized system of customary law and toward a world state.

According to Robert George, the argument between positivists and natural lawyers has largely been transcended, since it is now well understood that positivism aims at describing law, whereas natural law aims at justifying it. As a theory of justification, the "new classical theory" of natural law maintains that there are a number of self-evident "basic goods" that are constitutive of human flourishing, as well some moral principles that follow more or less directly from these basic goods. One of these goods is community, particularly the idea of a "complete" community capable of securing the overall well-being of its members. Given such contemporary international problems as nuclear proliferation and ecological degradation, George suggests, the natural law tradition is coming to regard the territorial state as an "incomplete" community, one incapable of securing the overall well-being of its members without the assistance of supranational institutions that can enforce multilateral agreements and other kinds of international law. But the tradition also emphasizes that many political, social, and economic problems admit of no single rational solution, and that dealing with them requires both circumstantial information and practical judgment. From the perspective of natural law, it is unreasonable to offer more than a very rough outline of the ideal constitution of a world government.

George argues that certain international arrangements are ruled out by natural law; for example, those based on racist assumptions. There must also be ways of limiting or resisting central authority, possibly including a right of individuals or communities to retain arms, as an obstacle to world tyranny. Most important, international institutions should be organized according to a principle of "subsidiarity," which permits more centralized agencies to handle problems only when less centralized agencies cannot do so. This principle would restrict the authority of a world government to those tasks that could not be dealt with successfully by national governments. It would also limit the scope of national government to those tasks that cannot be handled by regional governments, and so on. Subordinate levels of government would not be displaced, but would be provided with a political environment in which each can best perform its proper tasks. A world government would also have a duty to protect the right of communities to preserve their distinctive practices and cultures, as long as those practices were not morally evil. But although no legitimate national government would be displaced and cultural diversity would be protected, such a world state would not be a voluntary, contractual and his commentator, Chris Brown, agree with Tesón: only a prudential modus vivendi is possible between liberal and nonliberal states. They also take issue with John Rawls's recent attempt to describe a moral form of association between liberal states and well-ordered "hierarchical" states, that is, nonliberal states that are nevertheless committed to pursuing their ends peacefully and are committed to some conception of legal order and respect for human rights in their internal affairs. According to Brown, Rawls seems to solve the problem of international order by defining it away, for a well-ordered hierarchical state, so defined, would "have no great difficulty relating to liberal states, because it would actually be, in most respects, a liberal state." But, Brown argues, "few, if any, actual hierarchical states are 'well-ordered' to this extent."

For Brown, the main problem with a contractarian approach to justice is that it merely legitimizes principles of cooperation that are already given. Anything more than modest criticism of international inequality is impossible unless we detach principles of distributive justice from the contractarian framework—as Brown attempts to do. Brian Barry's chapter starts from the same idea, that is, that communal membership should not be regarded as having much relevance in evaluating the claims of justice that persons make on one another. Instead, Barry asks what connections, if any, moral cosmopolitanism (the view that all moral claims must be considered impartially) might have to institutional cosmopolitanism (the view that the authority of supranational institutions should be substantially enhanced). According to Barry, the idea of impartiality, properly construed, entails the principle that inequalities of rights, opportunities, and resources must be justifiable in terms that cannot be reasonably rejected by those who are least well off. From this perspective, the world appears deeply unjust in many ways, though Barry is most concerned with economic injustice. He argues that at environmentally sustainable levels of production, the distribution of wealth is a zero-sum game in which the rich are rich largely because the poor are poor. We are, however, currently beyond sustainable levels of production. Transfer payments to the poor are therefore required not only to relieve current poverty but to guarantee an ecologically balanced world for future generations by putting the brakes on the economies of rich nations.

Barry suggests that the demands of moral cosmopolitanism would probably be satisfied best by a world federal government (on the model of the United States), which taxes rich individuals wherever they live for the sake of poor individuals wherever they live (member states would also be free to levy their own taxes). But a world federal government is unimaginable without achieving a long-standing practice of transfers between states. This practice might be based on an international authority that attaches a levy proportional to GNP, or alternatively, that establishes user fees (such as charges for maritime transport or a tax on carbon emissions). This international authority would leave the method of raising the revenue to each state. Coercing recalcitrant states might not be a major problem once such a large-scale cooperative scheme had been established. As Barry acknowledges, however, the motive for starting the scheme must be moral; self-interest is not enough.

As a matter of nonideal theory, Barry thinks there is no argument for making transfers between states when those transfers are simply appropriated by a ruling elite. But there is an argument for putting the transfers into trusteeship and—subject to prudential reservations—for military intervention to displace corrupt governments. We are not simply excused from our duty to aid the least well-off by the fact that foreign governments are not doing everything they can to aid their poor. Barry also considers whether we would be obligated to give aid to a state if all its members voluntarily accepted an inegalitarian system. Such cases are purely conjectural, he suggests, because the poor will in fact always reject an inegalitarian social system if they are not kept in ignorance or coerced. But cosmopolitan principles set firm limits to permissible international diversity, and from a cosmopolitan perspective the existence of communal agreement on certain kinds of values and practices is morally irrelevant. Even if everyone in a particular society is happy with an inegalitarian system sanctioned by their religious beliefs, for example, it is never unreasonable for someone to reject such systems, which must therefore be regarded as illegitimate in principle.

David Miller challenges Barry's version of cosmopolitanism, which first equates cosmopolitanism with the impartial or moral point of view and then equates this view with the idea that each person is equally a subject of our moral concern, no matter how they are connected to us. According to Miller, this is an unrealistically demanding idea of what morality requires. More importantly, it does not really capture the moral significance of special obligations to particular persons and communities. Such obligations are not merely an efficient way to implement the requirements of universal morality. Their significance can only be captured by a different interpretation of the moral point of view itself. As Miller understands it, impartiality has to do with the even-handed application of rules that may, for good reasons, require treating different persons differently. Thus, the moral point of view should recognize not only general duties to strangers but also conflicting, and sometimes weightier, special obligations to compatriots. Miller argues that this "weak" cosmopolitanism—which in principle places special obligations to particular communities and general duties to humanity on a roughly equal footing—is preferable to Barry's "strong" cosmopolitanism, which consistently subordinates the particular to the general.

Miller also argues that principles of international justice should be "noncomparative," that is, should identify forms of treatment that each person is owed no matter what is happening to others. He interprets Barry's idea of an international duty to redistribute resources to protect the vital interests of persons and communities as a principle of this sort, since its purpose is to establish a welfare floor for individuals that is independent of judgments about their relative deprivation. But he thinks that Barry's ideas regarding the redistribution of nonessential resources do rest on comparative principles of justice—principles that require judgments of relative advantage. Miller argues against such redistribution on the grounds that it makes sense to apply comparative principles of justice only to persons who are already part of the same community, and there is no such inclusive world community.

At the level of nonideal theory, Miller criticizes Barry for ignoring the effects of economic and political systems on rates of population growth. The result, he argues, is that Barry's approach is a static one that ignores the possible effects of bad incentives. To avoid such outcomes, foreign aid policies should be linked to measures to limit population growth. Though populations may eventually stabilize once living standards reach a certain level, income redistribution could encourage a rate of growth so high that stabilization is never achieved. Miller suggests that a better approach would therefore be to lower the rate of population growth in poor countries while encouraging rapid economic growth. These ends might be pursued by establishing stable trading relationships, investing in appropriate technologies, and encouraging political stability. Miller's weak cosmopolitan ideal of international society imagines a diverse world of independent political communities, each able to protect the human rights of its members, but each pursuing its own conception of comparative justice in its own way.

Religious diversity has always been significant in the international order. This book includes commentaries written from the perspectives of Judaism, Christianity, and Islam, not only because the existence of millions of believers has implications for international relations upon which it is important to reflect, but also because thinkers within these traditions have concerned themselves with the theme of international society. In articulating how Jewish, Christian, and Islamic discourse handle this theme, these chapters sharply illuminate some of the presuppositions of secular moral and political philosophy.

David Novak directly addresses the question of the place of a religious tradition in a philosophical debate that proceeds on secular premises. Such a tradition cannot accept those premises without betraying its own theological commitments, but neither can it insist that these commitments be the basis of its discourse with outsiders. The best course, he suggests, is for those who speak from the standpoint of a particular religious tradition to articulate how that tradition understands the issues at hand, in this way entering into dialogue with other views without either conceding to secularism or refusing to look beyond its own horizon of concern. But the commitment to dialogue must be mutual: if those speaking out of a religious tradition acknowledge the propriety of secular viewpoints in public discourse, so must adherents of secular viewpoints acknowledge the propriety of religious participation in that discourse.

Judaism has contributed indirectly to a progressivist understanding of international society, but, Novak argues, its authentic contribution is apocalyptic because it is committed to the priority of divine judgment over merely human purposes and, especially, over human pride. It reminds us that a human effort like the creation of a more just international society cannot itself provide a way out of the human predicament. Jewish theology does, however, provide grounds for holding that, in this world, such a society must not contravene the pluralism of the human condition. A morally defensible international society must sustain human association without subordinating freedom to the tyranny of a teleocratic world state. This understanding entails a commitment to the rule of law—understood, however, in a way that does not concede the philosophical presuppositions of at least some forms of both legal positivism and natural law. But Judaism must reject the assumption (which underlies much social contract theorizing) that human agreement can provide a self-sufficient moral foundation for international society or indeed any human association. (The Covenant of the Jews with God is not a contract in the usual sense because it merely affirms what has already been freely granted by God.) It must also reject the worldliness that permeates those versions of cosmopolitanism that understand international justice to be a matter of economic redistribution.

Like Novak, Max Stackhouse seeks to define the appropriate role of theology in relation to a dialogue which, though it involves religious voices, seems to rest on secular premises. Implicit in his chapter is the suggestion that revealed religion, perhaps because it possesses an independent ground for confidence in its own understanding, can and should engage secular philosophy on matters of practical concern. Religion, though not of this world, exists in this world and should neither accept nor impose on itself any denial of its relevance to the world's concerns.

Like Judaism, Christianity regards law as ultimately religious, although civil, moral, and ecclesiastical forms of law can be distinguished for practical purposes. But unlike orthodox thought within the other faiths, most forms of Christian theology do not seek to make religious law the foundation for civil law. Instead of a Torah or *shari'a*, mainstream Christianity today offers a social philosophy or public theology addressing issues of public policy in religious terms while at the same time recognizing, as an aspect of human freedom, a distinction between the sacred and legal realms. Religion can seek to persuade but it cannot do more than that. It follows that although Christianity does not prescribe a particular understanding of international law, it does require that any such understanding be consonant with the inherent pluralism of the human condition. Thus, it must reject totalizing schemes for human improvement, including those that choose to express themselves in Christian terms. At the same time, it must express profound skepticism about the authority, even in purely human terms, of an international legal order understood in a manner that severs all links between the legal and the religious. If Christian faith is justified, Stackhouse asks, how can there not be such links?

The tension between reason and revelation is also evident in the dialogue between philosophy and Islam, though here the tension is exacerbated by the primacy of revealed religion in Islamic thought. The issues posed in contemporary Islamic discourse on international relations are, nevertheless, similar to those of Jewish or Christian discourse. As Sohail Hashmi observes, although Islam strikes many Westerners as hostile to Western values and to the international society they support, the Islamic debate is largely an internal one over how to reconcile the realities of the modern world with the truths of the ancient faith. One of these realities is the failure of Muslim states to live up to the moral principles of Islam. These principles, interpreted in startlingly diverse ways, are the basis for moral criticism focused largely on Muslim governments and their relations with one another, not on the larger international society. Hashmi's chapter carefully explains the sources of Islamic ethics and indicates the range of Islamic thinking on international ethics, providing the reader with knowledge that is indispensable if the exchange between Western philosophy and Islamic theology is to rise above the level of monologue.

Previous Ethikon volumes address general questions about the selection and comparison of ethical perspectives, so we have chosen not to repeat that discussion here.[1] Instead, we have sought to give the reader a clear idea of what is at issue in the current debate over the principles that ought to govern international society. We think that the ethical perspectives we have selected are important enough to warrant inclusion in this book, though it can certainly be argued that other perspectives should have been included. We also think that the perspectives that are represented here, though diverse in outlook and style, are worth looking at together. One of the aims of the Ethikon Institute is to promote dialogue among ethical perspectives, which means encouraging different voices to participate in the conversation. And conversation presupposes the participation of dissimilar, even irreconcilable, voices. Another Ethikon aim is to understand where conversation tends to break down, and this means that disagreement is something to be explored, not a reason for refusing to bring different views into contact. In short, while acknowledging that one can imagine other conversations about international society, we invite readers to join this one. Indeed, we think a good way to stimulate other such conversations is to offer an exchange of views between diverse ethical perspectives that is both spirited and respectful.

NOTES

1. See Terry Nardin and David R. Mapel, eds., *Traditions of International Ethics* (Cambridge: Cambridge University Press, 1992), ch. 1; Brian Barry and Robert E. Goodin, eds., *Free Movement: Ethical Issues in the Transnational Migration of People and of Money* (University Park, Pa.: Penn State Press, 1992), ch. 1; Chris Brown, ed., *Political Restructuring in Europe: Ethical Perspectives* (London: Routledge, 1994), ch. 1; and Terry Nardin, ed., *The Ethics of War and Peace: Religious and Secular Perspectives* (Princeton: Princeton University Press, 1996), intro.

PART ONE

Philosophical Interpretations

CHAPTER 1

Legal Positivism as a Theory of International Society

TERRY NARDIN

IN THIS chapter I discuss how the connected topics we have been asked to consider are understood within the family of ideas called "legal positivism." Though positivism purports to be a theory of law, some positivist theories do not give an adequate account of the rule of law. That is, they do not explain how a community ordered according to general rules is distinguished from one ordered by the arbitrary exercise of power. I therefore devote particular attention to a version of positivism—I'll call it "rule of law positivism"—that does provide a coherent account of the rule of law as distinguished from arbitrary rule. But the rule of law must also be distinguished from morality. Rule of law positivism is the form of legal positivism that most adequately distinguishes law from morality as well as from power.

To avoid misunderstanding, I wish to state at the outset that I am not seeking to justify rule of law positivism, nor am I advocating its adoption as a desirable program for reforming international society. Nor, in defending the cogency of rule of law positivism as a definition of law, am I implicitly recommending that definition. My intent in focusing on rule of law positivism is to remove certain arbitrary assumptions and internal inconsistencies from legal positivism, so as to present it as a distinct and coherent perspective on our topic.

WHAT IS LEGAL POSITIVISM?

The expression "legal positivism" has several meanings, of which three are especially relevant to international law. These may be listed in order of decreasing generality.[1]

According to the first, law is a distinct, autonomous social practice. The validity of legal rules, and therefore their authority or obligatory character, rests on criteria internal to a legal system and not on external foundations, divine or rational. Law properly so-called (positive law) is a set of rules distinguishable from revealed divine law, from rational morality (natural law), and from the moral conventions of any actual society. The content of actual legal and moral systems may overlap, and some legal systems may explicitly incorporate moral principles, but the validity of legal rules as law does not *depend* on their correspondence to moral principles unless explicitly provided for by law.[2] As John Austin puts it, "the existence of law is one thing; its merit or demerit another."[3] Because what counts as law is determined by criteria that differ from those used to distinguish moral rightness and wrongness (even where the legal system incorporates a moral test), there will always be discrepancies between morality and law. In this sense, at least, there is no *necessary* connection between morality and law.

Applied to international relations, this first, inclusive meaning of "legal positivism" yields the view that international law is rooted in the practices of international society—in the customs and agreements acknowledged by states as governing their relations with one another—and that its rules can be determined by examining evidence of actual diplomatic practice and not by deduction from basic principles of natural law. This view of international law emerged as orthodoxy toward the end of the eighteenth century among legal scholars who argued that, because it had its source not in reason but in state practice, the law of nations should be distinguished from natural law.[4]

The second meaning of "legal positivism" is that authentic law is law declared or "posited" (Latin *positum*, decreed) by a superior but this-worldly authority, a sovereign lawmaker. Since reason, which is the method of natural law, can generate many different and competing "laws," a choice among them must be made by some one person or body (the "sovereign") who is authorized to make this choice. Authentic law is the result of decisions by a sovereign to declare certain rules to be law, and *only* law issuing from the will of a sovereign is binding as law. Law is generated by an authoritative act of will and is embodied in statutes. This view of law is central to the meaning of legal positivism in eighteenth- and nineteenth-century European jurisprudence, and it fits comfortably with utilitarianism, a theory intended (as Bentham's name for it, "the theory of legislation," suggests) to guide legal reform.

Unlike the first definition, the second creates obvious problems for international law. For as soon as law is identified with rules originating in the exercise of sovereign authority, international law, which does not have such a source, becomes an anomaly requiring explanation.[5] The definition of law as declared by a superior power invites a dismissal of international law of the kind made famous by John Austin: that because a law is the command of a sovereign, and sovereigns are not subject to the commands of any earthly superior, international law is not law properly so-called but one species of "positive morality."

Notice that Austin uses the term "positive" here not only for rules set by superior authority, but also for those derived from a social practice. This is not the definition of positivism that is implicit in the expression "Austinian positivism," which identifies the view that law is the command of a sovereign. Those eighteenth-century positivists who argued that the task of international legal theory is to formulate the general norms implicit in state practice were not positivists in this latter, narrower, sense.[6]

The third meaning of "legal positivism" we need to be aware of is a by-product of efforts to defend international law against the view that law is an expression of sovereign will. According to the aptly named "consent theory," authentic international law is composed of rules to which states have given their explicit or tacit consent. Because no sovereign can be legally bound by the commands of another, international law can bind only by consent. If civil law is sovereign will expressed internally through legislation, international law is this will expressed externally through explicit agreement with other sovereigns (treaties) or by tacit agreement (custom). Related to this view of international law as resting on consent is the claim that international law is binding only on states: if states are the only subjects of international law ("international legal persons"), it follows that individuals, corporations, and other nonstate entities are *not* subjects of international law and have no rights or duties under it.

The expression "legal positivism" is most cogent when used in the first and most inclusive of these three senses. The others express subsidiary views within legal positivism inclusively defined. Whether authentic law must be declared by a lawmaker or also includes customary or common law is really a matter of intramural debate within legal positivism. Thus H.L.A. Hart, a positivist, can insist that law is not always the outcome of deliberate legislation, and that "legal positivism" means only that legal rules arise from social practices.[7] And what is sometimes identified as a debate between positivism and common law can be seen as a debate *within* positivism in this more inclusive sense.[8] Similarly, the proposition that international law is binding on a state only by its consent, or that only states have rights under international law, are matters about which positivists disagree and not views that define legal positivism as such.

Legal positivism in general understands as "law" any body of practices and rules creating not merely expectations but binding obligations for the members of a community. But because this understanding does not sharply distinguish law from the customs or moral practices of a community, many positivists argue that law proper is distinguished from morality by the existence of authoritative procedures or offices for recognizing and applying rules (as in Austin's command theory or Hart's theory of law as a "union of primary and secondary rules"[9]). The interpretation that I am calling "rule of law positivism" reaches the further conclusion that an authentic legal order must be distinguished from the diversity of social orders lumped together under the name "law." For example, the commands of a despot are sometimes regarded as law, but such commands are contrary to, not an expression of, the rule of law. Rule of law positivism holds that law is best understood as a system of noninstrumental or moral practices that have hardened into rules, and in which institutions for declaring and applying rules have evolved or been instituted. It therefore offers an alternative, *within positivism*, to the view that any expression of sovereign will whatever counts as law.

For positivists of all persuasions, the master question of international relations is whether authentic law can exist where institutions for declaring and applying law are absent or rudimentary. Austinians, as we have seen, arrive quickly at a negative answer to this question, but for others the answer is more complicated. Can the rule of law be realized in international society in the absence of civil institutions? Or is international relations inherently a domain of unreliable rules and therefore of power politics rather than the rule of law? Whether the rule of law is possible among states is an unresolved question on the agenda of international relations theory.

INTERNATIONAL SOCIETY

If law is a product of sovereign will, as some positivists argue, we must doubt not only the existence of international law but the reality of international society. In the absence of law, the international system is no more than a series of ad hoc transactions, not a real society of states. But if we adopt the more inclusive definition of positivism according to which law is a distinctive kind of social practice, we make room for international law and society. Because there are rights, rules, lawyers, lawsuits, judges, and judgments in the international sphere, international law must exist—however intermittent or ineffective this activity may be. And the definition links law and society conceptually: international society is not merely regulated by international law but *constituted* by it.

According to this argument, international society exists to the extent that states understand themselves to be related to one another as subjects of common rules—a common law—defining the terms of their coexistence. These rules prescribe obligations binding not only on states engaged in alliances, trade, and other forms of cooperation, but also on states whose relations with one another are hostile. Even states at war can be understood as belonging to a community of states, so long as the belligerents understand themselves to be constrained by international law.[10]

There are several connected ideas composing this conception of law as a social practice that need to be explicated. One is the idea of a body of law concerned specifically with relations between sovereign states—a common "law of nations" understood not merely as *ius gentium* but as *ius inter gentes*.[11] This idea of international law can be contrasted with, and understood to be the product of, two others: the idea of independent powers interacting with one another in a lawless state of nature, and that of a universal community of individuals united by a common law. According to the first, the world is an anarchy of separate states, each pursuing its interests and augmenting its powers without regard to the claims of other states. According to the second, the world is a single community—if not actually organized under one church or empire, at least potentially a *civitas maxima* or "world society." The fusion of these two ideas generates the idea of a *society* of *states*: a universal community whose members are not persons but communities of persons, an inclusive community of communities. For some, this idea of international society rests on a contradiction, one aptly summed up in the expression "the anarchical society."[12] A society of states is anarchic in the sense that it lacks a ruling authority, yet social because its members are united, despite this anarchic structure, by common rules.

Another important element of the social practice conception of law is the idea that international society is constituted by international law. On this point, positivists differ. While some see international law as rules made and observed by preexisting states, others argue that international law is constitutive of both states and the society of states. "Statehood" is a role defined by the rules that constitute international society.

Positivists who hold that international law arises only by consent think of international society as a kind of pact defined by mutual recognition and agreement. International society is *created* by treaties and other agreements voluntarily entered into for the sake of realizing common interests and shared goals. And international law is the limited and temporary *product* of these various transactions, not their continuous and permanent premise. Custom is law only to the extent that it expresses tacit consent.

One consequence of the widespread acceptance of this consent theory in eighteenth- and nineteenth-century international legal thought was the view that international law is binding only among states recognized as belonging to the society of states and participating in its practices. The result was a nearly exclusive preoccupation with European state practice and the consequent identification of international law as "the public law of Europe."[13] Because this law applied only in the European "family of nations," it did not govern the relations of Europeans with oriental sovereigns or uncivilized peoples.

In contrast to the voluntaristic positivism of consent theory, rule of law positivism makes general rules the basis of international society. What distinguishes a society of states from a jumble of ad hoc transactions is that its members acknowledge, as authoritative and binding, common laws that are antecedent to their particular transactions and agreements. Because these laws must be common to all, they are found only in customs binding on states generally, not in treaties, which bind only states that are party to them. Treaties are contracts within the law and as such cannot be fundamental to international law.[14] International law proper—general law applying to all (present and future) members of international society—is therefore always customary law. Customary international law regulates the relations of states in the absence of explicit agreement, prescribes procedures for reaching agreements and determining their validity, and limits what states may do by making treaties. Treaties are the outcome of particular transactions and also instruments of international cooperation, but customary international law cannot be understood in this way. Its rules are prior to these transactions, the noninstrumental presupposition of all international cooperation. Treaties are practically important but custom has conceptual priority.

It follows that the society of states is defined by general recognition of customary international law as authoritative, not by common interests or shared goals. Cultural similarity, geographical proximity, or a profusion of important transactions ("interdependence") may contribute to the efficacy of international law and may help to actualize the idea of international society in the relations of states, but they are not the basis of association. They may motivate states to cooperate with one another, but their relation to the idea of international society is contingent, not conceptual. It is the self-understanding of states as bound by common rules that constitutes the society of states.[15]

According to rule of law positivism, then, customary law is essential to the idea of an inclusive international society. Customary international law constitutes the society of states as such, but treaties establish particular relationships *within* international society. Even constitutional treaties like the League Covenant or the UN Charter establish only limited associations within international society, not international society itself. The "Constitution" of international society as a whole, on this view, is the unwritten constitution of customary international law, not the voluntary pacts and charters that certain states may occasionally enter into to establish particular, historic associations within the larger society of states.

Not surprisingly, these differences within the positivist camp over the relative priority of treaties and custom generate different views about what might be called the "constitutional structure" of world society. For some, this society cannot be a universal confederation or world state, for any such organization would be an entity created within international society. If this state were not universal, it would be just another state, though perhaps an immense and therefore hegemonic one, inside a more inclusive international society. But even were such a metastate to succeed in becoming universal, it could not bring about an *international* society, for with the creation of a universal state the society of states would disappear.

For others, a universal or nearly universal state is necessary if an inclusive system of world law is to acquire any real force. They would agree with Frederick Whelan that legal positivism points toward a world state rather than a society of states based on international law, because there can be no authentic and effective system of law without centralized institutions to declare and enforce it.[16] Those who hold the rule of law to be impossible without such institutions would reject as paradoxical Kant's idea that a permanent peace based on law could be secured by a loose confederation of republics in which states would retain some sovereign powers. For if the states belonging to the confederation are to be genuinely independent, they cannot concede their sovereign authority, while if the confederation is to be ruled by authentic law, it must be able to override the judgments of member states.[17] But whether international law can exist without supranational institutions is (as we shall see) a matter for continuing debate.

LEGALITY

The argument that the rule of law is a possible mode of international relations, one distinguishable both from morality, on the one hand, and the mere exercise of power, on the other, belongs to the strand of positivism I have labeled "rule of law positivism." Where the rule of law prevails, the scope of international law, as of law in general, is limited. Authentic laws constrain agents pursuing their own self-chosen goals, but they do not prescribe those goals. As Hobbes says, they are like the hedges that keep travelers on the roads but do not decide their destinations.[18]

Much of customary international law, as observed (and in recent years codified) by states, reflects this conception of the rule of law. The law of treaties, for example, is about the forms and procedures of treaty-making as a practice; it is not properly concerned with whether or not particular states make treaties or with the substantive content of their agreements. Similarly, diplomatic law concerns the forms and procedures of diplomatic practice; the law of war, the principles governing the initiation and conduct of war.

While the international legal system as it exists does, like other law, include instrumental rules intended to facilitate the pursuit of particular purposes, the production of particular outcomes, and the conferral of benefits on particular beneficiaries, these are intrusions of interest and power into the domain of the rule of law. For states to be related in terms of the rule of law is for them to be related on the basis of general rules, not particular transactions or enterprises.

Like other kinds of positivism, rule of law positivism sees law as a social practice consisting of the use and interpretation of rules. But it departs sharply from that strand of positivism that understands a rule to be an order or command. Whereas for Austin law is the command of the sovereign, for positivists like Hans Kelsen, H.L.A. Hart, and Michael Oakeshott, laws must be distinguished from commands. Commands are particular actions. Rules, in contrast, are always general. A rule is addressed to an indeterminate audience composed of all those who may at some future time fall within its jurisdiction, and it exists in advance of the situations to which it may come to be applied. Rules presuppose agents engaged in performing actions of their own choosing and prescribe attention to certain considerations in choosing these actions, not the performance of particular acts.

Far from explaining the character of law, commands are not intelligible apart from law. A command, properly speaking—that is, in contrast to a mere expression of power such as "your money or your life"—is an authoritative utterance whose validity lies solely in its lawfulness, that is, its rule-determined authority or authenticity.[19] Though Hobbes and Bentham are often classed with Austin as holding that law, and therefore legal obligation, arises from the exercise of power, this is a mistake. Unlike Austin, both authors clearly distinguish *authority* from *power* and connect obligation conceptually with the former; the power to enforce a law is related to its effectiveness, not its validity.

Laws, then, are rules, not commands. And where the rule of law is the mode of association, they are rules of a certain kind. They are not prudential or instrumental maxims containing information or advice about how to produce a desired outcome or result. They are *noninstrumental* rules. A non-instrumental rule is concerned solely with the propriety of actions, not their usefulness in achieving or avoiding particular outcomes. Its authority as a source of obligation rests on its validity as a rule, as determined by criteria internal to the legal system, not on its instrumental or prudential value. And the criteria according to which this validity is determined have nothing to do with a rule's conformity to a higher law or its effectiveness in producing a desired outcome.

With respect to these characteristics of the rule of law as a mode of relationship—that laws are rules, not commands; that they are noninstrumental rules, not prudential maxims; and that the validity of laws is established by criteria internal to the legal system—the same understanding of legality applies to international as to civil society. Against political realists, for whom the common rules of international society are merely useful tools for the pursuit of state purposes, as well as moral idealists, for whom these rules are expressions of a higher law, rule of law positivism argues that legality is realized in international affairs only where there is an authoritative body of noninstrumental rules: rules that are valid because they are part of the system of international law. And, as I shall explain more fully below, it is a distinguishing feature of positivism to insist that the laws that are valid within a given legal system are those identified by procedures internal to that system, not according to extraneous instrumental or higher law criteria.

If rules are to be the basis of association, however, those associated must know what the rules are. Rules cannot be used without being interpreted, and because interpretations can be disputed, some method of settling disputes is needed. Where those governed by rules are free to interpret them as they please, they can hardly be said to be governed by *common* rules. The resulting uncertainty undermines the premise of common life according to rules, which is that the rules be authoritative in the community they are supposed to govern.

What we need to resolve disputes over the interpretation of rules, positivists argue, is for interpretation itself to be governed by rules. In other words, we need a procedure for deciding, in an authoritative way, which interpretations are to count as correct. Such a procedure permits us to ascertain the authenticity of a disputed rule in the face of disagreements regarding its moral rightness or consequential desirability. A legal system, by specifying procedures for authoritatively fixing the meaning of its rules, makes it possible for agreed principles of conduct to be determined apart from disputes over the justice, fairness, reasonableness, or desirability of the obligations they prescribe. An authoritative—that is, valid or authentic—rule is one that has been declared through recognized procedures: a statute duly enacted and not ruled unconstitutional, a treaty properly signed and ratified, etc. The moral quality of a law may remain contentious, but the moral issue has at least been separated from the issue of legal validity.

According to legal positivism, then, law is an invention designed to remedy the inability of custom to settle disputes about the interpretation of rules by providing rule-governed procedures for determining their meaning. Law, properly so-called, emerges when a customary system of rules is augmented by procedures for providing authoritative determinations of what a rule means in cases of dispute—to declare which interpretations the rule shall be *law*. Positivism understands law to be a system of rules that has been provided with some way of distinguishing rules binding as law from other kinds of rules. Law requires a mechanism for identifying rules, for using them in particular situations, and for ensuring that they can be relied upon.

This conception of law as an institutionalized system of social rules explains why positivists are divided on the question of whether international law is really law. Among the doubtful, some argue that international law is defective because there is no superior power to compel obedience to its rules. Others focus on the absence in international society of official interpreters: legislators to enact or alter rules, or judges to say what the rules mean in specific situations and to decide whether or not they have been adequately observed. The most skeptical, like Hobbes and Oakeshott, have concluded that the institutions for declaring and interpreting international rules are so rudimentary as to preclude legal order at the international level. Foreign affairs, for skeptical realists of this kind, is guided by prudence, not law.

Other legal positivists, including Kelsen and Hart, are more confident that legal order can exist without such institutions. For them, the essence of legality lies in the reasonably consistent application of law, not in the particular institutions through which consistency is sometimes obtained. They argue that in international society, law is declared, interpreted, and applied in ways that, though less centralized and uniform than those prevailing within states, nevertheless do provide a significant degree of consistency. What we need, this line of argument suggests, are fewer *a priori* pronouncements on the impossibility of legal order in the absence of centralized legal institutions, and closer study of how uniformity, certainty, and impartiality are in fact pursued and to some extent achieved in international law.[20]

Justice

Legal positivists hold a variety of views about the meaning of "justice" and its relation to law. Some see justice as a substantive state of affairs, an outcome to be produced by means of legislation or a goal to guide judicial decisions. Justice here reduces to utility or desirability. Others stick to the traditional view that justice and utility are distinct ideas. On this view, that something is desirable or good does not make it just. Justice is not an *outcome* to be produced by action, and therefore it cannot be a goal of action. It is a *constraint* on action and can only be realized by acting within the limits that obligations impose on choice. Justice is therefore determined in relation to moral and legal principles. Conduct that disregards these principles is criticized as unjust, and this charge can be rebutted only in an effort to "justify" the censured act by showing that it does, after all, conform adequately to the appropriate principles.

Rule of law positivism may be seen as refining this nonconsequentialist conception of justice. To see how this works, we must distinguish between the justice of an act and the justice of a law. Some positivists, following Hobbes, have concluded that the justice of a *law* is nothing but its validity *as* law. Justice here is reduced not to utility but to legality. Because it makes law the sole standard of justice, however, this conclusion leaves little room for moral criticism: whatever is valid as law is also just. Rule of law positivism, in contrast, distinguishes "justice" (the moral rightness of a law) from legality (the validity or authenticity of a law). In doing so, it does not preclude consideration of the justice or moral rightness of a law. On the contrary, by distinguishing the justice of a law from its validity, it makes room for moral criticism of law. But it keeps this critical activity separate from the activity of saying what the law *is*, of determining valid or authentic law. On this view, the justice of a law does not pertain to the procedure by which it was created and with reference to which its validity is ascertained. A "just" law, strictly speaking, is not one that is properly enacted but one that is proper to have been enacted.[21]

For rule of law positivism, then, the justice of a law is not related to consequences that follow or are expected to follow from enacting or observing it. That a law will have desirable consequences, or that it will efficiently provide or fairly distribute substantive benefits, are matters of expediency, not justice. The only business of law with respect to these or any other outcomes is to prescribe constraints to be observed in seeking them. Much of the debate about international justice, from the standpoint of rule of law positivism, is really about desirable or undesirable states of affairs, not justice. The rule of law in international society, as in civil society, is concerned not with the consequences of state conduct but with its rightness in relation to diplomatic norms, the law of treaties, the laws of war, and other parts of customary international law. International justice concerns the circumstantial propriety, not the consequential desirability, of these laws.

Because it rejects utilitarian and other consequentialist theories of justice, and because it distinguishes the justice of a law from its validity, rule of law positivism may seem to come close to natural law. The reader may therefore be tempted, along with Frederick Whelan, to object that the version of positivism I have been expounding covertly imports substantive moral ideas into the idea of law and that, for this reason, it no longer belongs to the positivist family. If we believe the rule of law involves moral constraints on the exercise of power, rule of law positivism can be seen as providing an account of the moral *character* of law. But, in contrast to the tradition of natural law, it does so without making untenable assumptions or claims about the moral *foundations* of law.[22]

The difference between rule of law positivism and natural law can be illustrated by examining the question of whether law presupposes justice. For the rule of law positivist, the justice of a law must be distinguished from those features of the rule of law sometimes identified as "the inner morality of law" (in Lon Fuller's familiar phrase)—such as that there should be no secret or retrospective laws, no obligations other than those imposed by law, or no arbitrary exemptions or private laws.[23] These are not criteria of "just" law but of "law" itself; they are inherent in the idea of living according to rules, and therefore part of the idea of law insofar as law is understood to consist not of commands but of rules.[24] In other words, the "morality" of the rule of law is intrinsic to the rule of law itself. Both morality and the rule of law are ways of being related on the basis of rules, and both are disrupted by the arbitrary, inconsistent, or irrational application of rules. But it does not follow that to see the rule of law as the essence of law is to found law on morality or natural law. As Fuller well understood, law without legality or the rule of law is not merely unjust, it is not law.

The difference between rule of law positivism and natural law can also be seen in the positivist rejection of abstract moral ideals as criteria of legal validity. It is characteristic of natural law to identify justice with moral standards that are independent of the practices of actual communities, with the result that justice becomes an alternative to law and subversive of it. This situation can only be avoided if the moral standards that are used to evaluate a law are already in some way embodied in the legal order. For the positivist, the appropriate standards by which to measure the justice of particular laws are those already intimated by the system to which these laws belong. This concern with the coherence or integrity of a legal order also requires that we pay careful attention to circumstances, but it excludes, as a practical standard for determining the justice of particular laws, that these laws should conform to abstract, universal, and absolute moral standards. The constant appeal to extraneous moral standards in legal deliberation, whether under the name of nature, reason, rights, morality, necessity, justice, or the common good is more likely to undermine than to improve the rule of law.[25]

These arguments have force in international as well as in civil society. For the rule of law positivist, if *law* is to be the basis of international relations, the principles of justice used to criticize international law are best limited to those that have some connection with the customs and usages of international society. Criticism of international law that is concerned to sustain the rule of law will rely upon principles drawn from international experience—principles already immanent in international practice and closely connected with the kinds of obligations that are appropriately imposed by international law. The gradual incorporation into international law of a concern for human rights, for example, reflects a concern for legality as well as justice, whereas the retroactive assertion of sovereign rights to natural resources as a justification for expropriating foreign-owned companies does not. That assertion may reflect an abstract principle of justice proposed as an alternative to law, but not the rule of law.

Rule of law positivism is concerned to avoid the extremes of Hobbesian positivism, which makes legality itself the criterion of justice, and natural law, which makes justice into a criterion of legality. Against Hobbes, it denies that skepticism regarding moral claims must end in the conclusion that justice can have no meaning apart from law. Against natural law, it reminds us that legal order is grounded on recognition of the authority of laws, not on independent judgments of their justice or injustice. Law can supply a community's need for common rules only where it is valid or authentic law, that is, where its authority is established independently of its consequential desirability or moral rightness.

Authority

The positivist argument we have just considered, that the authority of a law is independent of its justice, is not a moral argument. It is an attempt to clarify discourse about legal authority by distinguishing legal validity from moral rightness or desirability. It is, therefore, a contribution to "analytical" rather than to "normative" jurisprudence. For positivism, to say that a rule is authoritative, and that it therefore gives rise to legally binding obligations, is to say that it is a valid or authentic rule within a particular legal system: where there is law, there is legal obligation. International law, too, is legally binding on states simply because it is law. The validity of its rules is determined by criteria and procedures that are internal to international law as a system of laws, not by external moral standards. No external explanation of the *legal* authority of these rules, or of the legal obligations prescribed by them, is necessary or even possible. One can ask whether there is a *moral* obligation to observe a particular rule of international law, but to do this is to raise a moral, not a legal, question. The rules of international law can have significant moral content and they can be criticized from a moral point of view, but their authority (validity, authenticity) as rules of international law does not rest on any "moral foundation."

Positivists disagree, however, about how the authority of legal rules is to be established. For some, the validity of a rule depends on the command or consent of a sovereign. But (as we have seen) if valid laws are an expression of sovereign will, international law can only come into being as the joint product of a multiplicity of sovereign wills. International law, on this view, is created by the "common consent" of the states composing international society.[26] A treaty is valid law for the states that are party to it because it is the product of the explicit consent of these parties, and customary international law is valid when it reflects the tacit consent of states. Other legal positivists challenge this consent theory of international law, arguing that the agreement of states, like the command of a sovereign, is a mere fact that can have legal consequences only if there is a rule specifying those consequences. In order to distinguish valid from invalid commands, agreements, or other expressions of will, one must rely on an existing criterion of validity that cannot itself be the outcome of the exercise of authority it is invoked to explain.

Further disagreement surrounds the issue of how these criteria of legal validity are themselves grounded or validated. Some positivists argue that in order to understand the authority of law we must postulate an ultimate source of legal validity. Kelsen, for example, traces the validity of particular laws back to a hypothetical "basic norm," the existence of which is logically presupposed by the idea of legal validity even if its existence cannot be empirically verified.[27] Other positivists argue that no such hypothesis is required because legal validity can spring directly from legal practice. In some systems, its source can be a validating "rule of recognition" implicit in the practice of public officials.[28] In customary law systems, however, there may be neither officials nor a rule of recognition but only the practice of the community members whose conduct is regulated by law. Customary law, in other words, is self-validating. It follows that the rules of customary international law are valid simply because they are recognized as valid by states. To establish their validity one searches not for a higher validating norm but for evidence in the conduct of states that would establish both a pattern of uniform practice and general acceptance of that practice as law (*opinio juris*). There is in international law no basic norm or rule of recognition for testing the validity of customary law, and no need for one, for all that such a rule could prescribe would be that states should recognize as valid the rules they recognize as valid. We can avoid this meaningless circularity by accepting the view that customary law simply exists, as a matter of empirical fact, in the practice of states.[29]

Finally, positivists are divided on the question of whether the rule of law in international society requires institutions for declaring and applying law. As we have seen, the rule of law presupposes some way of identifying a law and of authoritatively determining its meaning in particular situations. But there is confusion and disagreement about how these tasks are accomplished in international law. Those who regard civil institutions as a defining criterion of legal order conclude that in international society these tasks are not performed at all, and therefore that international law is not really "law." For those who regard the existence of such institutions as a condition contributing to the efficacy of legal order, international law is defective rather than nonexistent. International law may exist, on this view, but it exists only as an uncertain and largely ineffective system of rules. Thus Oppenheim, the leading English international law positivist around 1900, held that international law was "weak law" but "nevertheless still law."[30] Still others suggest that institutions for declaring and applying law are in fact present, in a special or hidden form, in international law.[31] Let us briefly consider these debates insofar as they are concerned with the institutions through which international law might be declared, adjudicated, or enforced.

Because a valid law is one that has been authoritatively declared according to a recognized procedure, positivists are inclined to hold that legal order requires a law-making office. Oakeshott, for example, argues that in a legal system the requirement that those governed by law must know what the laws are "is satisfied only where laws have been deliberately enacted or appropriated and may be deliberately altered or repealed"[32]—in other words, where there exists a legislative office of some kind to make, amend, and certify the authenticity of the laws. There may be customary law within a legal system, but such law can be revised at any time by legislative enactment and its validity rests on its compatibility with statutes currently in force. As Hobbes puts it, customary law is law only by the tacit acquiescence of the sovereign: what the sovereign power permits, it commands.[33]

Arguments of this kind have led some positivists to deny the possibility of international law and others to search for ways in which the legislative function is performed, in the absence of a legislature, in the international system. It may be argued, for example, that the victor who dictates terms to the vanquished is "legislating" for the latter, or that states "legislate" for themselves by becoming parties to a treaty and that very general treaties constitute "lawmaking treaties" or "international legislation." But these arguments stretch the meaning of the term "legislation" beyond the breaking point.[34] A better answer to skeptical critics of international law, for those who are persuaded that international law as a social practice exists, is that such critics mistake a common method for securing interpretive agreement with the idea of law itself. Legislative enactment may result in more effective laws, but it is not a criterion of the rule of law.

The debate over the importance of legislation is paralleled by a debate over adjudication. Legal order requires not only that those governed by law should know what the laws are, but also that these laws should be generally observed. What must be known, however, is not merely what the rules are in general, but what counts as adequate observance of a law in any given case. We need, then, a procedure for determining what the laws mean in particular situations and for resolving disputes about these meanings: hence the first Noahide commandment, that in any society judges are to be appointed. Here again positivists are divided, and along what will now be seen to be familiar lines: some taking the absence of international courts as a crippling defect of international law, others finding ways in which the judicial function is performed by such international tribunals as do exist as well as by domestic courts, and still others arguing that adjudication is neither a defining characteristic nor a necessary condition of legal order.

Positivists also disagree among themselves about the role of enforcement or sanctions in law. Many insist, with Austin, that laws must be enforced to be valid as law. The parallel argument regarding international law is that because international society lacks a coercive power to enforce its rules, these rules cannot give rise to binding obligations. Others reply, with Hart, that the Austinian argument confuses being "obliged" by superior power with being "obligated" to obey a rule. Hart continues a long-running argument in the positivist tradition when he argues that the command of a public official can give rise to an obligation only because the official is *authorized* to command. As Hobbes puts it, "law, properly, is the word of him that *by right* hath command over others"—a view Bentham echoes when he defines law as a command "backed by the *authority* of the sovereign."[35] On this view, coercion alone cannot create an obligation. Neither the authority of a ruler nor the obligations of a subject has anything to do with the ruler's power to compel observance of the laws. Law is enforced because it is obligatory, not obligatory because it is enforced.[36] Therefore, it cannot be held that the obligations of international law are not binding because they are not consistently enforced. It can, however, be plausibly argued that the absence of reliable enforcement tends to make international law ineffective. Bentham and Hart, for example, treat sanctions not as definitive of law but as one of the motivating forces contributing to an effective legal order.[37]

Diversity

The preceding discussion of legality and legal authority is directly related to the issue of diversity, for only a regime of noninstrumental rules, understood to be authoritative independent of particular beliefs or purposes, is compatible with the freedom of its subjects to be "different." Though legal positivists have often disagreed with this proposition, and many legal positivists have seen law as the instrument of shared beliefs and values, the positivist tradition in international law has for the most part not sought to understand international order in terms of cultural homogeneity. An obvious and enduring feature of international society is the ethnic, religious, and ideological diversity of its members, and legal positivists have generally understood international law to be a way of regulating, rather than erasing, this diversity. In contrast to utopian moral reformers who have proposed schemes for universal peace based on Christian, socialist, or democratic ideals, they have generally sought to understand rather than to transcend the messy pluralism of the international order. The tendency of legal positivism is therefore to reject the view that a peaceful, rule-governed international order is impossible in a multicultural world. On the contrary, it presumes that such an order is compatible with, even premised on, cultural diversity. By providing a framework for the coexistence of separate and culturally distinct communities, the "law of nations" seems to offer a way of limiting the destructive consequences of religious, ethnic, and other differences without demanding cultural homogeneity. It offers the possibility of international relations on the basis, not of a shared conception of the good, but of a practice of mutual forbearance.

So understood, the idea of a society of states is analogous to the idea of the civil state as an association of independent and therefore different individuals. At both levels, the device for facilitating peaceful association while preserving difference is the rule of law. Just as a civil society in which the rule of law has taken hold must accommodate, and is indeed premised on, the individuality of its members, so international society understood as a regulated association of independent political communities must tolerate the existence of differences among these communities. From the standpoint of a concern for coexistence under common laws, the precise constitutional shape of a society at either the civil or the international level is less important than that it can tolerate different beliefs, customs, and ways of life.

At both levels, membership in the community is a formal status that is compatible with the existence of substantive differences and inequalities. The rule of law within a state forbids making religion, language, or race criteria for citizenship, and international law cannot properly make them criteria for membership in the society of states. The international law definition of a "state"—a population living within a defined territory under its own laws and government—therefore says little about the composition or beliefs of that population's ethnicity or the substantive character of its laws. The formal equality ascribed to members of international society implies neither material equality nor cultural uniformity.[38] Where the rule of law prevails in international society, states can be Catholic or Protestant, monarchical or republican, European or non-European, capitalist or communist, developed or less developed, Sunni or Shiite—provided they acknowledge the authority of international law in their dealings with one another.

A positivism concerned with the rule of law in international society, then, will not demand religious, ideological, ethnic, or other substantive uniformity. It will be concerned solely with coexistence on the basis of common rules. The only requirement for membership in the society of states is that states should conduct themselves according to the rules of international law. States that cannot or will not observe these rules mark themselves as outlaws or barbarians. But this is a status they acquire not because of what they are but because of what they do. Cultural differences are tolerable, and must be tolerated, even when they lead to conduct that contravenes the common rules of international society. But that conduct need not be tolerated.

NOTES

1. Helpful discussions of the expression "legal positivism" include Roberto Ago, "Positive Law and International Law," *American Journal of International Law* 51 (1957): 691–733; H.L.A. Hart, *The Concept of Law* (Oxford: Oxford University Press, 1961), 253; and Aulis Aarnio, "Form and Content in Law: Dimensions and Definitions of Legal Positivism," *Philosophical Perspectives on Jurisprudence*, Acta Philosophica Fennica, vol. 36 (Helsinki: Philosophical Society of Finland, 1983), 76–93.

2. There are two versions of this positivist definition of law as a system of rules with its own criteria of validity. "Inclusive legal positivism" holds that a legal system can include moral considerations among the criteria used to determine the validity of legal rules. "Exclusive legal positivism" denies this claim. For discussion of the controversy and a defense of the inclusive position, see W. J. Waluchow, *Inclusive Legal Positivism* (Oxford: Oxford University Press, 1994), especially ch. 4.

3. *The Province of Jurisprudence Determined* (London: Weidenfeld and Nicolson, 1955), 184.

4. For example, Georg Friedrich von Martens, *The Law of Nations: The Science of National Law, Covenants, Power, Etc. Founded upon the Treaties and Customs of Modern Nations in Europe*, 4th ed. (London: Cobbett, 1829).

5. There exists no "positive law of nations which has the force of a law, properly so called, such as binds nations as if it proceeded from a superior." Samuel Pufendorf, *The Law of Nature and of Nations* (Oxford: Oxford University Press, 1934; first published 1672), bk. 2, ch. 3, sect. 23. Locke also notes the absence in foreign affairs of "antecedent, standing, positive laws." John Locke, *Two Treatises of Government*, ed. P. Laslett (Cambridge: Cambridge University Press, 1988; first published 1690), II, sect. 147.

6. Murray Forsyth, "The Tradition of International Law," in Terry Nardin and David R. Mapel, eds., *Traditions of International Ethics* (Cambridge: Cambridge University Press, 1992), 36–38.

7. For Hart's views on this question see, besides *The Concept of Law*, his *Essays in Jurisprudence and Philosophy* (Oxford: Oxford University Press, 1983).

8. Positivism and common law are distinguished by Gerald J. Postema, *Bentham and the Common Law Tradition* (Oxford: Oxford University Press, 1986).

9. Hart, *Concept of Law*, ch. 5.

10. As European publicists put it, perhaps hyperbolically, where there is law there is society and where there is society there is law: *ubi societas ibi ius*. John Westlake, *Collected Papers* (Cambridge: Cambridge University Press, 1914), 2; J. L. Brierly, *The Law of Nations*, 6th ed. (Oxford: Oxford University Press, 1963), 41. This postulated conceptual interdependence of international society and international law is characteristic of the entire internationalist or "Grotian" tradition, which embraces both natural law and positivist views.

11. On *ius inter gentes* as distinct from *ius gentium* see Richard Zouche, *An Exposition of Fecial Law and Procedure or of Law between Nations* (Washington, D.C.: The Carnegie Endowment, 1911; first published in 1650), 1–2; and Samuel Rachel, *Dissertations on the Law of Nature and of Nations* (Washington, D.C.: The Carnegie Endowment, 1916; first published in 1676), 157–58.

12. Hedley Bull, *The Anarchical Society: A Study of Order in World Politics* (London: Macmillan, 1977). For Bull, the idea of international society is not self-contradictory but corresponds to a distinctive form of social order.

13. Torsten Gihl, *International Legislation* (Oxford: Oxford University Press, 1937), 57–64. As Frederick Whelan observes, it is a parochial conception resting on a narrowly European "standard of civilization." See Chapter 2 below, under "Diversity."

14. Gihl, *International Legislation*, 20, 46–47; Gerald G. Fitzmaurice, "Some Problems Regarding the Formal Sources of International Law," *Symbolae Verzijl* (The Hague: Martinus Nijhoff, 1958), 157–60.

15. Terry Nardin, *Law, Morality, and the Relations of States* (Princeton: Princeton University Press, 1983), 68; see also 36–37 and 271.

16. See Chapter 2 below, under "Constitution."

17. For more on this difficulty in Kant's theory, see the chapters in this volume by Laberge and Tesón.

18. *Leviathan*, ch. 30.

19. Hart, *Concept of Law*, ch. 2; Michael Oakeshott, "The Rule of Law," in Oakeshott, *On History and Other Essays* (Oxford: Basil Blackwell, 1983), 129.

20. An early effort to explore how the rule of law can exist in the absence of civil institutions and therefore in a society of states is Henry Sumner Maine, *International Law* (New York: Henry Holt, 1888). See also Nardin, *Law, Morality, and the Relations of States*, ch. 7.

21. Oakeshott, "Rule of Law," 141.

22. According to Whelan, rule of law positivism is a "proposal" that a legal system "ought as a whole to be nonpurposive, consisting only of formal rules allowing for the peaceful coexistence of diverse and independent agents, whose various individual purposes and values are afforded equal respect." But what Oakeshott offers, as a theorist of rule of law positivism, is not a proposal but a philosophical definition designed to distinguish the rule of law from a teleocratic order whose laws are instruments used by the powerful to achieve their purposes. For Whelan's judgment, see Chapter 2 under "Justice."

23. Lon L. Fuller, *The Morality of Law*, Revised Edition (New Haven: Yale University Press, 1969), 39 and passim.

24. Michael Oakeshott, *On Human Conduct* (Oxford: Oxford University Press, 1975), 128.

25. Oakeshott, "Rule of Law," 142–44.

26. Lassa Oppenheim, *International Law*, vol. 1 (London: Longmans, Green and Co., 1905), 10.

27. Hans Kelsen, *General Theory of Law and State* (Cambridge, MA: Harvard University Press, 1945), 110.

28. Hart, *Concept of Law*, 113.

29. Torsten Gihl, "The Legal Character and Sources of International Law," *Scandinavian Studies in Law* 1 (1957): 53–71; Ago, "Positive Law and International Law," 691–733; and Hart, *The Concept of Law*, 226–31.

30. Oppenheim, *International Law*, 14.

31. Georges Scelle, "Le phénomène juridique du dédoublement fonctionnel," in Walter Schätzel and Hans-Jürgen Schlochauser, eds., *Rechtsfragen der Internationalen Organisation* (Frankfurt-am-Main: Klostermann, 1956), 324–42.

32. Oakeshott, "Rule of Law," 138. But see Friedman, Chapter 2 below, at p. 77.

33. Thomas Hobbes, *Elements of Law*, bk. 2, ch. 10, sect. 10; *Philosophical Rudiments*, ch. 14, sect. 15; *Leviathan*, ch. 26. Austin's view is the same; see *Province of Jurisprudence Determined*, 31–32.

34. Gihl, *International Legislation*, 26–53; Hersh Lauterpacht, *International Law*, vol. 1 (Cambridge: Cambridge University Press, 1970), 59, 196, 236–37.

35. Hart, *Concept of Law*, ch. 2; Hobbes, *Leviathan*, ch. 15; Jeremy Bentham, *Of Laws in General* (London: Athlone Press, 1970), 3. Emphasis added in both quotations.

36. Gerald Fitzmaurice, "The General Principles of International Law Considered from the Standpoint of the Rule of Law," The Hague Academy of International Law, *Recueil des cours* 92 (1957): 45.

37. Bentham, *Of Laws in General*, 133–35; Hart, *Concept of Law*, 27–35, 38–41, and 84. On the relation between validity and effectiveness, see Kelsen, *The Pure*

Theory of Law (Berkeley and Los Angeles: University of California Press, 1967), 211–14.

38. Pufendorf, *Law of Nature and of Nations*, bk. 8, ch. 4, sect. 20; Christian Wolff, *Jus Gentium Methodo Scientifica Pertractatum* (Oxford: Clarendon Press, 1934, first published 1764), Prolegomena, sect. 16.

CHAPTER 2

Legal Positivism and International Society

FREDERICK G. WHELAN

FOR POLITICAL theorists, legal positivism was founded by Thomas Hobbes, who offered a version of the doctrine that remains influential. Hobbes held that law was nothing other than the "command" or declaration of the will of a sovereign addressed to people under an obligation to obey; all genuine law had to be "posited" in this way, hence positive law. In a parallel formulation, Hobbes maintained that "it is not Wisdom, but Authority that makes a Law": valid law issued from legitimate authority, and neither its validity as law nor its obligatoriness could be challenged in the name of reason or of any extraneous standard supplied by (private) reason. Hobbes also held that effective law, promulgated and enforced by a sovereign, was a prerequisite for the existence of society. In a state of nature, the condition of human beings without sovereign authority, there was "no Society" in addition to many other disadvantages.[1] A lawless society was inconceivable. From these premises, it followed for Hobbes that since there was no higher-level sovereign, or no authoritative institutions standing above state sovereigns, there could be no international law, and hence no international society. Legal positivism in its original, Hobbesian form thus provides a simple, clear, and negative doctrine with respect to the topic of this book.

According to Hedley Bull, in contrast, we may speak of an international society of states, as distinguished from a mere "system of states," when a number of states, though independent, share a set of common interests, values, and institutions.[2] By these criteria, Hobbes would probably have argued that the existence of international society is unlikely, that empirical observation would probably confirm his deductive argument. In the absence of a world government of some kind, states could be expected to conduct themselves in an antisocial fashion, on the basis of competitive self-interest and power calculations. Of the institutions of international society discussed by Bull, some (war, diplomacy, and the balance of power) might exist in some form in a Hobbesian world on the basis of reciprocity or convention, but these practices and their rules would be much more unstable than if they reflected the shared purposes of a society in Bull's sense. Hobbesian legal positivism thus implies international realism as the correct descriptive and analytical theory of international relations.

John Austin, Hobbes's well-known follower in the development of legal positivism, agreed in a formal sense that there could be no international law "properly so-called" because there was no international political society with an habitually obeyed sovereign. Austin shared Hobbes's view that law was the command of a "political superior," capable of enforcing its will by means of sanctions;[3] at the very least, law had to have a "determinate source." Living in the nineteenth century, however, Austin could scarcely deny that there existed a well-developed body of rules and practices among European states that was called "international law." Austin solved this dilemma semantically by holding that these rules were not law but a form of "positive international morality." Unlike Hobbes, then, Austin believed that *moral* rules could exist and be practically effective, in some degree, in the absence of a sovereign, and by extension that *society*, including international society, could exist on the basis of positive morality, even without a sovereign and law. Although he accepted Hobbes's definition of law, he thus rejected other key elements of Hobbesian political theory, denying both that society presupposes law, and that morality itself is practically binding only within an orderly legal setting.[4] Austin's legal positivism, however, being a theory about law, had little to say about societies that rest on nonlegal foundations.

The most prominent twentieth-century legal positivists, H.L.A. Hart and Hans Kelsen, reformulate the doctrine in ways that allow them to regard international law as genuine (though defective) law, despite its ineffectiveness in comparison with national or intrastate law. They do this by dropping the definitional requirement that law must be the "command of a sovereign," although this change is less significant than it may appear. Contemporary legal positivists have been concerned to identify the characteristics of law and legal systems that differentiate these from other systems of normative rules such as custom and morality. For Kelsen, legal rules constitute a centralized system of norms, but their defining feature is their enforcement by coercive sanctions; for Hart, the key feature is the presence of "secondary rules" that identify a particular legal system and specify the officials who are to perform such functions as declaring and applying primary legal rules. Kelsen places more emphasis on enforcement, Hart on the "recognition," of valid laws. For both Hart and Kelsen, then, law properly understood implies, if not a sovereign, at least a system of acknowledged authority with recognition and enforcement capabilities. As Hobbes said, it is authority that makes law. It is the apparent weakness of the system of constituted authority in international society that makes international law defective for modern legal positivists, even if they are prepared to grant its existence.

Hobbes's theory addresses the conditions of a society of individuals under a sovereign; it also considers the idea of a society of sovereigns. Of what entities is contemporary international society composed? What are the criteria for membership in this society? Legal positivism has been more concerned with international law than with international society as such. International law in its traditional form, with its recognition of sovereign states as the sole subjects of law, indicates that in a legal perspective we should think of international society as a society of states. It is true that in recent decades other entities, such as international organizations and, for some purposes, individuals, have acquired standing in international law and recognition in world politics, complicating the question of international society or enlarging the range of possibilities. Nevertheless, since independent states are still the most important international entities, the following discussion of the legal positivist perspective on international society will largely be oriented to the idea of a society of states.

A society of states united in its members' mutual acknowledgment of international law is the ("Vattelian") conception of international relations that is expressed in classical international law and is conceptually related to classical liberalism. This conception views sovereign states as legal persons, relying on an analogy between states and natural individuals as bearers of legal status, rights, and obligations.[5] It may be justified by such a doctrine as Beitz labels the "morality of states,"[6] though this enterprise of justification lies well beyond the scope of legal positivism. If we think of a society as united by a common interest, it would seem that the minimal common interest of the society of states is the preservation of this society and the political order it creates in the world, and therefore also the maintenance of the system of international law that defines this society and assigns to sovereign states a privileged position in it.

The claim of states to form an orderly society may be in tension with other conceivable forms of international society or sociability. Movements expressing "transnational solidarity," as Bull points out, may undermine the society of states, though of course they need not: international Catholicism may have obstructed the emergence of the society of states in the early modern period, but it does not do so today. Other forms of transnational society (the community of scientists or the environmental movement, for example) may function in the framework of or alongside the society of states. Some groups that are left out of international society on this basis, however, or are disadvantaged by it (stateless minorities, for example), may challenge it with violence, in effect repudiating the claim made by states to a monopoly on the use of force or violence. The future course of fundamentalist Islam perhaps poses the most interesting question in this regard.

Society and Legality

The question of the nature of international society compels us to reflect on the meaning and sources of "society" as such, or of social order. Legal positivism indicates the role of law in creating social order. A society, it suggests, is a group of agents united in recognition of a set of laws, and agreement to abide by, and to be restrained by, these laws.[7] And it suggests that law can clearly be a source of order. International law could perform these functions for international society. Beyond this, since the members of international society (states) are artificial persons, they may be viewed as creations of the law, like corporations in domestic society. International law, by defining sovereign statehood and its legal status, therefore constitutes as well as regulates international society. Another important institution in the society of states is diplomacy, but the basic rules governing it are enshrined in international law, which therefore appears fundamental to international society in this respect as well.

Except in Hobbes's theory, however, legal positivism is not committed to the strong principle of *ubi societas ibi ius* that is maintained, according to Nardin, by some legal publicists, especially those in the Grotian tradition of international society.[8] This principle appears to assert either conceptual equivalence between society and a legal order, or that law is a necessary condition of society. It would seem, however, that "social" relations among people could exist on other foundations, such as custom, conventions, a common morality, or religious faith, all of which (though they could serve as sources of law as well) legal positivism would distinguish from law as such. Society could also rest on repeated economic transactions or simply on voluntary association expressed otherwise than economically, religiously, or legally. (An order, of some sort, among people and states can be attained in still other ways—through force, mutual deterrence, or a balance of power—though it could plausibly be denied that order produced in these ways should be thought of as "social.") Thus whatever its advantages for social order, it does not seem generally true that law is essential to the existence of society.

The case for the necessity of law may seem stronger for international society, especially if this is equated with a society of states whose members "understand themselves to be related to one another as subjects of common rules—a common law—defining the terms of their coexistence."[9] Certainly the modern, originally European, state system, with its distinctive juridical conception of sovereignty, developed in close conjunction with the modern European law of nations. But there are historical cases of international societies (ancient Greece and China, for example) that rested on religion or custom and apparently lacked any notion of international law.[10] Some Muslim thinkers maintain that an international society exists or should exist among Muslim states on the basis of their common religion (and perhaps on law also, but a law that is inextricably connected with religion in a manner that legal positivism cannot accommodate). The possibility that an international society might be a moral or religious community is surely foreign to legal positivism.

But legal positivism since Hobbes is not committed to the claim that a lawless society is an impossibility, or no society at all. It does not deny that other possibilities exist; as a doctrine about law, it simply has nothing to say about them. One could be a legal positivist with respect to one's understanding of law, and yet acknowledge that international society might more successfully rest on some other basis, particularly if one had doubts about the development of international law within a society of independent states. One would have to turn to other traditions for guidance, however.

Bull's analysis holds that international society requires rules, as a conceptual matter. Rules, however, can be of different kinds: legal, but also moral, religious, customary, prudential, or operational. Sometimes a rule will start as merely operational, then evolve into custom, and eventually attain the status of a recognized moral principle or international law.[11] Certain important rules of international politics, such as those governing the classical balance of power and, more recently, great power crisis management and arms control, appear to be merely operational rules or mutually useful conventions, not laws—and yet they express important common interests characteristic of a society.[12] Sometimes these distinctions are blurred, and it is not clear (and does not matter, for practical purposes) what precise status a rule has.

These points seem to be at variance with a basic contention of legal positivism—that legal rules are or should be essentially distinct from other types, and that a well-defined and autonomous legal system or authority is needed to identify them. Legal positivism acknowledges that a given rule can be both legal and moral (or customary, etc.), and that law can grow out of custom. But it insists that, if we are to speak of law, there must be a clear procedure for determining if a rule indeed has legal status. This is at odds with the developmental perspective sketched here, and seems arbitrary from the point of view of understanding international society.

In this section, I have questioned the claim that law is necessary to international society. We can also turn the question around and ask whether the existence of international law indicates the reality of international society, a point on which Bull and Nardin seem to agree. In some usages, as in classical political philosophy, to say that human beings are social is to deny that they are essentially selfish—to affirm that in some degree they are cooperative, can share common purposes, and work for a common good. Even essentially selfish people, however, can be fellow subjects of law, especially if it is enforced by an effective sovereign; and they can even agree to create a mutually restraining system of law, reflecting their minimal common interest in survival, as Hobbes showed.

Are independent states essentially selfish, as international realism claims? If so, the presence of international law does not mean that there is an international society, or any society in more than a minimal sense. Legal positivist techniques can help us to identify and describe international law, but they cannot tell us whether an international society in a stronger sense of the word exists. Contrary to the idea of *ubi societas ibi ius*, law might be neither a necessary nor a sufficient condition of society.

CONSTITUTION

A constitution or form of governance for international society could take a number of forms. We may think of the present arrangement—a society of independent states generally acknowledging international law, but with only rudimentary institutions for adjudication and enforcement—as a weak constitution. A stronger constitution, in varying degrees, might take the form of a confederation or union of states or even a world government. Legal positivism looks to law and a common legal system as the bond of international society; since international law could exist within any of these frameworks, it might be thought that legal positivism as such is indifferent among these possible constitutions.

Historically, however, legal positivism has been associated with the idea of sovereignty and with effective, de facto enforcement as criteria for genuine law. Although legal positivism sometimes claims to be simply a form of analytical jurisprudence, it has historically functioned as a normative doctrine or ideology supporting such objectives as legal neutrality and formality, and the modern centralized state as the provider of the rule of law.[13] I will argue, therefore, that the tendency of legal positivism is to favor the development of a world state or some other strong constitution for international society, thereby making its law less imperfect than it now is.

The doctrine of legal positivism was originally developed in conjunction with the rise of the modern state and its program to locate legislative supremacy and a monopoly of compulsory jurisdiction in its central government. Although twentieth-century legal positivists have omitted the reference to "the sovereign" that was so conspicuous in the Hobbes-Austin version of the doctrine, they continue to include authority and enforcement as hallmarks of valid law, and these concepts imply the need for a government with attributes of sovereignty, whether or not this term is used. Kelsen points to coercive sanctions as the distinctive feature of a system of legal norms in a way that is reminiscent of Austin's argument that actual compliance and enforcement are necessary aspects of true law. Hart relates law to the existence of a legal system defined by "secondary rules" that identify a set of actual officials and stipulate procedures by which the officials are empowered to perform such functions as recognition, change, adjudication, and enforcement of the primary legal rules. In considering whether law may be said to exist in a given setting (such as international society), Kelsen's theory tells us to look for the system of sanctions, which may be decentralized but must nonetheless operate; Hart also invites us to identify the "system," with its recognized officials and common practices, through which law is (at a minimum) authoritatively "recognized."

As an analytic theory, legal positivism provides criteria for determining whether a legal order exists, and for describing it. To the extent that legal positivism has a prescriptive dimension, however, it presumably recommends the development and perfection of legal orders in accordance with its analytic criteria.[14] Thus, when a legal order is imperfect, as in the case of international law, because its sanctions or its system of secondary rules are underdeveloped, the implicit program of legal positivism is to strengthen these institutions. The effect of such a program would be the development of a stronger government or constitution for international society, one that would ensure greater effectiveness for international law. Since legal positivism originated as a description of the civil law and the legal systems of sovereign states, it is not surprising that the doctrine implicitly wants international law to resemble state law, which it could do to the extent that something approximating a world state exists.

This argument diverges from Nardin's views. In *Law, Morality, and the Relations of States*, Nardin denies—in opposition to legal positivism as I have outlined it here—that legislation and enforcement are essential features of law or of a law-governed society. More problematically, he denies that the "certainty" or determinate quality of legal rules that is the product of authoritative adjudication is necessary. It is an error, he suggests, to demand of law in general the institutional arrangements and formal characteristics typical of law within states.[15] Legal positivism, however, tends to do precisely this, even if contemporary advocates have softened the original doctrine. Leaving aside the need for a "sovereign" legislator and enforcer, that is, even Hart insists at least on "rules of recognition" by which it can be established with some certainty what the law is, and these and other secondary rules must be supported by a "practice" or a functioning legal "system."[16]

In his chapter, Nardin correctly points out that legal positivism insists on the "autonomy" of law, but he neglects the institutional, as opposed to the conceptual, dimension of this autonomy, and avoids the problem of enforcement. The result is that the conception of "rule of law positivism" that he derives from within the legal positivist perspective consists merely of a standard for the content of international law. I suggest in contrast that a program that better reflects the historical spirit of legal positivism would aim to enhance the effectiveness of international law by improving it as a system, strengthening its courts and enforcement mechanisms and its authoritative recognition procedures. The tendency of such a program would be toward a world state with sovereign or quasi-sovereign attributes. Legal positivism remains Hobbesian at heart, even if we do not have to think simplistically in terms of the commands of a single and absolute ruler.[17]

In the absence of centralized political authority that could enforce law in the manner of a state, I offer two other comments regarding the character of international society. When they have not dismissed international law as illusory or as a form of "positive morality," legal positivists have concluded that it is a special—usually an imperfect or defective—kind of legal system. They often compare it to primitive law, which also exists in societies that lack a centralized state and therefore relies on decentralized sanctions.[18] Bull, drawing on Hart's analysis of law, suggests that international law resembles primitive law in that it is a set of primary rules without clear secondary rules of recognition, adjudication, and change.[19] Whatever its limitations, however, primitive law has existed and been effective in some societies.

If international law resembles primitive law, then international society perhaps resembles primitive society in other respects, including the nature of its constitution or enforcement machinery, which we should then consider more closely. I shall not pursue this here, except to note that stateless law may depend on a recognized practice of "self-help," including aid from one's neighbors or from law-minded bystanders.[20] Although a self-help system may be able to generate some degree of legal order, this concept points to two further difficulties of international law in a decentralized world of independent states: it cannot be enforced *against* the stronger states; and, in being enforced mainly *by* them, it is likely to be seen by some as a guise for promoting the interests of strong states. Either way, cynicism detrimental to international society may result. Alternatively, as in Kelsen's discussion, primitive-type law may depend on a variety of coercive actions (including informal sanctions) taken by the "community" as a whole against offenders.[21] Among these sanctions, public opinion has been noticed as a sometimes effective force in both primitive and international society, and might be thought of as a constitutional principle of international society, just as Kant and others have argued that publicity should be a constitutional principle of the liberal state.

Finally, mention may be made of the claim that, in the absence of a world state, international law depends on reciprocity and especially on the balance of power.[22] Vattel believed that the balance of power was a necessary foundation for the international society of Europe, and he accordingly sought to make it (and conduct designed to promote it) part of the law of nations. Alternatively, if the balance of power serves as a substitute for a sovereign in making possible the legal order on which international society rests, it may be thought of as an element of the constitution of international society. Bull considers the balance of power itself as an institution of international society, which seems plausible if it is an openly acknowledged policy thought to express a common interest of states.

Alternatively, the balance of power might be thought to arise from and to confirm Hobbesian or realist assumptions about the behavior of states. This would suggest the paradox that a phenomenon expressive of the antisocial nature of states (their love of power and domination) indirectly provides the constitutional framework for the society of states. There is also the lesser paradox that the balance of power, although it aims at international order, may have to be sustained by force; this simply parallels the point that law in general, at least in legal positivist analysis, requires coercive sanctions to supplement its normative force, even though its end is peaceful (noncoercive) relations among the members of society. These considerations point to the difficulty that international law might obstruct as well as promote world order. International law in some versions condemns state actions (such as preemptive wars) that may be necessary to sustain the balance of power, which would be self-defeating if indeed the balance of power is the necessary foundation for international law. International law may also cast doubt on "self-help" methods used to punish rogue states and in other aberrant cases, even though the long-term effect might be favorable to world order.

JUSTICE

Probably the most familiar feature of legal positivism is its insistence on a conceptual and practical distinction between law and morality, despite the similarity between these as alternative sets of norms, and the actual overlap and historical connections between them. Legal positivism is a form of analytical jurisprudence that sets out to define the essential features of law and to systematically describe actual systems of law. Over and above this, legal positivism insists that the only true law is actual—"positive"—law, and that all actual law that fulfills the theory's formal criteria is thereby valid, whatever its relation to morality. Legal positivism as such does not question the validity of moral principles; it need not be committed to moral relativism or any other metaethical position. Nor does legal positivism deny the possibility of such a project as "ideal jurisprudence," or what Bentham and Austin called the "science of legislation," in which actual law is evaluated by reference to morality, and proposals are made as to what the law ought to be. But legal positivism (the "science of jurisprudence") itself has no doctrines or proposals regarding such matters.

Although I argued earlier that it implicitly recommends the development of an effective legal system, legal positivism as such is therefore incomplete as a normative theory of law or more generally of political institutions and arrangements. Legal positivism might contribute to the analysis of a phenomenon such as international society; but insofar as we are interested in how international society ought ideally to be organized, and want to formulate prescriptions for its desirable development, legal positivism has little or nothing to offer.

Legal positivism frequently seems to repudiate morality (at least when moral considerations intrude into adjudication), but in fact it needs to be supplemented by ethical notions in order to be a complete theory. One can sense this felt need in the history of the doctrine: in the fact that Austin was a utilitarian (in ethics and politics) as well as a legal positivist, who assumed that judges would or should decide ambiguous cases in accordance with utility;[23] in the intellectually, as well as morally, unsatisfying quality of American legal realism, which faced an ethical void in which law appeared as sheer power;[24] and in Ronald Dworkin's project to exhibit moral principles embedded within legal traditions.

With respect to justice, a distinction must be drawn. One can plausibly argue that some form of legal or procedural justice is part of the concept of valid law, or of what would count as a "legal" system (as distinguished from a system of arbitrary political power or the nonlegal commands of a sovereign). Even Hobbes said that were a sovereign to punish an innocent person, or to condemn someone by an ex post facto law or without a hearing or other due process, his act could not properly be termed "justice" or legal "punishment" for a "crime," but would be a hostile act inflicted on an enemy.[25] Hart, too, upholds legal justice or the "principles of legality," such as deciding similar cases by "the same general rule, without prejudice, interest, or caprice."[26] Legal positivism thus endorses procedural justice within a legal order, and it could contribute to the development of this concept with special reference to international law.

But justice, as Hart emphasizes, is also a moral concept indicating the criteria for fair or fitting distributions of the goods of society, and it can in this sense serve as a standard for assessing the moral propriety of laws or of the content of an entire system of law. Some have attempted to work out theories of distributive justice for the international society of states, and the contemporary doctrine of human rights expresses a transnational idea of justice in the treatment of individuals. Ideas of justice like these, being moral conceptions, are extraneous to law and to that extent are outside the purview of legal positivism.

Moral principles can of course be incorporated into law or inspire the reform of legal rules. Principles of international distributive justice and human rights could therefore become part of international law; the latter, in some form, have arguably done so. One of the problems of international law, which legal positivists have pointed out, is that in the absence of well-defined rules of recognition or a legislature it is sometimes not evident when a moral or customary rule has in fact become part of law, and the procedures for such incorporation are ambiguous or controversial. Legal positivism is certainly interested in conceptions of international justice insofar as they have been accepted as legally obligatory. More importantly, legal positivist analysis might, through Hart's account of the importance of secondary rules, contribute to developing and specifying the procedures by which justice and other ideals are to receive recognition as international law.

Nardin describes a possible conception for international society, "rule of law positivism," which he believes can be defended from within the legal positivist perspective. To some extent, this conception appears to express norms of procedural justice that may be included in the idea of legality, and that legal positivism can therefore probably accommodate.[27] But although Nardin denies that rule of law positivism embraces an idea of justice in the moral sense, I believe that it does import a substantive, nonlegal norm into positivist analysis in a way that strict legal positivism cannot endorse. Rule of law positivism expresses the Oakeshottian idea that a large-scale legal (or social) order ought as a whole to be nonpurposive, consisting only of formal rules allowing for the peaceful coexistence of diverse and independent agents, whose various individual purposes and values are afforded equal respect. International society under this conception would be a *societas* and not a *universitas* with a common end.[28] This proposal seems at first glance to conflict with Bull's argument that international society, like any society as opposed to a mere system of interacting agents, should be defined in terms of the common interests and values of its members; it may be, though, that Bull is thinking only of such elementary (Hobbesian) common interests as peace, order, and agreement keeping, whereas Oakeshott and Nardin mean to rule out more specific or substantive purposes. The requirement of nonpurposiveness in international law is also questionable in light of the common assumption that a better-organized international society is desirable precisely in order to deal with pressing transnational problems, such as global environmental concerns, which would define common purposes.

In any case, it seems to me that rule of law positivism goes beyond the principles of legality as such to express a conception of what international law ought to be; it is therefore a contribution to ideal jurisprudence or normative political theory. However attractive a proposal it may be, it is not one that can be derived from or could be endorsed by legal positivism, which could equally well acknowledge the lawful quality of a system of international rules that united its subjects in a common purpose or common identity. The conception presented by Nardin is therefore better understood as expressing a particular ideal of justice or a just society in a supralegal sense.

This is an appropriate point to recall the condemnation of legal positivism offered by Friedrich Hayek, whose ideal of a "nomocracy" resembles Oake-shott's *societas* or the legal order of Nardin's rule of law positivism. According to Hayek, the formal or nonpurposive "laws of justice" that are characteristic of a liberal society or nomocracy tend to evolve from moral and customary rules. The kinds of laws that are explicitly enacted or posited by political authority, as in the legal positivist model, tend to be the rules of a "teleo-cracy," or of the state considered as an "organization," and are accordingly instrumental to the collective purposes that define the organization or are decided upon by its rulers. Modern legal positivists, Hayek says, have usually been public lawyers or "organization men . . . who can think of order only as organization," rather than as arising spontaneously among free agents under rules of justice. Legal positivism, historically associated with Hobbesian sovereignty and nineteenth-century utilitarianism, is in the twentieth century the legal ideology of socialism, constructivism, and "the omnipotence of the legislative power."[29] According to this interpretation, Nardin's conception of a rule of law for international society would probably derive more support from natural law or some other perspective rather than from legal positivism. The latter doctrine, by endorsing relatively strong and well-defined authoritative institutions, might lend itself to more purposive conceptions of international law and society than the arrangement that Nardin describes.

AUTHORITY

The authority of international law is clearly distinguished in legal positivism from its justice or moral goodness. I take the authority of law to be equivalent to what is often termed its validity, which in turn implies the presence of legal obligation on the part of the law's subjects. The validity of law depends on its source—on its promulgation through correct procedures by a legitimate sovereign or government, in line with Kelsen's "basic norm" of the system, or in Hart's version through its authoritative "recognition" by appropriate officials in accordance with generally accepted secondary rules. Rules of recognition, in turn, are simply established by standard practices within an acknowledged legal system, such as normally exists within a state (at least in periods of political stability); positivist analysis describes such practices but takes them as given, thus avoiding regress. Since the existence of such practices and such a system are less clear in international society, however, the validity or authority of international law is usually more questionable than that of national law. A legal positivist approach to international society would focus on the status of the secondary rules of international law and its authoritative institutions, seeking ways to strengthen them if a more robust international society is considered desirable.

In this section, I will comment on two issues having to do with both the determinateness and the scope of international law. First, in the positivist tradition of the past two hundred years, three sources of international law have been considered important: the customary practices of civilized states; treaties reflecting the express consent of sovereign states; and the consensus of jurists, statesmen, and diplomats professionally involved in the relations among states. Legal positivist analysis could attempt to work out the rules of recognition (not always unambiguous, to be sure) implicit in each of these sources. Of them, Nardin makes a case for the preferability of customary international law, but it seems to me there are two difficulties that should be weighed against the advantages of custom.

First, treaty law is normally more precise and clear than customary law (like statute law in comparison with common law), especially because what counts as customary practice in international society is controversial. This is a practical difficulty, but it is also a theoretical one in legal positivism, which seeks well-defined rules of recognition because it tends to associate the validity of law with its certainty, which is in turn a condition of the predictability of its enforcement. The determinateness of law is one of the things that typically differentiate it from morality and custom and give it special authority. Legal positivism of course acknowledges that custom can be a source of law, but only if customary rules are taken over, recognized, and given legal expression by clear procedures.[30] The underdevelopment of procedures and institutions for doing this internationally usually makes legal positivists as uncomfortable with custom as with morality as a source of international law.

Second, treaty law, being voluntaristic or consent based, clearly binds only those states that are parties to an agreement. Nardin holds that customary international law is more inclusive—a point in its favor.[31] In the natural law tradition, custom and consensus may be taken as evidence of a higher and generally obligatory moral law. But in the positivist tradition, custom is part of what used to be called the "voluntary law of nations," presumed to reflect the will or the implied consent of states and deriving its obligatoriness from this source. As a practical matter, the presumption of consent may indeed make customary law somewhat more inclusive than treaty law; but customary law cannot be held to bind states that do not actually follow the custom in question, and furthermore any state can renounce an alleged customary law by expressly dissenting from it. Customary law is not self-validating, as Nardin says, except for those who accept and follow it.

This point raises the question of the scope of international society, which may or may not be universal. If international society is constituted by the international legal order, then any state that renounces this law can opt out of international society, which in the positivist perspective must be a voluntary association in some sense. Whether one turns to custom or treaties, it seems impossible to guarantee that international law (and society) will be all-inclusive. Only a world state with legislative power could ensure this.

My second general observation concerns the problem of "hard cases" that is much discussed in relation to legal positivism. It is frequently the case in the real world that legal rules are ambiguous or that the law is unsettled: that what the law requires in a particular case is not clear. This poses a special difficulty for legal positivism because of its demand for certainty in law, and because when faced with adjudicating a hard case, judges are apt to seek guidance from extralegal considerations, thereby undermining the legal positivist's case for the autonomy of law. In international law, moreover, precisely because of the weakness of the secondary rules, what Hart calls the "core" of certain rules may be smaller, and the "penumbra" of uncertainty greater, than in national law.[32] The problem of how to deal with hard cases may therefore be especially troublesome in international law, detracting from its authority or legitimacy, and legal positivism's embarrassment on this issue may lessen its usefulness in constructing international society.

How should judges decide hard cases? The "realist" answer is simply that judges in effect legislate, imposing their own preferences or political beliefs. The view that the law is simply what judges say it is, while consistent with positivism (at least in its descriptive versions), has never been very satisfactory, and it is never openly admitted by judges, since it delegitimizes law by equating it with politics or power. This view would be especially corrosive of international law, and therefore destabilizing for international society, where the nationality of a particular judge would often be an invidious factor over and above those (such as ideology) that interfere with judicial impartiality domestically.

Hart's solution appears to be that judges should turn to considerations of public policy, at least when policy objectives can be inferred from the legal rule under consideration, or from relevant parts of the legal core.[33] It is questionable, however, whether most rules of international law embody social-policy purposes in the way that many domestic laws do; and it may be that references to policy aims would be contentious, or even that the concept of "policy" is altogether out of place in this context. Hart's assumption that laws advance society's collective purposes certainly appears to be in conflict with the formal requirements of Nardin's rule of law positivism.

Finally, although this is not a move of which legal positivism approves, judges can be guided by moral principles. Again though, depending on its basis, international society may not have a generally accepted morality to which judges could appeal, and it seems unlikely to have a legal tradition of the sort from which Dworkin believes appropriate principles can be extracted at the national level. I conclude that legal positivism's acknowledgment of hard cases, along with its lack of a solution that would command confidence in the international arena, constitutes a weakness in this perspective with respect to international society.

DIVERSITY

International society may consist, at a minimum, in a consensus among states on a set of rules and institutions that sustain orderly relations and a few other common interests among them. Bull argues strikingly, however, that international societies in the past have always rested on a deeper common culture among the member states—whether religion or the nineteenth-century European "standard of civilization"—that has provided a framework of basic values and mutual trust.[34] The international system, however, today contains many more, and more culturally diverse, states than in the past. Can this system constitute a stable international society? The contemporary system represents an expansion of the European states system, formally based on the idea of the sovereign state and international law as these were originally developed in Europe. Can such Western conceptions provide the necessary elements for a stable international society that embraces the entire world?

Since legal positivism suggests the crucial role of law in international society, a historical perspective on international law may be helpful. At the beginning of the nineteenth century, a positivist approach—one that derived international law inductively from the actual practices and agreements of states—displaced the more deductive and rationalistic natural law approach that had been dominant in the era of Grotius to Vattel. The natural law-based law of nations claimed to be universally valid, its European provenance a mere accident. Non-Westerners nevertheless sometimes reject it as parochial, based on distinctively European philosophical concepts, and resent what they see as its implicit denial of the claims of other cultures. Nineteenth-century positivist international law, in contrast, was openly parochial, recognizing as law only the rules observed by European states and admitting other states to the legal community only insofar as they measured up to the "standard of civilization" dictated by European customs.[35] Since legal positivism does not say what law ought to be, but only certifies the validity of actually existing law, the question for international society is whether a positivist analysis in the 1990s can confirm that an international legal system transcending Europe and accommodating the diversity of the world exists or is in the process of development.

Nardin defends an international variant of the contemporary liberal view that cultural diversity is both legitimate and valuable, and that a polity based on the rule of law is not only compatible with but requires tolerance of diversity. International law can accommodate states with different cultures, just as national law can regulate a multicultural society, especially if the law reflects the formality, procedural justice, and nonpurposiveness called for by rule of law positivism. The creation of a law that is neutral and "above moral conflict," and therefore compatible with diversity, has indeed been appreciated by liberals as the practical (though implicit) aim of legal positivism's separation of law and morals.[36]

Again, however, it seems to me that this argument combines conceptions of legality with a substantive liberal philosophical principle. Although liberals value the rule of law, this in itself does not prescribe tolerance of diversity, which reflects a value that may or may not be embodied in the content of law. Certainly there is nothing in legal positivism that specifically endorses diversity; legal systems that are friendly or hostile to this value can equally be embraced in its analysis.[37]

It is not clear if Nardin means to reject the thesis that international society requires a common culture, or, alternatively, to suggest that we should regard the consensus on law and the legal culture required to sustain international law as a viable practice as sufficient ingredients of a common international culture, one that is superimposed on cultural diversity at a lower and deeper level. The latter view is an optimistic one and seems to be supported by the almost universal acceptance of Western-style diplomatic conventions and by at least some elements of originally European international law. One should note that this scheme requires general acceptance of something like the legal positivist conception of law as autonomous (and thus thoroughly secular—not attached to religion—for example), and probably indeed of something like the Oakeshottian conception of a nonpurposive legal order. These ideas might seem to be rather specialized products of modern Western and liberal thought. One has to wonder if the apparent consensus, such as it is, represents in some cases merely a superficial elite culture of Westernism and modernism that we may expect to be challenged, when they have the means, by genuine representatives of non- or anti-Western societies.

The disintegration of communism, which in its early days repudiated international law and the existing society of states as bourgeois phenomena, has reduced the ideological diversity of the world. Genuine cultural diversity seems to exist, however, and may increase in its capacity to direct state policies and thus to challenge both existing international law as well as other possible foundations of international society.[38] Conflict between universalistic ideologies like liberalism and communism seemed particularly threatening to international society, since each denied the other's claim to legitimacy; cultural differences might or might not be more benign, depending on how hegemonic their aspirations. At the least, cultural rejection of Western-style international law could lead some states to opt out of a consensual international society to the detriment of this ideal. Religious fundamentalism, xenophobic nationalism, and the development of East Asian ("Confucian") civilization are probably the most important elements of diversity that will have a bearing on the nature and scope of international society in the near future.

NOTES

1. Thomas Hobbes, *Leviathan* (Harmondsworth, UK: Penguin, 1972), 312, 186; *A Dialogue between a Philosopher and a Student of the Common Laws of England*, ed. Joseph Cropsey (Chicago: University of Chicago Press, 1971), 55.

2. Hedley Bull, *The Anarchical Society* (New York: Columbia University Press, 1977).

3. Austin treats sovereignty and law entirely in terms of enforcement and obedience. More recent versions of legal positivism generally hold that legal norms are both coercive and normative.

4. John Austin, *The Province of Jurisprudence Determined* and *The Uses of the Study of Jurisprudence*, introduced by H.L.A. Hart (New York: Humanities Press, 1965), 133, 139–42, 200.

5. On the background to this classical conception, see Frederick G. Whelan, "Vattel's Doctrine of the State," *History of Political Thought* 9 (1988): 76–85.

6. Charles R. Beitz, *Political Theory and International Relations* (Princeton, NJ: Princeton University Press, 1979), pt. 2.

7. In Cicero's famous formula, a *consensus iuris* was a necessary part of the basis of a republic rather than society. Perhaps this is why the classical international jurists, such as Vattel, were fond of saying that the nations of Europe, sovereign yet joined in recognition of the *ius gentium*, formed a kind of great republic. It could also be said that they formed an international society.

8. Terry Nardin, "Legal Positivism as a Theory of International Society," Chapter 1 above, n. 10.

9. Nardin, Chapter 1 above, under "Society."

10. Bull, *Anarchical Society*, 142.

11. Bull, *Anarchical Society*, 67. This account of the evolution of rules is similar to Hume's account of the origins of the "rules of justice" and government in his *Treatise*, as I summarize that account in "Hume and Contractarianism," *Polity* 27 (1994).

12. Bull, *Anarchical Society*, 115.

13. On legal positivism as an ideology allied with liberalism, see Judith N. Shklar, *Legalism: Law, Morals, and Political Trials* (Cambridge, MA: Harvard University Press, 1964), pt. 1.

14. The common characterization of legal positivism as an "analytic" theory covers an ambiguity. Insofar as it is a descriptive theory, it cannot sustain its usual claim that law is distinct from morality, since the two are in fact often mingled in practice. Insofar as it is a conceptual or definitional (or, for Kelsen, a "pure") theory, it is normative in effect, and not merely analytical: to define law as "a system of sanctioned norms," for example, is to delegitimize or label defective so-called law that is insufficiently systematic, sanctioned, or normative, or to recommend that it acquire these features. See Philip Soper, *A Theory of Law* (Cambridge, MA: Harvard University Press, 1984), 37–38.

15. Terry Nardin, *Law, Morality, and the Relations of States* (Princeton, NJ: Princeton University Press, 1983), 132–38.

16. Hart notes the deficits, in these respects, of international law, thereby raising once again doubt about whether international law is *really* law at all by his own criteria. H.L.A. Hart, *The Concept of Law* (Oxford: Oxford University Press, 1961), 214, 218, 228–31.

17. Cf. Lyons's construction of an Austinian response to Hart, to the effect that its imperative quality and sanctions are what distinguish law from other normative rules; David Lyons, *Ethics and the Rule of Law* (Cambridge: Cambridge University Press, 1984), 45. Although its sanctions are weak, international law fits the Austinian model in that its rules are largely imperative or restrictive of the actions of states, rather than power creating.

18. Hans Kelsen insists on this analogy in *General Theory of Law and State*, trans. Anders Wedberg (Cambridge, MA: Harvard University Press, 1945), 338–41. See also Hart, *Concept of Law*, 89–90, and the discussion in Nardin, *Law, Morality, and the Relations of States*, 150–52.

19. Bull, *The Anarchical Society*, 135.

20. A version of this idea is expressed juridically in the diffused "right of execution" of natural law in Locke's state of nature.

21. If "community" sanctions in primitive law depend on the homogeneity of a tribal society, however, this analogy seems unhelpful for international society.

22. Bull, *Anarchical Society*, 108–110.

23. H.L.A. Hart, "Positivism and the Separation of Law and Morals," in his *Essays in Jurisprudence and Philosophy* (Oxford: Oxford University Press, 1983), 65–66.

24. Some legal positivists, including Kelsen, have sought to distinguish law from mere expressions of political power as well as from morality, that is, to shield it from politicization or ideological contamination. It is difficult to see how this can be achieved, however, insofar as law reflects the will (albeit generalized) of a political sovereign, and thus of whatever moral or ideological forces control the legislature.

25. Hobbes, *Leviathan*, 324–25, 339, 354.

26. Hart, *Concept of Law*, 157, 202.

27. Fuller, who makes principles of legality (the "inner morality of the law") central to his critique of legal positivism, claims that Hart's theory "systematically exclude[s]" this aspect of true law. Lon L. Fuller, *The Morality of Law*, rev. ed. (New Haven, CT: Yale University Press, 1969), 133. Hart denies this charge in *Concept of Law*, 202. "Neglects" might be a more accurate term.

28. Michael Oakeshott, *On Human Conduct* (Oxford: Oxford University Press, 1975), ch. 3.

29. Friedrich A. Hayek, *The Mirage of Social Justice*, vol. 2 of *Law, Legislation, and Liberty* (Chicago: University of Chicago Press, 1978), 46, 53.

30. Hart, *Concept of Law*, 45.

31. There is also the logical point that treaty law depends on the rule that *pacta servanda sunt*, which must be derived from a source more fundamental than treaties, whether custom, consensus, or morality (natural law).

32. We should recall Dworkin's rejection of Hart's statement of the problem, and his argument that hard cases may arise at the core of the law, reflecting disagreement on fundamental issues. See Ronald Dworkin, *Law's Empire* (Cambridge, MA: Harvard University Press, 1986), 39–43.

33. Hart, "Separation of Law and Morals," 68–69.

34. Bull, *Anarchical Society*, 16.

35. Parochialism is apparent less in Europeans' dealings with primitive peoples than in the misunderstandings and mutual offenses that occurred in their relations with other major civilizations such as China. The incident of Lord Macartney's refusal to kowtow in 1793 illustrates how opposing customs can obstruct the development of international society. See Gerrit W. Gong, *The Standard of 'Civilization' in International Society* (Oxford: Oxford University Press, 1984), 135.

36. Stephen Macedo, *Liberal Virtues* (Oxford: Oxford University Press, 1990), 82.

37. See Shklar, *Legalism*, 41–43.

38. See Samuel P. Huntington, "The Clash of Civilizations?" *Foreign Affairs* 72 (1993): 22–49. Huntington does not address the question of whether the various civilizations can agree on a common system of international law, though he does suggest that the idea of the rule of law is distinctively Western (40).

CHAPTER 3

Natural Law and International Order

ROBERT P. GEORGE

AMONG THE achievements of recent analytical jurisprudence is its virtual elimination of false oppositions between "natural law theory" and "legal positivism." Theorists of natural law such as John Finnis[1] and legal positivists such as Neil MacCormick[2] have developed refined understandings of relationships between law and morality in the light of which it no longer makes sense to suppose that a commitment to legal positivism logically excludes belief in natural law. Legal positivists, whatever their metaethical and normative commitments, recognize that nothing in the idea of legal positivism as such necessarily commits them to moral skepticism or cultural relativism; natural law theorists, acknowledging important respects in which law and morality are, indeed, "conceptually distinct," recognize concepts of law which, for valid theoretical purposes, systematically prescind from questions of the justice or injustice of laws or legal systems.[3]

The concern of the legal positivist is fundamentally with the accurate and theoretically interesting *description* of laws, legal institutions, and legal systems. His endeavor is to describe the social practices that constitute the phenomenon of law at various times and in various places. Thus, H.L.A. Hart begins *The Concept of Law* by advising the reader to regard his book "as an essay in descriptive sociology."[4] By contrast, the concern of the natural law theorist is fundamentally with *justification*, that is to say, moral evaluation or prescription. Insofar as laws, legal institutions, and legal systems are concerned, he is interested in their moral goodness or badness, their justice or injustice. Thus, John Finnis begins *Natural Law and Natural Rights* by declaring that

> there are human goods that can be secured only through the institutions of human law, and requirements of practical reasonableness that only those institutions can satisfy. It is the object of this book to identify those goods, and those requirements of practical reasonableness, and thus to show how and on what conditions such institutions are *justified* and the ways in which they can be (and often are) defective.[5]

In this chapter, I consider understandings of international order as they are, or could be, advanced by theorists operating within the tradition of natural law theorizing. I have, in other works, argued in support of the new classical natural law theory deployed by Finnis, though originally developed by

Germain Grisez in collaboration with Finnis and Joseph M. Boyle, Jr.; but I will make no effort in this chapter to defend that theory or the tradition of which it is a part. My goal, rather, is to provide a sound exposition of the natural law tradition, and of the new classical theory (which draws on the work of Aquinas and other theorists in the tradition, yet criticizes them in certain respects and enters into the broader debate about ethical theory), and to relate some of what the tradition and the theory have to say about international society.

Along the way, I will refer to pronouncements on natural law and international order in papal encyclicals and other official documents of the Roman Catholic Church. I cite these pronouncements, not because the Church or her officials have any special authority that it is appropriate to invoke in philosophical discussion or debate, but rather because the Church is, I believe, the principal institutional bearer of the tradition of natural law theorizing in the modern world. And, of course, the Church is herself an international institution and a longstanding actor in international affairs.

NATURAL LAW THEORY

The natural moral law, if there is such a thing, is a body of practical principles comprising two types or sets of noninstrumental reasons for action: first, reasons provided by "basic human goods" which make available to human agents rationally grounded options for choice ("practical possibilities"); and second, reasons provided by moral norms that exclude some of these practical possibilities as in one way or another unreasonable.[6] Moral norms, where they are in force, provide conclusive "second order" reasons not to choose certain practical possibilities despite one's "first order" reasons (or other motives) to choose them.[7] Natural law theories are accounts of basic human goods, moral norms, and the reasons for action they provide.

Plainly, natural law theorists are cognitivists or "objectivists" about morality. They are not accurately classified as either "teleologists" or "deontologists," however. Unlike deontologists, they give basic human goods a crucial structural role in their accounts of practical reasoning and moral judgment; at the same time, they reject the consequentialist methods of moral judgment favored by contemporary teleologists.

Any comprehensive theory of human good(s) will say something about the common good, just as any comprehensive theory of morality will say something about political morality. It is hardly surprising, then, that natural law theorists have something to say about law (including international law), economics (including international economics), and politics (including international politics). It is generally unhelpful, however, to attempt to classify natural law theories or theorists as "liberal" or "conservative," "capitalist" or "socialist," "individualist" or "communitarian," and so forth. The natural law tradition itself tends to be rather undogmatic about the proper solution to many of the political, social, and economic issues that divide people into such camps. For example, while modern popes have, in the name of natural law, defended certain "capitalist" principles, such as the market economy and the private ownership of property, they have at the same time allowed that a significant measure of economic regulation and governmental intervention in the economy can be permissible and may even be required as a matter of justice.[8] Furthermore, the popes have made no effort conclusively to settle questions of the proper scope of economic regulation and governmental intervention; nor have they provided precise guidelines as to when public ownership of this or that type of property is in order. Rather, they treat questions of this sort as prudential ones on which people may (within limits established by the requirements of justice and other moral principles) legitimately differ, and whose proper solution will, in any event, vary with the circumstances of any particular society at a given time. Sometimes a plurality of morally acceptable policy options will be available to political authorities in a community; other times, a uniquely morally correct option can be identified, but not without the degree of detailed knowledge of the facts on the ground that is likely to be possessed only by those actually on the scene.

The natural law tradition's well-known commitment to the idea of moral absolutes, forcefully reiterated by Pope John Paul II in his encyclical letter *Veritatis Splendor*, should not obscure the degree to which the tradition recognizes that many important issues of social and economic policy do not admit of a single uniquely correct solution that should, as a matter of natural moral law, govern in all places and at all times. In politics, as in personal affairs, the natural law may exclude only some (or, indeed, none) of the interesting options, leaving the matter to be settled by prudential judgment or, indeed, sheer preference. In one set of circumstances (in a great economic depression, for example) prudence might dictate a strongly interventionist economic policy, while in other circumstances (such as during periods of full employment or economic expansion) a policy of nonintervention or governmental withdrawal from certain sectors of the economy might be indicated. Relativities of this sort in fact abound when one considers the implications of natural law theorizing for international society.

THE NEW CLASSICAL THEORY

Before turning to the question of international order, however, let me fill out my sketch of natural law theorizing by describing in a little more detail the foundations of the new classical theory.

According to this theory, the first principles of natural law are not themselves moral principles. They are principles that extend to and govern all intelligent practical deliberation, regardless of whether it issues in morally

3. NATURAL LAW AND INTERNATIONAL ORDER **57**

upright choice, by directing action toward possibilities that offer some intelligible benefit (and not *merely* emotional satisfaction). Such principles refer to noninstrumental (and, in that sense, "basic" or "ultimate") reasons for action. Reasons of this sort are provided by ends that can be intelligently identified and pursued, not merely as means to other ends, but as ends-in-themselves (even when pursuit of some such end, in the particular circumstances in which one finds oneself, or by the only means available to one here and now, would be morally wrong).[9] Many philosophers refer to such ends as "intrinsic goods"; Grisez, Boyle, and Finnis call them "basic human goods."

Qua basic, such goods, and the fundamental practical principles which direct choice and action toward them, cannot be deduced from still more fundamental practical principles or from truths (such as putative facts about human nature that are not themselves practical principles or derived from premises that include practical principles).[10] They are, rather, underived and, strictly speaking, "self-evident."[11] They come to be known in noninferential acts of understanding wherein one grasps, in reflecting on the data of one's experience, the intelligible point of possible action (whether or not it is morally upright) directed toward the realization of (or participation in) the good in question by oneself or others (whether or not one happens to be interested in pursuing that good oneself here and how).

Following Aquinas,[12] proponents of the new classical theory identify a plurality of basic human goods, including life and health, knowledge and aesthetic appreciation, excellence in work and play, and various forms of harmony within each person and among persons (and their communities) and between persons (and their communities) and any wider reaches of reality.[13] These basic goods can be realized and participated in by an unlimited number of persons, in an unlimited number of ways, on an unlimited number of occasions. This multiplicity of basic goods, and of their possible instantiations in alternative interesting possible lines of action, entails great complexity in intelligent motivation. The incommensurability (that is, the rational irreducibility) of motives, at least one of which bears on an anticipated benefit whose unique goodness can come to be only through following practical reason's direction (which is often a nonexclusive direction) toward it, requires free choice—that is, a making up of one's indeterminate self to act on this motive rather than that one.

The plurality of basic human goods has a number of implications for how the new classical theory understands rational choice. Paradigmatically, one may have, and be aware of, a noninstrumental reason to do X, yet at the same time, have, and be aware of, a noninstrumental reason not to do X, or to do Y, the doing of which is incompatible with doing X. (In the limiting case, one makes a free choice between options, one of which is rationally grounded and the other of which is supplied by a purely emotional motive, like anger or repugnance.) Whichever option one chooses, one chooses for a noninstrumental reason; in that sense, the choosing of either option is *rational*.

Where it is the case that, of each of some set of incompatible options one
has a reason to choose it, yet one has no *conclusive* reason to choose one option
rather than the other(s), one chooses between options each of which presents
an undefeated reason for acting. Where one has, and is aware of, undefeated
competing reasons for acting, one's choice, though rationally grounded, is
rationally underdetermined.[14] In such cases, reason does not narrow one's
options to a single possibility. More than one practical possibility is not only
rationally grounded, but fully reasonable. Sometimes, however, a moral norm
(the Golden Rule of fairness) provides a *conclusive* reason not to choose one
(or some) option(s), despite one's reason to choose it (or them). In such cases,
at least one of one's first order reasons (that is, reasons provided by basic
human goods) is defeated by a second order reason (that is, a reason provided
by a moral norm) that provides a conclusive reason (and, thus, a moral obligation) to choose the undefeated option.

Still, one's first order reason, though defeated, is not destroyed or eliminated; the morally excluded option retains intelligible appeal. For one to
choose that option, while practically unreasonable (inasmuch as one's reason
for choosing it has been defeated by a conclusive reason not choose it), is not
utterly irrational; this is because one's action in choosing it, however immoral, is for the sake of some true good, and will, to the extent one succeeds,
instantiate some intelligible benefit for oneself or someone else. If, *per impos-
sibile*, a moral norm were to eliminate one's basic reason to choose a certain
option, then one's choosing that option would not merely be unreasonable,
but irrational, and, as such, intelligible, if at all, only as action motivated
purely by feeling or some other subrational factor.

According to the new classical theory, the basic human goods that motivate
and guide rational human choice are not "Platonic forms" somehow detached
from human persons; rather, they are constitutive aspects of the well-being
and fulfillment of flesh-and-blood individuals in their manifold dimensions,
that is to say, as animate, as rational, and as agents through deliberation and
choice. Basic human goods provide reasons for action precisely, and only,
insofar as they are constitutive aspects of human well-being or flourishing.

Taken together, the first principles of practical reason that direct action
toward these goods and reasons outline the (vast) range of possible rationally
motivated actions, and point to an ideal of "integral human fulfillment," that
is to say, the compete fulfillment of all human persons (and their communities) in all possible respects. Of course, no choice or series of choices can
actually bring about integral human fulfillment; it is an ideal rather than an
operational objective. Nevertheless, it is morally significant inasmuch as the
first principle of morality (which, contrary to the representations of some
expositors and critics of the new classical theory,[15] is no mere ideal) directs
that choice and action for the sake of basic human goods be compatible with
a will toward this ideal.

Given its abstractness and generality, the first principle of morality must be
specified if it is to be useful in actually guiding people's choosing. Its specifica-

tions take account of the (necessarily subrational) motives people may have for choosing and otherwise willing incompatibly with a will toward integral human fulfillment; to act on such motives (that is, in defiance of moral norms) is to permit one's reason to be fettered by emotion and, typically, harnessed to it for the purpose of producing rationalizations for immoral conduct. The specifications of the first principle of morality guide action by excluding options that seem reasonable only if one's reason has been thus fettered.

These specifications are not, however, the most specific moral norms. They state propositions such as "do unto others as you would have them do unto you," and "evil may not be done that good may come of it," rather than more specific norms (of which they are, to be sure, principles) such as "thou shalt not steal," and "thou shalt not kill the innocent and just." They are, as it were, midway in generality between the first principle and fully specific norms. Finnis refers to these moral principles as "requirements of practical reasonableness"; Grisez and Boyle (and Finnis in his collaborative writings with them) refer to them as "modes of responsibility." They provide conclusive second order reasons not to choose certain practical possibilities, despite one's first order reasons (and one's more or less powerful emotional motives) to choose them.

Moral principles, according to the new classical theory, are norms for free choice. In freely choosing, that is to say, in choosing for (or against) reasons provided by basic human goods, one integrates the goods (or the damaging and consequent privations of the goods, that is, the evils) one intends—whether as ends or as means to other ends—into one's will, thus effecting a sort of synthesis between oneself as an acting person and the objects of one's choices, that is to say, the goods and evils one intends. (This is in no way to deny that free choice is exercised and self-constitution effected also by the accepting of side-effects.) Hence, one's free choices are self-constituting: they persist as virtues or vices in one's character and personality as a choosing subject unless or until, for better or worse, one reverses one's previous choice by choosing incompatibly with it, or, at least, resolves to choose differently should one face the same or relevantly similar options in the future.[16]

Noting the different ways that different types of willing bear on human goods and evils, proponents of the new classical theory distinguish as distinct modes of voluntariness "intending" a good or evil (as end or means) from "permitting" or "accepting" (as a side effect) a good or evil that one foresees as a consequence of one's action but does not intend (that is, which serves as neither an instrumental or noninstrumental reason for one's choice and action). Although one is morally responsible for the bad side effects one knowingly brings about, one is not responsible for them in precisely the same way one is responsible for the evils one intends. And sometimes no moral norm excludes one's bringing about as a side effect of an action one has a reason (perhaps even a conclusive reason) to perform, some evil that one could not legitimately intend. On the other hand, often one will have an obligation in justice or fairness to others (and thus a conclusive reason supplied by a moral norm) not to bring about a certain evil that one knows or believes would probably result, though as an unintended side effect, from one's action.

"Common Good" and "Complete Community"

Aristotle treated the *polis* as the paradigm of a complete community, that is, one capable of securing the overall well-being and fulfillment of its members. Later theorists working in the tradition he established retained the term "politics" for the affairs of a complete community, but treated the territorial state as the truly "complete community" and the politics of such states as "politics" in its focal sense. Similarly, they treated the territorial state as the paradigm of a legal system and the law of such states as "law" in its focal sense. Yet again, they treated the common good of the territorial state as the paradigmatic case and focal sense of "the common good." Of course, the tradition of natural law theory recognizes that any group or association can have a "politics," a "law," and a "common good." To the extent, however, that a community is "incomplete," that is to say, less than fully self-sufficient, it has a politics, law, and common good in a derivative or, in any event, nonfocal sense.

What does it mean, though, to speak of a "common good" in any sense? Finnis's primary definition has gained wide acceptance among natural law theorists: "a set of conditions which enables the members of a community to attain for themselves reasonable objectives, or to realize reasonably for themselves the value(s), for the sake of which they have reason to collaborate with each other (positively or negatively) in a community."[17] In light of this definition, we may ask: Is there a common good of the "international community?" Indeed, is there an international "community" at all?

A central feature of medieval and modern natural law theory is belief in a universal human nature. In the absence of such a belief, the tradition could not speak meaningfully of a *common* good of members of different tribes, clans, nations, or races, or, indeed, of an international *community* at all. Even with such a belief in place, however, the mainstream of the tradition has tended to treat the international community, and its politics, law, and common good, as nonparadigmatic. Increasingly, however, natural law theorists are coming to view the territorial or national state as crucially "incomplete," that is to say, incapable of doing all that can and must be done to secure conditions for the all-round flourishing of its citizens. Finnis states the implications of this change in view for the natural law theory of the international order:

> If it now appears that the good of individuals can only be fully secured and realized in the context of international community, we must conclude that the claim of the national state to be a complete community is unwarranted and the

postulate of the national legal order, that it is supreme and comprehensive and an exclusive source of legal obligation, is increasingly what lawyers call a "legal fiction."[18]

In other words, the national state can no longer (if it ever could) secure the conditions of its citizens' overall well-being (that is, their common good) without more or less systematically coordinating its activities with other nation states and, indeed, without the active assistance of supranational institutions,[19] at least some of which must possess powers to enforce multilateral agreements and international law. Hence, it has become necessary to develop institutions that will enable the international community to function as a complete community and, therefore, as a community whose politics, law, and common good are paradigmatic and focal.

One need not accept any of the distinctive claims of the natural law tradition in order to recognize the urgent need for international cooperation, and, indeed, for the (further) development of international institutions, to deal with modern social, economic, and political problems. The distinctively modern problems of nuclear and other weapons of mass destruction, not to mention global environmental problems such as ozone depletion, oceanic pollution, and mass deforestation, simply do not admit of effective solutions without substantial international cooperation. Moreover, international action is necessary to combat mass starvation and other evils, whether they are the intended or unintended consequences of human action or the result of earthquakes, hurricanes, or other natural catastrophes, as well as to promote the economic development of poor nations and to protect human rights.

Does this mean that natural law theory, as applied to the problems of today, envisages the institution of a world government? The answer is, I think, "yes"; however, it is subject to certain clarifications and, perhaps, qualifications. Ideally, a central political authority would attend to the common good of mankind in, for example, avoiding (or at least limiting) war, protecting the physical environment, preventing starvation and other forms of misery, promoting economic development, and protecting human rights. Such authority would be justified, as is political authority generally, by its capacity efficiently to generate and implement fair and otherwise reasonable solutions to the community's "coordination problems."[20] At the same time, it must be observed that concentrating power, and particularly the force of arms, in a central government that is not subject to effective countervailing power is obviously risky. To be sure, some risks are entailed by the creation of any central authority; and risks of this sort are often worth bearing. At the same time, ways must be found to lessen the risks, by, for example, constitutional schemes that divide, check, and limit governmental powers. Moreover, the risks of permitting individuals and communities subject to a world government to retain armaments must be weighed prudentially against the risks of disarming them. The concerns that prompted late-eighteenth-century Americans to entrench in their federal constitution a right of the people to keep and bear arms may not be anachronistic.[21] Perhaps those in power in a world government should not be left entirely secure against the possibility of armed resistance, should their rule degenerate into tyranny.

"Determinatio" in International Society

According to natural law theory, just and good positive law, including constitutional law, is always in some sense derived from the natural law. As Aquinas observed, however, this derivation is accomplished in at least two quite different ways. In the case of certain principles, the legislator translates the natural law into positive law more or less directly. So, for example, a conscientious legislator will deal with grave injustices, such as murder, rape, and theft, by moving according to an intellectual process akin to deduction[22] from the moral proposition that, say, the killing of innocent persons is unjust to the legal prohibition of such killing. In a great many cases, however, the movement from natural to positive law in the practical thinking of the conscientious legislator cannot be so direct.

It is easy, for example, to understand the basic practical principle that identifies health as a basic human good and the preservation of human health as an important goal. A modern legislator will therefore easily see, for example, the need for a scheme of coordination of vehicular traffic to protect the health and safety of drivers and pedestrians. The common good, which it is his responsibility to foster and serve in this respect, clearly requires such a scheme. Ordinarily, however, he will not be able to deduce from the natural law a uniquely correct scheme of traffic regulation. The natural law does not determine once and for all the perfect scheme of traffic regulation or establish one or another set of tradeoffs (so much convenience or efficiency for so much safety, for example) as uniquely or definitively right. A number of different schemes—attended by different and often incommensurable costs and benefits, risks and advantages—may be consistent with the requirements of natural law. So the legislator must exercise a certain creative freedom in authoritatively choosing from among competing reasonable schemes. He must move, not by deduction or any intellectual process akin to it, but rather by an activity of the practical intellect which Aquinas called *determinatio*.[23]

Unfortunately, no single word in English adequately captures the meaning of *determinatio*. "Determination" has some of the flavor of it; but so do "implementation," "specification," and "concretization." The key thing to understand is that in making *determinationes*, the legislator enjoys a creative freedom that Aquinas analogizes to the freedom exercised by an architect. An architect must design a building that is sound and sensible for the purposes to which it will be put. Ordinarily, however, he cannot identify a form of the building that would be uniquely suitable. A range of possible designs will likely satisfy the relevant criteria. Obviously, a design with "doors" no more than three feet high is unlikely to meet an important requirement for a functional building. No principle of architecture, however, sets the proper height of a door at six feet two inches as opposed to six feet eight inches. In designing a particular building, the architect will strive to make the height of the doors make sense in light of a variety of factors, some of which are themselves the fruit of *determinationes* (the height of the ceilings, for example); but even here he will typically face a variety of acceptable but incompatible design options.

Contemporary legal theory has brought to light the importance of authoritative legal enactments as norms for regulating and coordinating human action for the common good.[24] More often than not, such enactments are not direct "deductions" from the natural law; rather, they are *determinationes*. Whether they are products of legislation or multilateral agreements, the norms of international law that have been, or could be, put into force to regulate and coordinate the activities of states, corporations, and other actors in international affairs for the sake of the common good would, in the majority of cases, be *determinationes*. For example, in the case of a particular international environmental problem, the natural law may well require that some action be taken, but not prescribe any particular scheme among the range of possible reasonable schemes for dealing with the problem. Nor, perhaps, will the natural law dictate a uniquely correct solution if, in the case, a choice must be made between tolerating a certain amount of environmental pollution and sacrificing a certain measure of economic development. Where tradeoffs of this sort must be made, natural justice requires only that choices be made by fair procedures which take fully into account the rights and interests of all parties who will be affected.

Indeed, key questions about the proper constitution of the international order are themselves matters for *determinatio*. They do not admit of uniquely correct answers. Rather, choices must be made from among a range of reasonable constitutional schemes. Natural law requires that one of these schemes be selected for the sake of the human goods to be fostered and protected by international authority; however, there is no scheme of international authority that is uniquely required as a matter of natural law.

Is natural law theory completely relativistic, then, on the question of the proper constituting of the international order and on other questions pertaining to the common good of international society? No. The principles of natural law rule out certain possibilities, usually on the ground that they are unjust. For example, a constitutional scheme based on racist suppositions would be excluded as a matter of natural law. So, too, would any scheme that unfairly distributed the burdens and benefits of international cooperation in dealing, to stay with the example, with ecological problems. The relativism of the natural law theory of international order is limited. It follows from the belief that the principles of natural law, which exclude certain possibilities as unjust or otherwise immoral, will not necessarily narrow the possibilities for a just and upright ordering of international society, or a fair and effective solution to global environmental problems, to a single uniquely correct option.

I repeat, however, that a substantively acceptable scheme for constituting a society, or the international society, or for solving other problems pertaining to the common good of national or international societies, might nevertheless be judged according to natural law theory to be morally unacceptable on the ground that the procedures used to select that scheme from among the range of possible reasonable schemes were themselves unjust. For example, wealthy and powerful nations might arbitrarily or otherwise unjustly exclude poor and weak nations from participating effectively in decisions affecting the organization of international society. Or the interests and preferences of developing nations might be left out of account in making tradeoffs between, say, environmental protection and economic development.

"Subsidiarity" and International Order

I have suggested that contemporary natural law theory envisages a world government that would function as the central authority in a "complete community." Does this mean that natural law theory is "statist"? I think not. I have already noted that risks, as well as benefits, would attend the creation of any world government, and have spoken of the recognition by natural law theory of the need to lessen these risks, where possible, by checking and limiting the powers of that government. In addition to prudential considerations, however, natural law theory proposes principled grounds for decentralizing power wherever practicable.

Recall Finnis's definition of the common good as "a set of conditions which enables the members of a community to attain *for themselves* reasonable objectives, or to realize reasonably *for themselves* the value(s) for the sake of which they have reason to collaborate . . . in a community" (emphasis supplied). Under the natural law account of human good(s), it is important not only that basic human goods be realized, but that people, and peoples, realize these goods *for themselves*, that is, as the fruits of their own deliberation, judgment, choice, and action. On the basis of this consideration, the tradition of natural law theorizing has identified and endorsed the principle of "subsidiarity."[25] The meaning and implications of subsidiarity were nicely stated by Pope Pius XI in his 1931 encyclical letter *Quadragesimo Anno*:

> just as it is wrong to withdraw from the individual and commit to a group what private initiative and effort can accomplish, so too it is an injustice . . . for a larger and higher association to arrogate to itself functions which can be performed efficiently by smaller and lower associations. This is a fundamental principle. . . . Of

its very nature the true aim of all social activity should be to help members of a social body, and never to destroy or absorb them.[26]

As applied to the question of international order and a possible world government, the principle of subsidiarity would restrict the authority of any world government to those problems which cannot be successfully dealt with by national governments, just as it restricts the authority of national governments to those problems which cannot be successfully dealt with by regional governments, of regional governments to those problems which cannot be dealt with successfully by local governments, of local governments to those problems which cannot be dealt with successfully by neighborhood groups and other private associations, and of such groups and associations to problems which cannot be dealt with successfully by families.

Toward the end of his 1963 encyclical letter *Pacem in Terris*, Pope John XXIII reflected on the implications of the principle of subsidiarity for the precise question of constituting international society. He unambiguously affirmed the idea of an international or "world-wide" public authority which would serve "the universal common good"[27] by coming to grips with problems that "the public authorities of individual states are not in a position to tackle . . . with any hope of a positive solution."[28] This universal public authority would, he said, "have as its fundamental objective the recognition, respect, safeguarding and promotion of the rights of the human person."[29] But, he insisted,

> the world-wide public authority is not intended to limit the sphere of action of the public authority of the individual state, much less to take its place. On the contrary, its purpose is to create, on a world basis, an environment in which the public authorities of each state, its citizens and intermediate associations, can carry out their tasks, fulfill their duties and exercise their rights with greater security.[30]

In the understanding of Pope John, and the tradition in which he speaks, world government is, in principle, limited government. Although such government is envisaged as the central authority of a complete community, it is not meant to displace regional, national, or local authorities. Indeed, a world government may legitimately exercise power only where regional, national, or local authorities are not competent to solve the problems at hand.

Of course, the application of the principle of subsidiarity is more a matter of art than of science; and, in the modern world, the principle must be applied under constantly shifting conditions. In many cases, problems that are appropriately dealt with at one level in the conditions prevailing today may more appropriately be dealt with at another level (higher *or lower*) in the conditions prevailing tomorrow. And often enough it will prove impracticable to shift authority to deal with a certain problem from one level of government to another, or from governmental to private hands, or vice versa, at every point at which it would be ideal to do so. Natural law theorists are confident that the principle of subsidiarity can guide the practical thinking of conscientious statesmen, but they do not pretend that it can be applied mechanically or with anything approaching mathematical precision.

A CONTRACTUAL ASSOCIATION OF NATIONS?

If the tradition of natural law theorizing envisages world government as limited in the scope of its just authority by the principle of subsidiarity, and if it maintains that such government must refrain from displacing national governments (and, indeed, subnational governments) or interfering with the exercise of their authority in matters within their competence, does the tradition conceive of international society as a contractual association of nations?

Certainly no nation is under an obligation of natural justice to submit to the jurisdiction of a world government that is in itself unjust, or which was brought into being by procedures which excluded that or any other nation from fair participation in the *determinationes* embodied in its design. The substantive or procedural injustice of an international authority can provide an undefeated reason (and, indeed, under some circumstances, a conclusive reason) for a nation to refuse to submit to the jurisdiction of that authority. The fact that the international common good demands the institution of (limited) world government does not impose on any nation the obligation to accept the first offer of world government that comes along.

At the same time, the tradition of natural law theorizing does not suppose that a nation may justly fail to submit to the jurisdiction of a just world government which has been, or is being, created in accordance with basically just procedures. The tradition does not view international cooperation to secure the worldwide common good as somehow optional for states or peoples. The reality of international problems demanding international responses imposes on every nation, as a matter of natural justice, a duty to cooperate with other nations to secure the international common good. Thus, submission to the jurisdiction of a just world government is not morally optional in the way that participating in a contract is ordinarily morally optional. The common goods to be achieved (and common evils to be avoided) by the institution of a central international authority provide *conclusive* reasons for nations to submit to the jurisdiction of a just world government. For any nation to resist the jurisdiction of such a government is contrary to the international common good, and, as such, constitutes the sort of practical unreasonableness in political affairs that the natural law tradition treats as a paradigmatic case of injustice.[31]

None of this should be taken to imply, however, that there would be no place for bilateral or multilateral treaties and other contracts between nations in a properly constituted international order. Nor should it be taken to mean that the contractual *form* is inappropriate for the establishment of a world government or other international political institutions.

CULTURAL DIVERSITY

For the natural law tradition, the obligation of international authority to respect cultural autonomy, and therefore to permit cultural diversity, is rooted in the principle of subsidiarity and in the diversity of basic human goods and of the reasonable ways that individuals and communities instantiate these goods in their lives. Contemporary natural law theory recognizes that dramatically different cultures can provide people with the resources they need to live fulfilling and morally upright lives. This recognition is perfectly compatible with the natural law tradition's historic rejection of cultural relativism. To say that some cultures are morally bad (or, more precisely, that certain practices deeply rooted in, or central to, some cultures are morally bad) is not to say that there is only one culture that is morally good.

In speaking of the obligation of international institutions to assist the economic and social development of impoverished nations, Pope Paul VI in his 1967 encyclical letter *Populorum Progressio* was careful to highlight both the principle of subsidiarity and belief in legitimate cultural autonomy and diversity:

> We hope ... that multilateral and international bodies ... will discover ways that will allow peoples which are still under-developed to break through the barriers which seem to enclose them and to discover *for themselves, in full fidelity to their own proper genius*, the means for their social and human progress.[32]

According to Pope Paul VI and the natural law tradition, international cooperation, and even the institution of international authority, for the sake of the universal common good, entails neither statism nor cultural uniformity. Indeed, it is important to protect the human values to be realized by people, and peoples, precisely in their acting "for themselves" and "in fidelity to their own proper genius."

Natural law theory rejects the idea that we must choose between cultural chauvinism and cultural relativism. Far from supposing that the natural moral law imposes a single cultural norm to which all peoples should aspire, contemporary natural law theorists maintain that respect for the integrity of diverse legitimate cultures is itself a requirement of natural justice. They hold that international law and government must, to the extent possible, not only permit diverse national and subnational communities to control their own affairs, but also respect (and, if necessary, help to protect) the right of such communities to preserve, by legitimate means, their distinctive languages, customs, traditions, and ways of life.

This in no way implies that international authority acts illegitimately in forbidding and repressing violations of human rights, even when they are sanctioned by cultural norms. The question here, of course, is what constitutes a violation of human rights. Natural law theorists are by no means in agreement among themselves on this question; and everyone recognizes cer-

68 ROBERT P. GEORGE

tain "hard cases." Natural law theorists generally do agree, however, in recognizing a wide-ranging legitimate cultural diversity, and in holding that the repression of cultural practices by public authority is justified only for the sake of preventing fundamental injustices or other grave evils.[33]

NOTES

1. See John Finnis, *Natural Law and Natural Rights* (Oxford: Oxford University Press, 1980), esp. chs. 1 and 12, and Finnis, "The Truth in Legal Positivism," in Robert P. George, ed., *The Autonomy of Law: Essays on Legal Positivism* (Oxford: Oxford University Press, 1996).

2. See Neil MacCormick, "Natural Law and the Separation of Law and Morals," in Robert P. George, ed., *Natural Law Theory: Contemporary Essays* (Oxford: Oxford University Press, 1992).

3. Hence, natural law theorists need not object to "positivism" in either of the two major senses discussed by Terry Nardin in Chapter 1 above. At the same time, it is worth noting that natural law theorists lay particular emphasis on the proposition—denied today by few legal positivists—that the description of social phenomena cannot be utterly value free. As Finnis has observed, "there is no escaping the theoretical requirement that a judgment of *significance* and *importance* must be made if [descriptive] theory is to be more than a vast rubbish heap of miscellaneous facts described in a multitude of incommensurable terminologies." Finnis, *Natural Law*, 17.

4. H.L.A. Hart, *The Concept of Law* (Oxford: Oxford University Press, 1961), vi.

5. Finnis, *Natural Law*, 3 (emphasis supplied).

6. As I explain below, it is possible to distinguish moral principles of varying levels of generality. Taking these varying levels into account, one can speak of natural law as consisting of more than two sets of principles.

7. For a fuller explanation, see Robert P. George, "Does the Incommensurability Thesis Imperil Common Sense Moral Judgments?" *American Journal of Jurisprudence* 37 (1992): 185–95.

8. For example, Pope Paul VI, in harmony with the tradition of papal social teaching inaugurated in the late nineteenth century by Pope Leo XIII in *Rerum Novarum*, taught that "without abolishing the competitive market, it should be kept within limits which make it just and moral, and therefore human." *Populorum Progressio*, par. 61.

9. I explain the idea and significance of ultimate reasons for action in "Recent Criticism of Natural Law Theory," *University of Chicago Law Review* 55 (1988): 1390–94.

10. In this respect, the new classical theory differs markedly from familiar neoscholastic accounts of natural law, such as the one propounded by Thomas Higgins, *Man as Man: The Science and Art of Ethics* (Milwaukee, WI: Bruce Publishers, 1958).

11. For a careful explanation of the much misunderstood claim that the most basic practical principles are self-evident, see Joseph Boyle, "Natural Law and the Ethics of Traditions," in George, ed., *Natural Law Theory*, 23–27.

12. *Summa theologiae*, I-II, q. 94, a. 2., on which see Germain Grisez's path-breaking article, "The First Principle of Practical Reason: A Commentary on the *Summa Theologiae*, I-II, q. 94, a. 2," *Natural Law Forum* 10 (1965): 168–201.

13. See John Finnis, Joseph M. Boyle, Jr., and Germain Grisez, *Nuclear Deterrence, Morality and Realism* (Oxford: Oxford University Press, 1987), 279–80; also Germain Grisez, Joseph Boyle, and John Finnis, "Practical Principles, Moral Truth, and Ultimate Ends," *American Journal of Jurisprudence* 32 (1987): 107–108.

14. See Joseph Raz, *The Morality of Freedom* (Oxford: Oxford University Press, 1986), 339.

15. See, for example, Ru'ssell Hittinger's exposition and critique in *A Critique of the New Natural Law Theory* (Notre Dame: University of Notre Dame Press, 1987), 50–51.

16. On the lastingness and character-forming consequences of free choices, see John Finnis, *Fundamentals of Ethics* (Washington, DC: Georgetown University Press, 1983), 139–44.

17. Finnis, *Natural Law*, 155.

18. Finnis, *Natural Law*, 15.

19. See Second Vatican Council, *Gaudiem et Spes*, par. 84.

20. On the justification of political authority in the natural law tradition, see Finnis, *Natural Law*, ch. 10.

21. The Second Amendment to the Constitution of the United States: "A well regulated Militia, being necessary to the security of a free State, the right of the people to keep and bear arms, shall not be infringed."

22. See St. Thomas Aquinas, *Summa theologiae*, I-II, q. 95, a. 2.

23. *Summa theologiae*, I-II, q. 95, a. 2. In describing *determinatio* as "an activity of the practical intellect," as I do here (and have done elsewhere), I do not mean to deny that *determinatio* crucially involves *choosing*. My point is to affirm that the choosing is guided by "an intellectual process which is not deductive and does involve free choice (human will) and yet is intelligent and directed by reason." John Finnis, "On 'On the Critical Legal Studies Movement,'" *American Journal of Jurisprudence* 30 (1985): 23.

24. See Edna Ullman-Margalit, *The Emergence of Norms* (Oxford: Oxford University Press, 1980).

25. From the Latin *subsidium*, "to help."

26. *Quadragesimo Anno*, par. 79. According to John Finnis, "an attempt, for the sake of the common good, to absorb the individual altogether into common enterprises would be disastrous for the common good, however much the common enterprises might prosper." Finnis, *Natural Law*, 168.

27. *Pacem in Terris*, par. 139.

28. *Pacem in Terris*, par. 140.

29. *Pacem in Terris*, par. 139.

30. *Pacem in Terris*, par. 141.

31. My focus on the question of world government here is not meant to obscure the natural law tradition's recognition of mutual obligations among nation states even prior to the creation of central authority. This recognition is certainly evident in the idea of the *ius gentium*, as it figures in the thought of classical and Christian theorists of natural law. These thinkers stressed the obligation of states to cooperate to solve common problems and provide assistance to one another.

32. *Populorum Progressio*, par. 64, emphasis supplied. The phrase "for themselves" reflects Pope Paul VI's commitment to the principle of subsidiarity; the phrase "according to their own proper genius" reflects his belief in legitimate cultural diversity, not only as a matter of past practice, but something that rightly continues as peoples progress.

33. I am grateful to Joseph Boyle for his extremely helpful suggestions regarding the argument of this chapter. An earlier version appeared in Kenneth Grasso, et al., eds., *Catholicism, Liberalism, and Communitarianism* (Lanham, MD: Rowman & Littlefield, 1995).

Some Thoughts on Natural Law and International Order

RICHARD B. FRIEDMAN

IN HIS chapter, Robert George presents a stimulating restatement of "the new classical theory of natural law" and its bearing on various problems of international society. In this response, I shall confine myself to raising some questions about George's views and indicating some alternatives that may be plausibly associated with what George calls "the natural law tradition." This response is, then, brief and provisional, with no attempt made to provide sustained argument but only to identify an agenda of issues worth discussing.

THE NEW CLASSICAL THEORY

This theory would seem to be composed of five basic elements, which are, in sequence: basic human goods, the first principle of morality, the moral ideal, the specifications of the first principles of morality, and the most specific moral norms conceived as exclusionary norms (or the laws of nature, as they were called in the tradition, for example, "Kill not"). Here, then, is a theory with a definite structure, beginning in a particular conception of the kind of foundation a political theory must possess (the good) and concluding with a particular conception of the kind of arrangements that should order a society of human beings (law).

Three clusters of questions will be raised, focused on the foundation and the conclusion.

To start with: is there a tension between two theses George advances about our knowledge of the basic human goods, namely the incommensurability thesis and the self-evidence thesis? If reasonable people can reasonably disagree about the priority or ranking of the basic human goods, why can't they reasonably disagree over which goods are basic? (Note that the space in which free choice can be expressed is determined by this division between what is self-evident and what is incommensurable.) In any case, are the basic goods self-evident? And is their self-evident quality conceptually required by their being noninstrumental? It is worth observing that when Aquinas reaches the crucial section of the *Summa theologiae* that treats human happiness (I–II, qq. 5–17), he treats the problem of which goods belong to complete human happiness not as self-evident, but as posing a series of disputed questions to be argued out in relation to an intricate set of criticisms and countercriticisms; and he locates human liberty ("man's *dominium* over his own acts") not in the incommensurability of various goods, but in the consideration that man as a rational creature can recognize that he is incapable of being fully satisfied by any natural goods or all of them together and that consequently he has the power to resist their attraction.

There is an additional problem about the notion of basic human goods springing from a pivotal claim made by George. He claims that it is an essential characteristic of the basic goods that they can be shared by all humans without contention. "These basic goods," he writes, "can be realized and participated in by an unlimited number of persons, in an unlimited number of ways, on an unlimited number of occasions." The status of this striking claim within the theory seems ambiguous. Is it supposed to be a demonstrable *conclusion* about the world in which humans pursue these goods, that there is nothing in nature that hinders full and harmonious participation? Or does this claim belong to the foundation of the theory in the sense that it constitutes the effective *criterion* for distinguishing basic goods from nonbasic goods: a good qualifies as a basic if and only if it can be shared without conflict. If it is operating as a gatekeeper, then the division between nonbasic and basic goods is coextensive with the division between conflictual and non-conflictual goals. But is this self-evident or otherwise demonstrable by natural reason alone? On either interpretation of the status of George's claim, a serious problem is posed for a theory that purports to be grounded in nature. It also opens up an interpretive issue about the continuity of the natural law tradition: whether there was a rupture in the seventeenth century between the Thomist and the modern "Grotian" versions of natural law theory over the naturalness of conflict or, in the idiom of the times, whether the state of nature was a state of war. This issue is bound to have repercussions when the theorist turns attention to the international arena, as may be seen in the later stages of George's paper where he envisages the international order as a "complete community."

The role played by the notion of an exclusionary norm in the new classical theory of natural law also raises questions. This notion is a construct of Joseph Raz, invented to explain what it means for a law or some other kind of norm to function as an authoritative reason for action in the deliberations of those subject to the norm.[1] It was then adopted by John Finnis, and may be recognized as a valuable addition to natural law theory.[2] The parallel in the natural law tradition was the precept-counsel distinction employed continuously by natural law thinkers from the thirteenth to the seventeenth centuries. I am, however, unable to discern the basis of the exclusionary function of norms in the new classical theory. It cannot be based on the voluntarist concept of law, as the will of superior authority, since notoriously voluntarism makes the identity of the norms that are exclusionary a wholly contingent matter. This will not do for a natural law theory that aspires to stabilize a particular set of moral norms as norms for all mankind. But it is also hard to see how it could be based on the intellectualist concept of law, which views law as what is rationally necessary to the achievement of certain ends.[3] The difficulty here is that the role given to the exclusionary norms in the new classical theory is not merely to override the pursuit of selfish, conflictual, or nonbasic goods, but also, in George's words, to "defeat . . . reasons provided by basic human goods." It would seem to follow that the exclusionary character of the norms cannot consist in their being instrumental rules rationally necessary to achieve the basic goods, since they can override the direct pursuit of these goods. Where then do they get their authority? I think the dilemma involved here is a crucial issue for a natural law theory, since it suggests the inadequacy of both the voluntarist and the intellectualist concepts of law. Yet I also believe the natural law tradition has the intellectual resources to furnish a solution, even though I am unable to discern an answer in the new classical theory, in any of its formulations so far.

NATURAL LAW: WHAT? NATURAL LAW THEORY: WHAT?

At the very outset of his paper, George praises contemporary analytical jurisprudence for removing "false oppositions between 'natural law theory' and 'legal positivism,'" and then goes on to establish a division of labor between the two. On the one hand, he declares that positivism is concerned with "the accurate and theoretically interesting *description* of laws . . . [as] social practices," adding that there is "nothing in the idea of legal positivism as such [that] commits them [positivists] to moral skepticism or cultural relativism." On the other hand, natural law theory is said to be concerned "with *justification*, that is to say, moral evaluation or prescription," that is, with the "approximation" of laws and legal institutions "to an ideal of 'integral human fulfillment.'" From the standpoint of this division of labor, the conceptual work of jurisprudence is allotted to the positivists, while the natural lawyers receive the normative work, and the long-running argument between the two schools is effectively defused.

That this division of intellectual labor within jurisprudence has a certain immediate appeal cannot be denied. Yet doubt creeps in and cannot be readily assuaged. Are there not some issues at stake in the long-running debate between positivism and natural law theory that cannot be accommodated to this distribution of tasks?

At the very least, the difficulty is that the notion of a natural law theory in play here is too broad and undifferentiated. An ideal of natural justice may indeed be essential to a natural law theory, but there are other philosophies in which it is also essential, yet which do not conceive of a system of natural justice as taking the form of a regime of law in which all the inhabitants of society are subjects (that is, the persons between whom the laws apply)—as, for example, in Plato's *Republic* and *Statesman*.[4] Again, natural law theory may indeed reject moral skepticism and cultural relativism in favor of moral realism and common values ("basic human goods"), yet what it distinctively affirms is something more: the existence of a worldwide legal community to which all individual rational agents belong. As Cicero puts it:

> Those who have reason in common also have right reason in common. But since right reason is law (*lex*), we men must regard ourselves as associated (*consociati homines*) with the gods in law. But further those who have law in common (*communio legis*) have justice in common. And those who have these things in common must be held to belong to the same city (*civitas*). . . . Hence we must now conceive of the whole universe as one common city (*civitas communis*) of which both gods and men are the members.[5]

How this complex syllogism and each of its components is to be construed is, of course, much debated; how it could possibly be given a philosophical defense is yet another subject of debate. However that may be, the crucial point is that, for Cicero, the naturally just society consists of a particular kind of association among a particular category of beings, namely a worldwide city of law that extends membership to all rational being in virtue of their nature, not their conventional status in this or that particular city; and the question for conceptual jurisprudence is, then, whether the notion of law *required here* can be understood according to positivist theory, either in Austin's reductive version of law as force or in Hart's social practice version. So my doubt persists: given this more specific and differentiated Stoic conception of natural law, might there not be some deep and ineliminable opposition between positivism and natural law theory that cannot be defused in the manner suggested by George?

Yet another doubt springs from this Cicero passage (although this is to jump ahead): doesn't Cicero's Stoic understanding of natural law as the cosmic city of law cast doubt on George's contention that "the mainstream of the [natural law] tradition" regarded the international community as "nonparadigmatic," and instead treated some form of municipal society such as the polis or territorial state as the paradigm of a "complete community"? Indeed, from the standpoint of this passage, it appears that the only complete community would have to be a worldwide *civitas communis*—though what institutional form this would take is a still further question.

Another question connected with all of the above: if the preceding discussion associates natural law too closely with Stoicism, it would prove helpful to learn about the alternative understanding of natural law embraced by the new classical theory.

"THE COMPLETE COMMUNITY" AND "THE REAL PROBLEMS OF INTERNATIONAL ORDER"

In the last half of his chapter, George gives us his view of the real problems of international order, and his starting point is the Aristotelian notion of a complete community. The latter is defined as a community "capable of securing the overall well-being and fulfillment of its members" or "the common good." George next proceeds to make three historical claims about the locus of complete community according to the natural law tradition. The polis was taken by Aristotle as the embodiment of the complete community, but later theorists of natural law "treated the territorial state as the truly 'complete community,'" while the entire "mainstream of the tradition" considered the international community as "nonparadigmatic." George then challenges the contemporary relevance of this mainstream outlook, contending that the state can no longer be accepted as a complete community because of its inability "to deal with modern social, economic, and political problems." He therefore declares that "it has become necessary to develop institutions that will enable the international community to function as a complete community," and he accordingly concludes by calling for "world government" as necessary to the realization of complete community at the global level. The only qualifications he permits are "the principle of subsidiarity" and a certain degree of political participation by all existing states in the establishment of the world government. George thus articulates a stadial conception of historical progress, from polis to state to world government, as successive embodiments of Aristotelian complete community.

This is troubling from the standpoint of both the new classical theory of natural law itself and the natural law tradition.

The most striking feature of George's reasoning here is his reversion to an almost unqualified consequentialism as the proper mode of normative argument. George dismisses the state and passes directly to the new global embodiment of the complete community by reference entirely to practical problem-solving. Nor does "the principle of subsidiarity" introduce a non-consequentialist criterion into the argument, since that principle is concerned with the effectiveness of problem-solving at different levels. What appears to be happening to the new classical theory of natural law here is that the teleological component of the theory is doing all the work, while the natural law component has been shunted to the sidelines. Although there is much talk of exclusionary norms in the initial formulation of the theory, they have dropped from sight at the suprastate level. This disappearing act can be seen in George's selection of the real problems of international order, or rather in what he ignores. There is no mention of the painfully difficult legal problems of the international arena, no concern with international law nor with the possibility (certainly suggested by the natural law tradition) that there may be a necessary connection between "the law of nations" and "the law of nature," no concern with "international anarchy" in the sense of the failure, or at any rate the difficulty, of bringing the use of force under the governance of law (precisely as exclusionary norms ruling out the instrumental use of force for the state's own purpose), no interest in "world government" as a specifically juridical institution to fill the holes in a quasi-legal order, and, finally and most remarkably, no interest in exploring any of the rich fund of ideas about the character of the international world generated within the natural law tradition from the Stoics and Cicero to Vitoria, Suarez, and Grotius.

George's approach thus seems to me markedly one-sided. It is one thing to stress the crisis proportions of the social, economic, and political problems of the international world, quite another thing to abandon the legal problematic of the international arena in what purports to be a theory of law. One is left wondering: why this loss of balance among the components of the new classical theory of natural law when it comes to address problems of international society? I am not sure, but the next section will suggest the possibility of a restructuring of the approach adopted by the new classical theory to international order.

AN ALTERNATIVE APPROACH

It is generally recognized that the natural law tradition from the Stoics and Cicero down through Vitoria and Suarez to Grotius and Pufendorf is pervaded by a concern with the international scene. George ignores this prominent feature of the tradition in favor of the approach to "the international order" he finds in the new classical theory, and I think this indifference is rooted in his conception of natural law theory. So the purpose of this final section is to sketch an alternative conception of what natural law theory is/was all about. This sketch will include a distinct account of the identity of the problem to which natural law theory is addressed and a different perspective on the way in which the international scene enters into natural law theory—not as an afterthought, but as something essential. (Throughout these pages, the modern term "international" is used with reservation for reasons that will surface as the discussion unfolds.)

The following remarks will also prove to have a bearing on one key aspect of the approach to cosmopolitanism taken by some of the contributors to an earlier Ethikon volume and to this volume.[6] It is hardly necessary to point out that the original version of cosmopolitanism was the Stoic notion or "dream"[7] of a cosmic city of rational individuals associated in terms of common law (*koinos nomos*), which tradition came to regard as the initial formulation of natural law theory. So it is both striking and puzzling to discover, in various discussions of cosmopolitanism by Ethikon contributors, that cosmopolitanism has been dissociated from any connection with natural law, or for that matter with any concern with the nature of legal order, and treated as a separate tradition of thinking about the international world and its problems. (Consider Charles Beitz's statement, taken over by Brian Barry, that "there is no necessary connection between moral cosmopolitanism and institutional cosmopolitanism."[8] Does this mean no necessary connection with law?) This is an approach to cosmopolitanism that the following sketch will call into question, even if it cannot be elaborated here.

I wish, then, to distinguish rather swiftly between two models of natural law theory and their respective problematics. Both have recurrently received expression in the natural law tradition, although to my knowledge no attempt has been made to differentiate them, let alone to work through the implications of each in comparison to the other.

The first may be called the vertical model of natural law theory. It conceives of natural law (*ius naturale, lex naturalis,* etc.) as a set of higher order rules or norms hierarchical and controlling over positive law, constituting an objective standard of justice that sets a limit to what positive law may rightfully require of those subject to it. The specific focus of this vertical model is the content of the positive law of a legal order, and the problem it is concerned with is the variability of this content. Positive law is recognized as something conventional, made what it is by an act of will or agreement by those authorized to make it, and consequently having only a contingent, not a necessary, connection with justice or morality. From this standpoint, the job of natural law theory is to provide a "limit to selectivity," as Niklas Luhmann puts it,[9] which is not itself conventional and hence not eligible to be altered by an act of will.

This vertical model is the one George is working with in his presentation of the new classical theory. This may be seen in two respects. First, there is the provenance of natural law theory for George. He explicitly locates that theory in the context of a complete community, polis, or state characterized by a sovereign government ruling its subjects by issuing positive laws to them. And he declares without argument that this is the provenance within which the mainstream natural law thinkers developed their theories. Second, the job George assigns to natural law theory is to supply a standard of justice for judging positive law, a standard anchored in something nonconventional, the basic human goods, and therefore impervious to change by human power. George's teaching thus possesses the structure of the vertical model.

George's accommodation to legal positivism should not obscure his adherence to this vertical model. Legal positivism is a theory about law as a "social practice," centered on the fact that every legal order provides some criterion or method for identifying its own laws; and the basic thesis of positivism is that since this criterion is conventional in character, it follows that a rule can be picked out as a valid legal rule that is immoral. No conventional criterion of legal validity can guarantee the justice of the content of law. George is perfectly willing to give positivism this point because it leaves the vertical model of natural law theory and its problem of content-variability undisturbed. Indeed, if anything, positivism highlights the problem of content-variability. Thus George dismisses the standard textbook view that natural law theory is in competition with legal positivism because, as he sees it, the specific issue about law that is at stake for natural law theory is unaffected by this concession to positivism.

The vertical model of natural law theory is addressed to the problem of the variable content of positive law, and it is unquestionable that this model has repeatedly received expression in the long history of natural law theorizing. (This is most obvious when natural law is presented in a theological framework in which the higher-order norms are regarded as divine commands.)

Unfortunately, however, the assumption has frequently been made that natural law theory has always been, or even necessarily must be, cast in this vertical mode.[10] A full-scale criticism of the roots of this assumption is badly needed, if the philosophical issues surrounding the idea that "law exists in rational nature" are to be fully understood and addressed. But here it will have to suffice to point out that there is another aspect to the conventional character of a positive legal order: that law is open to variation along another dimension besides its content; that concern with the problem posed by this second aspect of the conventionality of law was central to the natural law tradition; and that all this gives a different structure to natural law theory.

Suppose we say that human beings enjoy a legal relationship with one another when their conduct toward one another is regulated by an authoritative set of rules. They are the subjects or juridical persons who are jointly obligated and protected by these rules. Each is obligated in the sense that the rules are "exclusionary" (to stick with George's useful concept): it is never a legally acceptable reason for refusing to observe a rule to claim that obedience frustrates the pursuit of the basic human goods or, more generally, is not an effective means to the achievement of one's ends. And each subject is protected by these same rules in the sense that all the other subjects of this legal relationship are also obligated by these authoritative rules in their conduct toward him. Thus "subject" necessarily means "fellow-subject": to be a subject or juridical person is to stand in a distinct type of relationship with all who are also subjects. On this view of legal relationship, recourse to physical force is not ruled out as necessarily unlawful, but it is subordinated to law. Force can be lawfully employed only as a response to a legal wrong, and never for some purely instrumental reason; that is, it can be lawfully employed only as a sanction for violation of law itself determined according to law, or to "enforce" an existing law. Law therefore not only mediates the relationship between subjects but also stands between these subjects and their government, if they have one.

From this angle, the point to be emphasized is that legal relationship is constitutive of a certain type of social relationship. It is a social relationship distinguished by the existence of authoritative rules interposed between the associates and by the exclusion of the instrumental use of force. There is of course the further question, much discussed and debated in contemporary legal theory, as to whether legal order also includes, as necessary constituents, socially differentiated institutions or procedures for identifying, promulgating, and securing obedience to the rules that are law. The addition of differentiated institutions to perform these jobs obviously makes the social relation of law more complex and evolved. I have no quarrel with those who take the affirmative on this question, as long as the affirmative answer does not supersede and then drive out the conception of law as a distinct social relation between subjects. Given this proviso, then, as far as I can tell, nothing that follows in the discussion hinges on this question and the analysis can go forward.

So next suppose that the criterion of admission to this legal relationship is itself a matter of convention. The juridical category "subject" or "person" is itself determined by the social practice of law by reference to some conventional criterion such as birth, descent, kinship, or a particular religion. The legal order engages in the official classification of humans as to their legal status. Perhaps there are different statuses barring different "legal effects," but among the different statuses there is the fundamental division between those who have legal standing and those who lack it altogether. The social practice of law provides not only a criterion for identifying the rules that are law and distinguishing them from what is not law, but also a criterion for identifying who or what qualifies as a subject and distinguishing subjects from those who are not subjects. Legal identity is then a matter of convention, and legal order can be recognized to be capable of variability across the range of its subjects as well as its rules.

Now if these two suppositions are put together—the idea of legal relationship as a distinct social relationship and access to it as conventional—then the result will be obvious. The enjoyment of legal relationship will be reserved to some humans, while others will be closed out of it. Any one who fails to meet the conventional test will not count as a subject, that is, as a fellow-subject, whose interactions with those who do count as subjects is mediated by law. He will be neither obligated by nor protected by the authoritative constraints of the legal order. The restrictions distinctive of legal relationship will not apply: the use of force directed at him will not be subordinated to law and will not have to be justified as a response to a legal wrong committed by him; he will be exposed to the instrumental use of force and to whatever fate those who prove stronger may choose to impose on him.

What a conventional criterion of admission to legal community establishes, if strictly adhered to, are two logically exhaustive and mutually exclusive relationships among humans. There is the relationship between those who qualify as subjects under the conventional standard, and this is a legal relationship governed by the restriction distinctive of this relationship; and there is the relationship between those who together form the conventionally constituted legal community and the assorted humans who do not qualify, and this relationship is not a legal relationship, and so it is released from all legal constraints. Law will not fill the human world, but will run out at the threshold determined by the operative convention. There will be two domains of law and nonlaw existing side by side, both inscribed in the jurisprudence of the conventional community.

It is of special importance to note that the parties or entities that face each other in the convention-generated extralegal domain are neither "individuals" nor "states." What a conventional criterion of access to legal relationship yields is a single authentic legal community on the one side facing a variety of nonlegal outsiders on the other side. The fact that some or all of these other humans who are excluded from the authentic legal community nevertheless count as juridical persons within their own legal communities, according to some different particularistic convention, is irrelevant. Given strict conformity to the particular convention of each legal community, juridical personality is nontransferable. The fact that others have achieved and maintained a viable legal order of their own has no legal effects in the home community, although it may possess significance, from a so-called realist perspective, as a matter of power and expediency. A conventional criterion dissolves the other's social existence as something carrying normative weight. The outsider's community cannot be conceived as a "state" understood as itself a subject of some wider legal relationship without introducing some other criterion besides the prevailing convention and indeed transcending all such particularistic conventions.[11]

This extralegal zone may therefore be recognized to have another feature, and this is that there can be no place in it for the distinction between peace and war as mutually exclusive legal statuses or for the distinction between just and unjust war. Both presuppose legal relationship between subjects, the violation of which constitutes a legal wrong justifying a decision to move from peace to war and so to have recourse to types of actions unlawful in the legal condition of peace. In this nonlegal domain, generated by some conventional criterion of legal personality, recourse to force is not subordinated to law, need not be justified as a response to an antecedent wrong, and may be resorted to for any expediential reason. To sum up, then, strict conformity to a conventional criterion of admission to legal relationship yields an extreme condition in which both personality and peace are dissolved, and the derivation of this extreme situation is out of certain features of a legal world dominated by a particular conception of community.[12]

This "sketch" is becoming increasingly complex (and perhaps contentious). But enough has been said to make clear the direction of argument and the main points. The argument I am making is that, first and foremost, the conventional character of law cannot be confined to content-conventionalism. There is also scope-conventionalism, and this is so because law can be made to vary along two dimensions—not only which rules are valid law but which humans are juridical persons. Further, when these two types of conventionalism are prised apart, a distinct problem about the solution of law to justice may be identified—distinct, that is to say, from the problem addressed by the vertical model. Third, the provenance of "natural law theory" addressed to the problem of scope-conventionalism will be displaced onto the international scene: there will be a shift of attention from the *internal* relationship within a complete community between the content of positive law and the persons obligated to obey it to the *external* relationship at the interface between the conventional legal community and all who are defined by the reigning convention as "outsiders." And finally, a natural law theory centered on this relationship will be associated with a distinctive conception of "natural law" as the notion of legal relationship, properly so-called, embracing all who by nature are capable of being governed by law and so being fellow-subjects with one another. In short, natural law here will be Cicero's and Grotius's *humani generis societas* for which the division between those creatures who have law in common and those who do not is determined by nature, not convention.

Unfortunately, no attempt can be made here to exhibit the centrality of this problematic to specific texts in the natural law tradition, in particular to the original versions of natural law theory developed by the Stoics and by Cicero. There is simply not space to undertake the requisite inquiry. Moreover, the reconstruction of Stoic theory is beset with interpretive difficulty, due to the massive loss of the chief Stoic writings and to the absence of any sustained presentation of Stoic "cosmopolitanism" before Cicero, who may well have transformed it. Not surprisingly, both the content and context of Stoic theory remain subjects of continuing controversy in modern scholarship, with the key questions of the identity of the members of the cosmic city of law and the nature of "nomos" very much at the forefront of debate.[13] For several different reasons, the foregoing sketch of the problematic of natural law theory must therefore be regarded as merely a hypothesis for inquiry and an aid for rethinking what the natural law tradition was all about.

One last comment, however, may be in order regarding the general theme of this chapter, "natural law and international order." The preceding attempt to sketch the problem of scope-conventionalism will, I hope, have provided a distinct perspective on the pervasive concern with the international scene in the natural law tradition. This concern is no accident or afterthought, as it appears when the provenance of natural law theory is taken to be "complete community."[14] The issue of scope-conventionalism creates a special problem of international relations and international law, and the suggestion of this chapter is that when attention is turned to such key texts as Plutarch's *Alexander* 328–29, Cicero's *De officiis*, Vitoria's *De Indis*, or Grotius's *De iure belli ac pacis*, the context of theory will be recognized as a world in which positive law has run out, because some conventional criterion of juridical personality dominates the self-understanding of human community.

NOTES

1. See Joseph Raz, *Practical Reason and Norms* (London: Hutchinson, 1975), 37–45, 47–48, 74, 89, and other writings.

2. John Finnis, *Natural Law and Natural Rights* (Oxford: Oxford University Press, 1980), 234–35, 255, 308–309, 345, 352.

3. Cf. Finnis, *Natural Law and Natural Rights*, ch. 2, sect. 6.

4. This distinction between natural justice and natural law is explored by Gisele Striker, "The Origin of the Concept of Natural Law," *Proceedings of the Boston Area Colloquium in Ancient Philosophy* 2 (1987): 79–101.

5. Cicero, *De legibus* 1.23.

6. Charles R. Beitz, "Cosmopolitan Liberalism and the States System," in Chris Brown, ed., *Political Restructuring in Europe: Ethical Perspectives* (London: Routledge, 1994), 123–36, and Brian Barry in Chapter 9 below.

7. Plutarch, *Alexander* 329A–B.

8. Beitz, "Cosmopolitan Liberalism," 125.

9. Niklas Luhmann, *A Sociological Theory of Law*, trans. Elizabeth King and Martin Albrow (London: Routledge and Kegan Paul, 1985), 150–53.

10. For a particularly influential statement of this assumption, see G.E.M. Anscombe, "Modern Moral Philosophy," *Philosophy* 33 (1958): 1–19. Finnis and George deny that natural law theory must be situated in a theological framework, but they fail to recognize that the appeal of a theological framework depends on the assumption that natural law theory must be cast in the vertical mode.

11. As an aid to reflection, see Lucien Levy-Bruhl, "La Condition du Romain a l'étranger," in *Quelques problèmes du très ancien droit Romain* (Paris, 1934), as well as his "Theorie de l'esclavage" in the same volume and also reprinted in M. I. Finley, ed., *Slavery in Classical Antiquity* (Cambridge: Heffer, 1968).

12. See Bruce Lincoln, "War and Warriors: An Overview," in *Death, War, and Sacrifice: Studies in Ideology and Practice* (Chicago: University of Chicago Press, 1991), for an analysis of the extreme situation.

13. For a sampling of the disparate views on offer in the contemporary debate, see Malcolm Schofield, *The Stoic Idea of the City* (Cambridge: Cambridge University Press, 1991); Andrew Erskine, *The Hellenistic Stoa: Political Thought and Action* (London: Duckworth, 1990); Philip Mitsis, "Natural Law and Natural Right in Post-Aristotelian Philosophy: The Stoics and Their Critics," in Wolfgang Haase, ed., *Aufstieg and Niedergang der romischen Welt*, T. 2, bd. 36, teilbd. 7 (Berlin: W. de Gruyter, 1994), 4851–900; Paul A. Vander Waerdt, "Zeno's Republic and the Origins of Natural Law," in Vander Waerdt, ed., *The Socratic Movement* (Ithaca, NY: Cornell University Press, 1994), 272–308; and Striker, "Origin of the Concept of Natural Law."

14. In distinguishing the two models of natural law theory, I do not mean to imply absence of essential connection between them. But this is an issue that cannot be examined here.

CHAPTER 5

Kant on Justice and the Law of Nations

PIERRE LABERGE

FOR HEDLEY BULL, there are three traditions of thought on international politics: "the Hobbesian or realist tradition, which views international politics as a state of war; the Kantian or universalist tradition, which sees at work in international politics a potential community of mankind; and the Grotian or internationalist tradition, which views international politics as taking place within an international society."[1] Our theme, the constitution of international society, might not therefore appear very Kantian. All the less so since international society in this "Grotian" or internationalist sense is a "society of states,"[2] not a society of "individuals linked across national boundaries" or understood "in cosmopolitan terms."[3] And Kantianism is considered "the most cosmopolitan of . . . traditions."[4]

Yet Kant would have understood the term "international society" in an internationalist sense; his "law of nations" deals with the rules of international society understood as a society of states.[5] Informed that "the 'Constitution' of international society . . . is the unwritten constitution of customary international law,"[6] he would say that his concern is elsewhere: is this constitutive customary law and the law of nations in general *just*? Just, that is, in keeping not with an actual contract, but with a norm, or with the "Idea" of an original contract, to employ Kant's distinctive terminology. The idea of a contract is to other contracts somewhat like what Terry Nardin calls a "practical association" is to a "purposive association."[7] "In all social contracts," Kant writes, "we find a union of many individuals for some common end which they all *share*." In the original contract, however, we find a "union as an end in itself which they all *ought to share*."[8]

Because the idea of the original contract is the idea of a union of individuals, the "ultimate units of concern" of a just law of nations are, of course, "human beings, or persons, rather than . . . nations, or states."[9] Kant writes on the law of nations as a cosmopolitan. But then what of Kant's cosmopolitan law, if his view of the law of nations is already of cosmopolitan inspiration? Is it not, after all, the introduction of cosmopolitan law (*ius cosmopoliticum*) beside civil law (*ius civitatis*) and the law of nations (*ius gentium*) that makes the Kantian (and then the Fichtean) division of public law original?[10] To understand the relations between these three laws, and, more generally, to cover our topic-related questions, we already foresee that the best firing angle is

83

Kant's views on justice. And to deal with Kant's theory of international justice requires some treatment of his theory of justice in general.

It will then immediately appear that, on one major point, Kant does not belong to the "Kantian tradition" as understood by Bull: "on the universalist view, the interests of all men are one and the same; international politics is . . . a purely cooperative or non-zero-sum game."[11] Nothing could be less Kantian. Commenting on Hobbes's proposition, "the natural state of men is the war of everybody with everybody," Kant quarrels only with the word "war," to which he prefers "state of war."[12] For Kant, there is no more "automatic harmony" between human beings than there is, for the neorealist Kenneth Waltz, between states.[13] It seems to me that it would be more appropriate to place Kant in the Hobbesian tradition. At least at the beginning.[14]

KANT's THEORY OF JUSTICE

Kant systematically developed his theory of justice for the first time in his "Doctrine of Law," which is the first part of *The Metaphysics of Morals* (1797),[15]—cited hereafter as MM. His essays "Theory and Practice" (1793)[16] and "Perpetual Peace" (1795)[17]—the latter cited hereafter as PP—deal only with public law and therefore only with political justice. The fact that Kant treats justice in his "Doctrine of Law" rather than in the *Foundations of the Metaphysics of Morals* (1785)[18] or the *Critique of Practical Reason* (1788),[19] his two classics in moral philosophy, requires that we situate his conception of justice, on the one hand, vis-à-vis his conception of law and, on the other hand, vis-à-vis his conception of morality. Nobody, I believe, has better fulfilled this double task than Otfried Höffe. I will therefore often borrow from him in the next few pages.[20]

Law, one might say, is positive law, the subject matter covered in the "faculty of law." It is no more the business of the "philosophy faculty" than is biblical hermeneutics (the subject matter covered in the "theology faculty"). The jurist *as such* (because of course the same person can be a jurist and a philosopher) "does not look to his reason for the laws that secure the Mine and Thine, but to the code of laws."[21] The question, *Quid sit juris?*—What are the positive laws and how should they be applied in given cases?—has to remain her private ground. But the question "What is just?"—What are *just* positive laws?—belongs to the philosopher, more specifically in this case to the professor of natural law. The "faculty of law" teaches positive law while the "philosophy faculty" teaches the "criterion," the "immutable principles for any giving of positive law" (MM 55). This criterion, these principles, are the principles of justice. What are they?

First and foremost, the imperative: "so act externally that the free use of your choice (*Willkür*) can coexist with the freedom of everyone in accordance with a universal law" (MM 56). As a principle of justice, this imperative is the criterion "for any giving of positive law." But what has it to do with morality? Here an important distinction is in order. This imperative is moral since it is neither technical, nor pragmatic, but categorical. In another sense, it is not moral since it does not demand virtue.

That it is not pragmatic has to be underscored. It does not require the maximization of either total or average well-being. The point of justice is to reconcile the freedom of each with everyone's freedom, even if the maximization of well-being is thereby put in jeopardy. While a hypothetical (technical or pragmatic) imperative is always an "if" principle, a categorical imperative is always an "even if" principle.[22] The criterion of justice is categorical, and therefore moral.

But this moral imperative is, in another sense, not moral since it requires a concern for everyone's freedom only from the positive laws. Justice demands that laws be just, but not that one submit to them because they are just. It does not demand virtue (MM 194). Let us assume that Michel Rocard was right when explaining on French TV that Desert Storm was a police operation required by international law. After all, one cannot let one state swallow another. The fact, if it is one, that the US led Desert Storm to protect western oil supplies is of no interest for Kant's idea of justice.

Now, to understand the categorical imperative of justice one has to take into account the problem it has to solve; one has to identify what Rawls, following Hume, calls the "circumstances of justice."[23] Kant does this at paragraph B of the introduction to his "Doctrine of Law" (MM 55–56).[24]

The first "circumstance of justice" is the coexistence of free agents in a common world, therefore their "unavoidable" influence on each other (MM 121, translation revised). And the relevant freedom of these agents is not their internal, but their external freedom, their "independence from being constrained by another's choice" (MM 63). Such a freedom is compatible with what the *Foundations* calls "heteronomy of the will."[25] Kant goes as far as to say that the problem of justice would arise even between devils, provided they were intelligent (PP 112).[26]

A second "circumstance of justice" is the relation of one's free choice to that of others, not to their needs. Beneficence, although a duty, does not belong to the realm of justice. Rawls takes pride in the fact that his theory of justice makes sense of the French trio, *liberté, égalité, fraternité*.[27] Kant's own theory does not take *fraternité* into account.

Hence the problem of justice lies in the coexistence of free agents in a common world and in the conflicts which therefore inevitably arise. In such a world, as in the original chaos of Kant's cosmogony, rest cannot last more than an instant. Such a state of nature is a state of war for Kant, as it is for Hobbes. Everyone is at the mercy of everyone else. The strongest can be killed "by secret machination or by confederacy with others."[28] An intelligent devil could not but will to abandon this condition. He (or she) could not but will to exchange his freedom to kill for his right not to be killed.[29]

His life as a condition of her external freedom, and to that extent his external freedom itself, would then coexist with the life and therefore with the external freedom of his peers "in accordance with a universal law," in this case, thou shall not kill. Hence, the imperative of justice as formulated above.

The ban on killing is part of the solution to the problem that faces everyone in the state of nature if and only if that solution is universal, that is, only if it limits each person's external freedom equally, thereby securing everyone's life and external freedom. Only such an equal limitation of freedom can be preferred to the state of nature and war by every devil. Only justice can be willed universally.

But is it the case that everyone's external freedom is limited and thereby secured? What if devil B tries to "make an exception" for himself (PP 112, translation revised) and prevents devil A from exercising his external freedom within the limits which make possible the coexistence of their external freedoms? Devil B would then overstep these limits and devil A should be authorized to coerce him in return, within the limits he oversteps. Otherwise, the limitation of devil A's external freedom would no longer secure his external freedom. Kant therefore concludes: "right and authorization to use coercion . . . mean one and the same thing" (MM 58).

But must devil B wait until he "has learned by bitter experience" (MM 122) the disposition of devil A to try to exempt himself from the law? Would it not be prudent, and devils are prudent, to preempt?[30] But if the security of B's freedom is made possible by the limitation of A's freedom, while the limitation of A's freedom is provided by B, one hardly sees any improvement vis-à-vis the state of nature and war. Indeed, devils A and B are still in the state of nature. Nevertheless some improvement has been achieved insofar as they now know what will be the task of public law. Public law should secure everyone's freedom by securing an equal limitation of everyone's freedom, by guaranteeing private law or natural justice (MM 120–21).[31]

Until now we have abstracted from a difficulty. We have presented Kant's theory of justice as if there were only an "internally" mine or thine. But private law also deals with an "externally" mine or thine (MM 63). My body obviously falls under what is internally mine. My clothes fall under what is externally mine. They can hardly be considered as internally mine, since, although they are mine, someone else can wear them. More generally, external things and chiefly land, on the one hand, and another's performances promised through contracts, on the other hand, fall under the externally mine or thine (MM 259, 261).

But is there, now for justice or natural law, a new problem specifically associated with the "externally" mine or thine? For instance with land? Is it not sufficient once again to limit equally everyone's freedom in order to secure it: I give up taking over your piece of land if you give up taking over my mine? But, as Leslie Mulholland points out, such a renunciation presupposes that we already agree on the boundaries of our respective pieces of land.[32] (This difficulty does not arise concerning our bodies.) Our claims may differ and my neighbor may believe that I claim a limitation of his freedom beyond what is required to make our freedoms coexist. And vice versa.

Let us assume that, far from being devils, we are both virtuous, as well disposed and law-abiding as we can be. How will we settle our unavoidable conflicts of claims? Through war? Why would the loser accept the outcome? Will he not sooner or later resume the hostilities? The solution is to substitute the decision of a "competent judge" for victory as a procedure of settling conflicts—a solution Kant was so fond of that he borrowed it for his critical philosophy and its tribunal of reason. This "competent judge" presupposes a legislative power and an executive power, just as the conclusion of a practical syllogism presupposes major and minor premises (MM 312–13). It is not easy to be more specific about this analogy.[33] Be that as it may, the legislative power's function is to express the general will. Legislation for which it is impossible "to have an object of my external freedom as mine" would wrong me; that is to say, it would limit my external freedom more than is required by the imperative of justice (MM 68–69). But for legislation to avoid so doing without thereby wronging others, it is necessary to express the general will. The general will alone can, in principle, multilaterally absolve the unilateral original acquisition of land from the unilateral limitation of freedom it implies (MM 267–68).

The three powers and their separation—in other words, the republican constitution (PP 95–96)—make possible the substitution of judicial decision for victory and thereby the coexistence of free agents claiming an externally mine or thine. Without them, every externally mine or thine is only "provisional," not "conclusive," and will remain so until the republican constitution "extends to the entire human race" (MM 78, 87).

If an externally mine or thine has to be granted to avoid excessively limiting my freedom, and if such an excessive limitation of my freedom cannot be avoided without excessively limiting your freedom unless the state of nature is abandoned in favor of a public state and a republican constitution, then one must leave the state of nature, *exeundum e statu naturali*.

It has been suggested that this new imperative rests exclusively on the impossibility of securing an externally mine or thine without a state. It would rest exclusively on this difficulty if and only if we were virtuous, however. But we assumed this condition of virtue only to make it appear that, because of this peculiar difficulty, we would have to abandon the state of nature even if we were all virtuous.

Under this assumption, however, we could not see that the decision of the competent judge has to be supported by the use of coercion (MM 124). To abandon the state of nature was to go to a judge without a sword. But what if we are not virtuous? What if we are devils, or, as Kant believed, a bunch of liars and cheaters?[34] Or at least, what if we are virtuous without being sure that our peers are also virtuous? In such a world, will we abide by the decision of the judge, even when we dislike it, without being sure that our peers would do the same?[35] And in such a world would not a feeling of insecurity be justified as far as the internally mine or thine is concerned? And justified also without the peculiar problem the externally mine or thine presents us with?

Kant's theory of justice demands the equal limitation of everyone's freedom as a general solution to the problem of their coexistence in a common world. It recognizes that the problem of such a coexistence is made more difficult by the special problem of an externally mine and thine. It demands the substitution of the decision of a judge for victory as a solution to this peculiar problem. It demands, moreover, that this decision be enforceable to solve the problem of the instability of both the particular and the general solution. In a word, Kant's theory of justice demands a republican constitution, the substitution of *enforced* judicial decision for victory.

A final remark on Kantian justice and reciprocity. Just *laws* are constitutions securing everyone's freedom by equal limitations of everyone's freedom. They thereby make possible the coexistence of free agents in accordance with universal laws. They can be willed by intelligent devils. The just *person*, however, submits to these laws, not merely from interest, as devils do, but out of reverence for those laws that can be willed by intelligent devils. Now would devils submit to such laws if they believed that their peers will cheat? Of course not. That would be against their interest. Would devils submit to those laws if they believed that their peers will also submit? Of course not. That would not be in their best interest. But will a just person submit to the law if she believes that her peers will not? In other words, is reciprocity a condition of her submission? Some interpreters of Kant believe that it is not. Since the just person obeys out of reverence for the law, she is ready to be prey. But Kant's view, I think, is different. "I am therefore not under obligation," he writes, "to leave external objects belonging to others untouched unless everyone else provides me assurance that he will behave in accordance with the same principle with regard to what is mine" (MM 77; see also 122). The virtuous person does not differ from the intelligent devil in that she would not excuse herself from obeying the law were her peers to *disobey* it. She differs in that she would not excuse herself from obeying the law were her peers to *obey* it. She will defend herself against the noncompliance of others but will not take advantage of their compliance.

Kant's justice culminates in what he calls "distributive justice" (MM 121). But as Gregor puts it, Kant's theory is not a theory of

> distributive justice in the sense of fairness in the distribution of goods and burdens. Kant himself is not concerned with this problem; by a state of distributive justice he means only a condition in which there are courts to determine effectively what belongs to each party in a dispute about rights.[36]

There is a libertarian flavor in all this which does not look promising for a Kantian theory of global or transnational justice which could "take needs seriously." This is why some distinguished students of Kant endeavor to go beyond Kant's theory of justice as presented so far. The most interesting example is Onora O'Neill's.

One could interpret her Kantian theory of justice as rooted in an amendment to the first "circumstance of justice" as presented above: the coexistence of agents influencing each other in a common world. For her, the problem of justice still "arises only for a plurality of at least potentially interacting agents . . . who share a world" and the question of justice still reads: "what principles can a plurality of agents . . . live by?" Moreover, her test of universality looks pretty close to the one we are now familiar with. "Put quite generally," she writes, "principles of action that hinge on victimizing some, whether by destroying, paralyzing, or undercutting their capacities for agency for at least some time and in some ways . . . cannot be universally adopted." After all, as we have seen, the freedom to kill cannot be universally adopted as a principle by a "nation of devils" (provided they are mortal devils, of course). The same is true of "a principle to coerce."[37] The freedom to coerce (distinct from the permission to coerce the would-be coercer) cannot be universally adopted by a nation of devils. In general, such principles cannot be adopted by all intelligent devils because they can be adopted by *none* of them. None of them accepts anything but the equal limitation of everyone's freedom to kill, to coerce, etc. (if it is enforced), owing to their assumed equal vulnerability.

Nevertheless, O'Neill's test of universality differs from the one we applied with Höffe to the nation of devils. The freedom to coerce "cannot be universally adopted" not because *no one* can adopt this principle, but because "*some*"[38] cannot adopt it. What has been abandoned is the assumption of equal vulnerability. The unavoidable *abstraction* of principles of justice ought not be confused with the avoidable *idealization* of the free agents referred to in the first circumstance of justice. These agents are "finite, needy" beings,[39] their vulnerability is indeterminate, as is their rationality. They are not idealized, equally vulnerable superstars like Kant's devils. The description of the first circumstance of justice has to be amended accordingly.

Renunciation of idealization and of the premise of equal vulnerability makes it possible for a Kantian theory of justice to take needs seriously. The abstract, but nonidealizing principle of noncoercion has to be applied to people of unequal vulnerability. It is easier to make an unrefusable offer to the hungry than to the well fed. Not to coerce the needy is more demanding. "Justice to the weak demands more than justice to the strong."[40] But will not the strong, even the benevolent strong, be inclined to take advantage of a position of strength? May we believe, asks the soft-spoken Fénelon, that "une nation qui peut subjuguer les autres s'en abstienne pendant des siècles entiers?"[41] Institutions should therefore be created which will reduce the "powerlessness and vulnerability"[42] of the most needy and vulnerable.

The just Kantian society is one whose constitution is republican. The scope of republican law is no more than liberty and equality, unless one succeeds in freeing Kant's theory of justice from its idealizing twist. The prototype of a basic structure incompatible with republican law is therefore a hereditary nobility. It is not possible for all to agree to a law stating that "a certain class of *subjects* must be privileged as a hereditary *ruling class*."[43] Such a law would lack legitimacy and authority.

But, to our surprise, Kant does not conclude that we have a right to rebel against it. For this reason, though he does defend the right to write in favor of constitutional reforms, the "freedom of the pen," Kant believes that, even when just (*rechtmässige*) to only a low degree, a constitution, as legal (*rechtliche*), is better than none at all, or than "the anarchic condition which would result from precipitate reform" (PP 120).

The original contract is a norm, not a fact (as Danton misunderstood it to be).[44] But it is a standard which humanity will come closer and closer to meeting if it ever begins to meet it. But from the very moment there are public laws, that is (to speak like Kant) something "rechtlich," even if it imposes something as unpalatable as hereditary nobility, there is inchoately a constitution in keeping with the Idea of the original contract, of a "rechtmässige," that is, a republican, constitution. It is as if law were a promise of justice, because, after all, there cannot be law without at least a modest amount of justice or possible coexistence.[45]

Finally, since "right and authorization to coerce . . . mean one and the same thing," there cannot be an authoritative law without enforceability and— since private enforceability would lead us back to the state of nature—without public enforceability.

KANTIAN CONCEPTIONS OF INTERNATIONAL JUSTICE

The "philosophy faculty" does not ask the question "What is the law?" but "What are just laws?" It is the same with international law.

In *A Theory of Justice*, John Rawls argues that principles for the law of nations can hardly be agreed on without prior agreement on common principles for the basic structure of society.[46] Kant agrees.

Rawls gathers under the veil of ignorance "representative persons" from a society conceived as "closed" or autarkical. Charles Beitz, drawing upon theorists of international interdependence, has objected that no society is autarkical.[47] Be that as it may, Rawls could have chosen an impeccable example of an autarkical society: the society of men and women living on earth. The Rawlsian principles of justice could have been chosen by parties from whom the veil of ignorance conceals their membership in different states, by concealing in the first place the empirical fact of a plurality of states. After all, though the problem of justice cannot arise without a plurality of agents in a common world, it can arise without a plurality of states. *A Theory of Justice* using such an opaque veil of ignorance would have been the same, minus Section 58.

The Kantian principles of justice summarized in republicanism could also be chosen in ignorance of the fact of a plurality of states. Does not Kant mention the rotundity of the earth already in his exposition of private law (MM 83)? On the basis of its modest presupposition—a plurality of free agents (of undeterminate vulnerability, O'Neill would emphasize) in a common world—Kant's general theory of justice does not and cannot take into account the plurality of states. It is a theory for the inhabitants of the earth. From its point of view, the law of nations disappears, civil law and cosmopolitan law coincide, every mine or thine appears "conclusive."

But, with the revelation of a plurality of states, we leave ideal theory. Hence the uneasiness, indeed the impatience, of every liberal theorist of global justice before these irksome intruders, the states. On the one hand, they exist in a state of nature and of war (PP 92) analogous to the state we could agree to leave as individuals under the veil of ignorance. And they are drawing us with them into a state of nature and of war. Our mine and thine cannot become "conclusive," but must remain "provisional" until our national boundaries cease to be provisional (MM 87). On the other hand, not all the constitutions of our states fit our principle of justice, the idea of republicanism. Which principle(s) should we adopt under these "less happy conditions?"[48] Kant now needs a nonideal theory.

The principle of this nonideal theory, I suggest, is provided by Kant's suggestion that

> the law of nations is a law in a state . . . of war, that is, in the absence of public justice. Its only principle, therefore, is that all actions of a nation toward others conform to the necessary conditions of public justice, that is to the conditions under which alone a league of nations (*Völkerbund*) is possible, . . . for even if no public justice is given, nations are nevertheless bound by [the principle by] which public justice would be possible."[49]

This applies more specifically to the law of war (*ius in bello*). But its principle holds, I take it, for the whole of the law of nations. It is upon such a principle for the law of nations that the parties could agree after they had been informed of their distribution in different states. I would paraphrase this principle in the following way: states ought to govern their interactions in such a way that these interactions, at worst, do not make impossible, and, at best, favor the future coexistence of everyone's freedom with everyone's freedom agreed on in the ideal theory. At least in this sense, a Kantian is mainly concerned with *individuals* when evaluating the justice of the law of nations. The law of nations ought to be such that it does not hinder, and even promotes, the advent of the law, both civil and cosmopolitan, agreed on in ignorance of the fact of a plurality of states.

Is Kant more specific on the principle(s) of the law of nations? Let us recall Kant's articles for perpetual peace. The "Preliminary Articles" are:

> 1. No treaty of peace shall be held valid in which there is tacitly reserved matter for a future war.
> 2. No independent states, large or small, shall come under the dominion of another state by inheritance, exchange, purchase, or donation.

3. Standing armies (*miles perpetuus*) shall in time be totally abolished.

4. National debts shall not be contracted with a view to the external friction of states.

5. No state shall by force interfere with the constitution or government of another state.

6. No state shall, during war, permit such acts of hostility which would make mutual confidence in the subsequent peace impossible.

And the "Definitive Articles":

1. The civil constitution of every state should be republican.
2. The law of nations shall be founded on a federation of free states.
3. The law of world citizenship shall be limited to conditions of universal hospitality (PP 85–105).

In "Perpetual Peace," Kant mentions explicitly only one principle of the law of nations, namely the second definitive article. Nevertheless, at least the sixth preliminary article obviously pertains to the law of nations, since it is concerned with the law of war (*ius in bello*), which is also covered by the law of nations according to the "Doctrine of Law" (MM 150). Moreover, I interpret the first five preliminary articles as pertaining to the law of war understood in a broader sense. Although they are concerned neither with the rules to be observed during hostilities (as the sixth article is) nor with the rules to be observed during a "state of war" in the strict sense of a state following a declaration of war (in this sense France and Germany were already in war during the "drôle de guerre"), they are concerned with rules to be observed in the state of war which is the state of nature (PP 92). This is not to say that the observance of the second definitive article will draw them out of such a state of nature and war into a civil state (PP 101–102), but at least it will bring them to a kind of intermediary state which Kant calls a "federal state (*foederativer Zustand*)" (PP 133, translation revised). To this already complex picture, one must finally add that Kant distinguishes between strict and more permissive preliminary articles for perpetual peace (PP 91) and, more importantly, considers the federation of free states, the league of nations on which to found the law of nations, as no more than the "surrogate" of a "world republic" (PP 102).

Such a world republic would realize the law, both civil and cosmopolitan, that the parties were able to agree on in their first round of discussions. In the second round, their problem has become the following: what kind of law of nations will make possible the creation of this civil and cosmopolitan law? Kant's answer is a law of nations founded on a federation (*Foederalism*) of free states, the league of nations. But the eighteenth-century states were not already there. Some conditions needed to be met (and some without any delay) for such a treaty (*foedus*) or league itself to be made possible, that is, acceptable. Like those "preliminary conditions (sometimes designated preliminary articles) which are demanded by the victorious party . . . as a fundamental basis for negotiation, where the other party sues for peace."[50] These preliminary conditions are indeed the six preliminary articles for a perpetual peace.

The following questions immediately arise: (1) Why is the treaty of free states or the league of nations a mere surrogate of a world republic? (2) If the treaty is not more than that, why does not the second definitive article for a perpetual peace demand more? (3) Why does the second article demand such a treaty at all? (4) How are the preliminary articles conditions of the second definitive article? (5) Why the third and first definitive articles for a perpetual peace?

1. Why is the treaty of free states a mere surrogate of a world republic? The ideal theory demands the republican constitution, that is, the substitution of an enforceable judicial decision for victory as a procedure of settling conflicts. It demands that individuals leave the state of nature and war. But the ideal theory does not take the existence of states into account. The nonideal theory does. For it, the problem is how to escape the state of nature and war among individuals who happen to be members of different states which are themselves in a state of nature and war. And the answer is that individuals will not leave the state of nature and war if states do not, and that states will not if they don't give up victory in favor of enforceable judicial decision. "There cannot be any [other] reasonable way," Kant insists (PP 51).

A treaty or league of free states cannot, therefore, be more than a surrogate for a world republic with its enforceable judicial decision. Kant criticizes his own second definitive article for a perpetual peace, for the very reason the neorealist Waltz criticizes it[51] and that World Federalists of all stripes criticizes the UN Charter. There is no way out of the state of nature and war among states (and, Kant would add, therefore among individuals) without an enforceable judicial decision, without a world state. States cannot get out of the state of nature and war for cheap. From the "Idea for a Universal History" of 1784[52] to the "Doctrine of Law" of 1797 (MM 156), Kant stuck to this position.[53]

2. Why, then, does not the second definitive article, which requires a federation of free states, instead demand a world republic? A first answer is suggested by Kant himself. With a world republic, there would be no law of nations anymore (PP 98). But one may counter: so what? In the same vein, a second answer could be: if the second article demanded a world republic, the first and third definitive articles would become obsolete. The first reads: "The civil constitution of every state should be republican." But what would "every state" mean in a world state? And why a cosmopolitan third article in the realm of a law both civil and cosmopolitan? But again: so what? Three definitive articles would be replaced by only one! So much the better!

A more plausible answer, and one again suggested by Kant, is that under their idea of the law of nations, states do not want a world republic (PP 101). Why, then, bother drafting a second definitive article to which states are opposed, an article, which, to be implemented, lacks only, as Frederick the Great would put it, "le consentement de l'Europe et quelques autres bagatelles semblables"?[54] The nonideal theorist, after all, has to take into account "less happy conditions."

That the nonideal theorist is not a political "moralist" does not make out of him a "despotizing moralist" (PP 120) who demands a republican constitution and a world state right here and now. He is a "moral politician," a kind of Aristotelian Kantian.[55] If he does not accept as fate the opposition of states to the establishment of a world state, he nevertheless takes it into account. He demands the league of nations not as the solution (only a world republic would be that), but as a scheme which will bring states closer to a world republic[56]—just as a "pluralistic security community" may lead to an "amalgamated security community," according to Karl Deutsch.[57]

Nevertheless, this third answer to our second question is not, I think, the most important. The nonideal theorist takes into account not only the unwillingness of states to establish a world state (a matter of prudence), but also the legitimate reluctance of at least some of them (a matter of justice). The imperative *exeundum e statu naturali* does not apply to states in the same way it applies to individuals, for states "already have an internal legal (*rechtliche*) constitution and have thus outgrown compulsion from others to submit to a more extended lawful constitution according to their ideas of law" (PP 100, translation revised). This difference not only forbids a state to *coercively* submit another to its own constitution (for Iraq to swallow Kuwait, for example) on the ground that the state of nature among states should be abandoned. It may also give to states a reason not to *voluntarily* cosubmit to a common constitution. A nonrepublican constitution, as *rechtliche* although not fully *rechtmässige*, is already an achievement. A republican constitution is a remarkable achievement. To cosubmit "to a more extended lawful constitution" is a risk.[58] The extended constitution may prove less just than the one already enjoyed. As the monetary policies of different countries have to be brought closer before a monetary union becomes possible, so have conceptions of domestic justice to be brought closer before a world state becomes possible.

3. But granted that a league of nations and the law of nations founded on it is only a surrogate, why is it better than nothing at all? It is like asking why, in the absence of a world state, the prohibition by UN Charter Article 2(4) of the use or threat of force in international relations is better than nothing at all.

Of course there are at least two differences between the Kantian league of nations and the United Nations as bound by Article 2(4). On the one hand, since most states are members of the United Nations, the United Nations cannot be understood as a defensive alliance against outside aggression (MM 155).[59] One might suggest that the Kantian league resembles NATO more than the UN. But the Kantian league, like the Fichtean one, is destined to cover the earth (PP 101) and will then cease to be an alliance. On the other hand, one might argue that the Kantian league is a treaty between republican states. I will deal with this difficulty below.

Be that as it may, there are important similarities. The United Nations and the Kantian league are treaties (PP 131). "Foederalism" comes from "foedus," as F. H. Hinsley points out.[60] Contrary to a state constitution, the Kantian league not only has the original contract as a norm, it is itself an international contract. Moreover the Kantian treaty is negative: it "averts war" and forbids attempts against the freedom of states (PP 100–102). So it almost coincides with Article 2(4) of the UN Charter.

Now why is the Kantian league, why is Article 2(4), better than nothing? Because to agree on the norm not to use force (except in self-defense) is already better than not to agree on such a norm. That justice is incomplete without the sword does not argue for the sword without justice, but for justice with the sword.

4. How are the preliminary articles conditions of the second definitive article? The ideal theorist demands that individuals leave the state of nature and war. The nonideal theorist realizes that this is not possible unless states themselves leave the state of nature and war. She also realizes that for the time being such an exit is not only politically impossible, but threatening for the level of justice some may already enjoy. As a surrogate for a world republic, a law of nations founded on a league of nations, that is something like Article 2(4)—and Article 51 on the "inherent" right of self-defense—of the UN Charter, is the norm. But under what preliminary conditions is it possible for states to renounce the use of force? These conditions of a federation of free states are set in the six preliminary articles, first and foremost in the three strict ones.[61]

A state that tacitly reserves matter for a future war does not renounce the use of force and makes it impossible for other states to renounce it. Hence the first preliminary article, which condemns such reservations allowed by the existing law of nations (PP 125).

States will not renounce the use of force if other states are allowed to intervene by force in their domestic affairs. Hence the fifth preliminary article forbidding forcible intervention. After all, would states have agreed to Article 2(4) in the absence of Article 2(7) against intervention by the UN and a fortiori by states acting unilaterally in matters which are essentially within their domestic jurisdiction? One could not accept Goerres's plan for a revolutionary intervention without becoming the objective ally of Gentz preaching for a monarchist counterrevolution.[62] One could hardly promote a Reagan Doctrine without making easier the life of supporters of a Brezhnev Doctrine. The relation between the second definitive article and the fifth preliminary one could then read: no Article 2(4) without Article 2(7).

It is impossible to trust in states that do not abide by the law of war. And it is impossible to renounce the use of force vis-à-vis states you don't trust. Moreover, the league itself is fragile and war may occur in spite of it (PP 102). War has then to be conducted according to rules, the law of war, which will not put in jeopardy the minimal mutual trust necessary for the restoration of the league. Hence the sixth preliminary article.

5a. Why a third definitive article for a perpetual peace concerning cosmopolitan law? The cosmopolitan law is also a surrogate. To discover its precise contribution "under less happy conditions," let us suppose we already have a law of nations founded on a treaty of all states. The cosmopolitan law then appears as a kind of concession dragged out of the law of nations as a law of "coexistence" in the name of the principle of justice agreed on in ideal theory, that is of the Idea of a world republic.[63] It tells us: even if the states of our world league of nations are sovereign, everyone has "an innate right to be on the land (to occupy a place on earth) on which nature or chance (therefore without . . . choice) has put" him or her.[64] I understand "chance" here to mean birth and "nature" to mean other kinds of situations one has been put into without any choice, such as the condition of a refugee. One cannot refuse to receive a citizen of the world if this cannot be done without causing her destruction (PP 102). Refugee law is the most obvious contribution of cosmopolitan law to the law of nations. It is true that Kant takes the opportunity provided by cosmopolitan law to condemn colonialism,[65] but, in so doing, he sets limits to cosmopolitan law, and explains what it is not, not what it is.

5b. Why a first definitive article of perpetual peace requiring republican government? In Professor Tesón's view,

> the Kantian theory . . . necessitates amendment of the conditions of admission and permanence in the United Nations. Articles 4 and 6 of the Charter . . . should be amended to include the requirement that only democratic governments that respect human rights should be allowed to represent members, and that only democratic states will be accepted as new members.[66]

This is not the Kantian view as I have presented it so far, but it is the view of Carl J. Friedrich,[67] and a very natural and respectable one indeed in the light of Kant's first definitive article: "The civil constitution of every state should be republican."

Let us call this the "Friedrich-Tesón" view and the one presented so far the "progressive-conservative" view. The latter is not purely conservative: it respects states because it respects persons. That is, it respects states because this is taken to be the right track to a world republic. But the Friedrich-Tesón view respects states not only because it respects persons, but also because states respect persons. "Political legitimacy is thus seen as the proper foundation of state sovereignty."[68] One cannot deny that the two views belong to the Kantian tradition. What I have already said supports the progressive-conservative view. What supports the Friedrich-Tesón one?

What does not support it is Friedrich's reading of the word "free" in the formulation of the second definitive article: that the law of nations should be founded on a federation of "free states." Free here does not mean republican, but sovereign. Nevertheless the convergence of conceptions of domestic justice needed for a league of nations (and a law of nations) to become obsolete and disappear, and for a world republic to come into being, is obviously a convergence toward the republican conception. That is why the first definitive article is also an article for perpetual peace. There will be no perpetual peace without a world republic and, as a penultimate target, a world treaty of republican states. Nevertheless, a progressive-conservative might answer, this penultimate target disqualifies, as antepenultimate targets, neither a world of republican states without a treaty nor a world treaty with some nonrepublican states. (Michael Doyle interprets Kant's league as an "as if" league of republican states, as a league of republican states, one might say, without a treaty.)[69]

The best argument for the Friedrich-Tesón view is the fragility of a league which is not panrepublican. In the absence of an enforceable sentence, when states agree to submit their conflicts to arbitration, they cannot, if they win, trust the other party to abide by the arbiter's decision.[70] Hence all kinds of temptations to preempt make the league unstable. If Article 2(3) of the Charter on the peaceful settlement of conflicts does not work, Article 2(4) cannot hold. Without an enforceable judicial decision, no peaceful settlement of conflicts without trust and, therefore, without trust, no stability of the league.

Kant believes—with some hesitation (MM 160)—that trust and thereby stability can be provided if the parties enjoy republican constitutions. And he gives, as an illustration of the practicability of the idea of the league of nations, the advent of the powerful French republic whose constitution "by its nature must be inclined to perpetual peace" and provides "a fulcrum to the federation with other states" (PP 100–101).

The embryo of the league is then provided by the rally of republican states around a powerful republican state. This embryonic league resembles NATO and the world league developed from it will resemble a world league as Friedrich and Tesón want it. Will a progressive-conservative be left speechless by this admittedly strong argument? Unfortunately not, because Kant gives in the "Doctrine of Law" another illustration of a league, namely "the assembly of the States General at the Hague" and of "the ministers of most of the courts of Europe" in the first half of the eighteenth century (MM 156). Would not a world league developed from such an embryo be more in tune with the progressive-conservative view?

All in all, then, Kant's complex, if not inconsistent, view is perhaps the following:

A. A world league of nations open to all states, republican or not, and a law of nations founded on it, that forbids the use of force, and therefore intervention in matters which are within domestic jurisdiction, is what the nonideal theorist demands, even if it is not his penultimate target.

B. A panrepublican world league of nations is the penultimate target of a nonideal theorist, the target being a world republic. And even if one believes a world republic to be impossible, as Kant himself sometimes seems to believe (MM 156, "an unachievable idea"), or one considers it too big a risk, any Kantian believes that a panrepublican league of nations would be more stable than a league whose member states are not, or are not all, republican. And therefore that a world league of nations developed from a republican rally around a powerful republican state would be more stable than the treaty of the United Nations—a view explicitly challenged by the neorealist Kenneth Waltz.[71]

C. At the antepenultimate stage, states whose conception of justice is already republican and who, "comme tout le monde," have an "inherent right" to self-defense, will profit from their peace-inclined constitutions and the existence of a strong republic to build a defensive alliance. Within such republican alliances, the principles of publicity (PP 129–35) are less reluctantly complied with, and security and confidence-building measures are both easier to accept and self-enhancing.[72] This is why "liberal democracies don't make war on one another" (or hardly ever),[73] as recognized by Michael Doyle and Bruce Russett.[74] The UN as a progressive-conservative league, and NATO as a Friedrich-Tesón one, might both be embryos of the world panrepublican league.

D. Since republican states are less of a threat even for nonrepublican states, as Kant (though not Doyle) believes,[75] would a republicanizing war fought to achieve international security and to end all wars be legitimate? A war for perpetual peace? The answer is no. Kant cannot be revolutionary in foreign affairs while being a reformist in domestic affairs.[76] Moreover, "it is the peculiarity of morals specially with respect to principles of public right . . . that the less it makes conduct depend on the proposed end, that is, the intended material or moral advantage, the more it agrees with it in general" (PP 125–26).[77] A war for peace as an end does not bring us closer to peace. Therefore republican alliances and their wars should remain defensive.

The "philosophy faculty" does not ask: What is the law of nations? What are its sources? This is the function of the "faculty of law." Rather it asks: What ought the law of nations to be? What would be a just law of nations? And the Kantian answer is: a just law of nations is one that provides the necessary conditions for a world republic to come (and the necessary conditions for these necessary conditions).

Had Kant been asked to speak on the law of nations as if he were a "faculty of law" professor, however, he might have said that there is an international society of states acknowledging a law of nations, but this society is European. "One has worked on [a law of nations] only in Europe, but not much progress has been made."[78]

The sources of this European law of nations are to be found in treaties, for instance in peace treaties ("Perpetual Peace" is a pastiche of such a treaty), but also in custom. This is acknowledged by Kant when he proposes that cosmopolitan law be developed as "a supplement to the unwritten code" of the law of nations (PP 105).

Kant might not have objected to the thesis that the European international society is constituted by a customary law of nations, but, as a good Kantian, he would have insisted that this law be reformed and this society expanded. If such expansion and reform succeed, the stage will be set for a world republic, that is, for the disappearance of the law of nations and international society. The idea of justice or original contract therefore is the norm of such reforms and expansion. But historical contracts, treaties like the league of nations, will be needed to stimulate the development of the customary law of nations. One can conceive the transition to a world republic as a transition from a world in which the customary law of nations, although influenced by treaties, also makes treaties possible, to a world in which an agreed-on world republican constitution is the basis on which a law both civil and cosmopolitan will develop as customary.

The scope of the law of nations, as founded on the league of nations, is the liberty and equality of states, since the league unites "free states" to secure their freedom (PP 100). According to the Friedrich-Tesón view, respect for a state's freedom is grounded on that state's respect for its citizens. "Internal legitimacy is what gives states the shield of sovereignty against foreign intervention."[79] According to the progressive-conservative view, respect for a state's freedom, although not grounded on this state's respect for its citizens, is nevertheless grounded on respect for individuals. Even if a law of nations were aimed at meeting needs, one wonders how global needs could be met without the coercive institutions of a world republic. However this may be, some Kantians do not assign to the world republic itself the task of meeting needs. They see the world republic as a federal state which, of course, is no longer a federation of free states since it is provided with coercive institutions. Nevertheless these institutions intervene as little as possible, and are no more than "night watchmen," uninvolved in the social or cultural policies of the former free states turned world provinces.[80]

What is the authority, one might ask, of the law of nations founded on the league? A treaty has been signed and *pacta sunt servanda*. But why? Because compliance is to the advantage of even the strongest states? Hardly. Why would states then always comply with a rule which is not advantageous to every state anyway? Because compliance is on the right track to a world republic which is advantageous to every individual? But authority is then founded on legitimacy without being backed by public coercion—an unstable situation. (I leave aside the increased stability provided when all states of the league have republican constitutions.) One understands why Kant believed that a world republic with its enforceable sentence was the only "reasonable way" out of the state of nature and war. And one understands why, so as not to despair, Kant needed a philosophy of history according to which nature brings nations where they do not want to go (PP 111).

Kant is not a cultural relativist. For him, the norm of every constitution, including a world one, is the republican constitution (PP 93–94). A world league of republican states is the penultimate target of the nonideal theorist. Meanwhile, republican states, the only states whose constitutions are "created in such a way as to avoid, by their very nature, principles permitting offensive wars,"[81] will see fit to build a defensive alliance. For the Friedrich-Tesón view, the league of nations is coextensive with this alliance. For the progressive-conservative view, however, until all states become republican, NATO and the UN should exist side by side. And the UN has no chance of surviving without the principle of nonintervention, even against despotic states. This makes constitutional plurality permissible as the price to pay on humanity's road to a world republic, with its law both civil and cosmopolitan. Finally, Kant praises linguistic and religious plurality as a tool used by nature to protect us from the advent of a despotic (vs. republican) world State (PP 113). The constitution of a world republic would therefore have to take this plurality into account.

NOTES

1. Hedley Bull, *The Anarchical Society* (London: Macmillan, 1977), 24.

2. Bull, *The Anarchical Society*, 13.

3. Terry Nardin, *Law, Morality, and the Relations of States* (Princeton, NJ: Princeton University Press, 1983), 5.

4. Terry Nardin and David R. Mapel, "Convergence and Divergence in International Ethics," in *Traditions of International Ethics*, ed. Terry Nardin and David R. Mapel (Cambridge: Cambridge University Press, 1992), 310.

5. Even Kant's most uninternationalist expressions are used most of the time in an internationalist sense. For instance, *"weltbürgerliche Societät"* in *Kants gesammelte Schriften*, Band 23 (Berlin: Walter de Gruyter, 1955), 352.

6. Terry Nardin, Chapter 1 above.

7. Nardin, *Law, Morality, and the Relations of States*, 3–24.

8. *Kant's Political Writings*, ed. Hans Reiss, trans. H. B. Nisbet (Cambridge: Cambridge University Press, 1971), 73.

9. Thomas Pogge, "Cosmopolitanism and Sovereignty," *Ethics* 103 (1992): 48.

10. Interpreters have found it difficult to see the precise distinction between the law of nations and cosmopolitan law. The author of one of the most recent books on Kant's "Perpetual Peace" writes: "At first sight, one does not easily see why Kant took a third definitive article to be necessary." See Georg Cavallar, *Pax kantiana* (Vienna: Boehlau, 1992), 225 (my translation). And already in 1800, Wilhelm Traugott Krug was of the view that the "ius cosmopoliticum, which some have recently expounded as a part of public law, is truly only a part of the ius gentium." See Krug "Anmerkung zur Philosophie des Rechts" (1800), in A. Dietze and W. Dietze, eds., *Ewiger Friede?* (Munich: C. H. Beck, 1989), 168 (my translation). According to still another interpretation, cosmopolitan law is founded on a federation of all states, while the law of nations is founded on a federation of fewer than all states. See Karl Vorländer, *Kant und der Gedanke des Völkerbundes* (Leipzig: Felix Meiner, 1919), 43–44, and Mary Gregor, "Kant's Theory of Property," *Review of Metaphysics* 41 (1988): 758. But cosmopolitan law would then be no more than a global edition of the law of nations. There would be no place in it for the concept of a citizen of the world.

11. Bull, *The Anarchical Society*, 25–26.

12. Immanuel Kant, *Religion within the Limits of Reason Alone*, trans. T. H. Greene and H. H. Hudson (New York: Harper and Row, 1960), 89.

13. Kenneth N. Waltz, *Man, the State, and War* (New York: Columbia University Press, 1957), 182.

14. On this question, see the important article of Karlfriedrich Herb and Bernd Ludwig, "Naturzustand, Eigentum und Staat: Immanuel Kants Relativierung des 'Ideal des Hobbes,'" *Kant-Studien* 84 (1993): 283–316.

15. Immanuel Kant, *The Metaphysics of Morals*, trans. Mary J. Gregor (Cambridge: Cambridge University Press, 1991), 33 (revised translation).

16. See *Kant's Political Writings*, 61–92.

17. Immanuel Kant, "Perpetual Peace," in Kant, *On History*, ed. and trans. Lewis White Beck (New York: Macmillan, 1985), 85–135.

18. Immanuel Kant, *Foundations of the Metaphysics of Morals*, trans. Lewis White Beck (New York: Macmillan, 1959).

19. Immanuel Kant, *Critique of Practical Reason*, trans. Lewis White Beck (New York: Bobbs-Merrill, 1956).

20. Mainly from Otfried Höffe, *Kategorische Rechtsprinzipien* (Frankfurt: Suhrkamp: 1990), 63–69. Also from Höffe, *Politische Gerechtigkeit* (Frankfurt: Suhrkamp, 1987), 382–455, and Höffe, *Den Staat braucht selbst ein Volk von Teufeln* (Stuttgart: Reclam, 1988), 55–78.

21. Immanuel Kant, *The Conflict of the Faculties*, trans. Mary J. Gregor (Lincoln: University of Nebraska Press, 1979), 37.

22. Pierre Laberge, "L'espèce de cercle dont, à ce qu'il semble, il n'y a pas moyen de sortir," *Dialogue* 21 (1982): 748.

23. John Rawls, *A Theory of Justice* (Cambridge, MA: Harvard University Press, 1971), 22.

24. See again Höffe, *Kategorische Rechtsprinzipien*, 127–34.

25. Kant, *Foundations*, 59.

26. See Höffe, *Den Staat braucht selbst ein Volk von Teufeln*, 56.

27. Rawls, *Theory of Justice*, 105.

28. Thomas Hobbes, *Leviathan* (1651), ed. C. B. Macpherson (London: Penguin Books, 1968), 183.

29. See Höffe, *Politische Gerechtigkeit*, 382–406, and review by Pierre Laberge, *Dialogue* 32 (1993): 412–15.

30. Kant, *Religion*, 22.

31. See Höffe, *Politische Gerechtigkeit*, 433–38.

32. Leslie A. Mulholland, "Kant on War and International Justice," *Kant-Studien* 78 (1987): 31.

33. But see Bernd Ludwig, *Kants Rechtslehre* (Hamburg: Felix Meiner, 1988), 159–61.

34. Pierre Laberge, "Das radicale Böse und der Völkerzustand," in François Marty and Friedo Ricken, eds., *Kant über Religion* (Stuttgart: Kolhammer, 1992), 114–15.

35. Mulholland, "Kant on War and International Justice," 32.

36. Gregor, 762. See also Jules Vuillemin, "La justice par convention; signification philosophique de la doctrine de Rawls," *Dialectica* 41 (1987): 164.

37. Onora O'Neill, *Constructions of Reason* (Cambridge: Cambridge University Press, 1989), 212–16.

38. O'Neill, *Constructions of Reason*, 216.

39. Onora O'Neill, "Transnational Justice," in David Held, ed., *Political Theory Today* (Oxford: Polity Press, 1991), 296.

40. O'Neill, *Constructions of Reason*, 217.

41. Quoted by Charles Dupuis, *Le principe d'équilibre et le concert européen* (Paris: Perrin, 1909), 27.

42. O'Neill, "Transnational Justice," 302.

43. *Kant's Political Writings*, 79.

44. *Kant's Political Writings*, 83.
45. See Höffe, *Politische Gerechtigkeit*, 165–71.
46. Rawls, *Theory of Justice*, 110.
47. Charles R. Beitz, *Political Theory and International Relations* (Princeton, NJ: Princeton University Press, 1979), 143–53. Beitz bases his argument against the premise of autarky on the theory of interdependence in Robert O. Keohane and Joseph Nye, eds., *Transnational Relations and World Politics* (Cambridge, MA: Harvard University Press, 1972).
48. Rawls, *Theory of Justice*, 246.
49. *Kants gesammelte Schriften*, Band 19 (1934), 598 (my translation).
50. Coleman Phillipson, *Termination of War and Treaties of Peace* (London: T. Fisher Unwin, 1916), 95.
51. Kenneth N. Waltz, "Kant, Liberalism and War," *American Political Science Review* 56 (1962): 338.
52. Immanuel Kant, "Idea for a Universal History from a Cosmopolitan Point of View," in Kant, *On History*, 19.
53. I have to confess that most Kant scholars are of a different view. For instance Sidney Axinn, "Kant on World Government," in G. Funke and T. Seebohm, eds., *Proceedings of the Sixth International Kant Congress* (Washington, DC: University Press of America, 1989), 243–51.
54. Quoted by Pierre Hassner, "Les concepts de guerre et de paix chez Kant," *Revue française de science politique* 11 (1961): 653.
55. See Pierre Aubenque, "La prudence chez Kant," *Revue de métaphysique et de morale* 80 (1975): 156–82.
56. Cavallar, *Pax kantiana*, 201–13.
57. Karl W. Deutsch, et al., *Political Community and the North Atlantic Area* (Princeton, NJ: Princeton University Press, 1957), 162–63.
58. See Georg Geismann, "Kants Rechtslehre von Weltfrieden," *Zeitschrift für philosophische Forschung* 37 (1983): 382.
59. See Andrew Hurrell, "Kant and the Kantian Paradigm in International Relations," *Review of International Studies* 16 (1990): 193.
60. F.H. Hinsley, *Power and the Pursuit of Peace* (Cambridge: Cambridge University Press, 1963), 66.
61. The preliminary articles themselves are not conditioned by the first definitive article as Philonenko takes them to be. See Alexis Philonenko, *Essais sur la philosophie de la guerre* (Paris: Vrin, 1988), 40.
62. Cavallar, *Pax kantiana*, 124–28.
63. On this interpretation of cosmopolitan law, see Bernard Gilson, *L'essor de la dialectique moderne et la philosophie du droit* (Paris: Vrin, 1991), 117.
64. *Kants gesammelte Schriften*, Band 23:314 (my translation).
65. Cavallar, *Pax kantiana*, 225–34.
66. Fernando R. Tesón, "The Kantian Theory of International Law," *Columbia Law Review* 92 (1992): 100.
67. Carl J. Friedrich, "L'essai sur la paix," in *La philosophie politique de Kant* (Paris: Presses Universitaires de France, 1962), 156.
68. Tesón, "The Kantian Theory of International Law," 92.
69. See Pierre Laberge, "Kant et la paix," in G. Funke, ed., *Akten des 7. Internationalen Kant Kongress* (Bonn: Bouvier, 1991), 207.
70. Mulholland, "Kant on War and International Justice," 32.

71. Waltz, "Kant, Liberalism and War," 338–39. See, for an attempt to meet this challenge, Pierre Laberge, "L'application du principe 'exeundum est e statu natuarli' aux relations interétatiques," in H. Robinson, ed., *Proceedings of the Eighth International Kant Congress* (Milwaukee: Marquette University Press, 1995), 243–55.

72. See Laberge, "Das radicale Böse und der Völkerzustand," 120–21.

73. Melvin Small and J. David Singer, "The War-Proneness of Democratic Regimes, 1816–1965," *Jerusalem Journal of International Relations* 1 (1976): 67.

74. Michael W. Doyle, "Liberalism and World Politics," *American Political Science Review* 80 (1986): 1151. See also Bruce Russett, *Grasping the Democratic Peace* (Princeton, NJ: Princeton University Press, 1993). For a well-balanced assessment of the democratic or liberal peace thesis, see Chris Brown, "Really Existing Liberalism and International Order," *Millennium* 21 (1992): 312–28.

75. Kant, *The Conflict of the Faculties*, 155.

76. Georges Vlachos, *La pensée politique de Kant* (Paris: Presses Universitaires de France, 1962), 546–82.

77. See Mulholland, "Kant on War and International Justice," 40.

78. *Immanuel Kants Menschenkunde*, ed. Fr. Ch. Starke (Hildesheim: Olms, 1976), 124.

79. Tesón, "The Kantian Theory of International Law," 92.

80. See Geismann, "Kants Rechtslehre von Weltfrieden," 383, and Cavallar, *Pax kantiana*, 212.

81. Kant, *The Conflict of the Faculties*, 153.

CHAPTER 6

Kantian International Liberalism

FERNANDO R. TESÓN

ONE CAN distinguish two ways of approaching the work of a philosopher. One is to clarify what the philosopher is saying. This is an enterprise of philosophical exegesis—the classic task of the scholar. The other is to reconstruct the philosopher's view, so as to provide a coherent and rationally defensible interpretation of that view. The difference is important, because the reconstructive approach implies sometimes disagreeing with the philosopher and improving upon his or her arguments. The first approach asks "what did X mean?" while the second asks "what coherent and defensible system of thought can be devised using X's main insights?"

Without denying the value of exegesis, I am decidedly a proponent of reconstruction. To articulate the most coherent and defensible Kantian view of international relations calls for a delicate microsurgery on the Kantian texts. This reconstruction is sometimes required for reasons of consistency, but sometimes, more crucially, for moral reasons. In my view, the Kantian tradition in political philosophy (domestic *and* international) is the tradition of autonomy-based freedom, the rule of law, the empire of reason, and the primacy of individual dignity over nationalist, state-centered concerns. Kant must be read with the concerns of this tradition in mind.

THE KANTIAN QUESTION AND THE KANTIAN ANSWER

Pierre Laberge poses the Kantian question in these terms: What is the just arrangement of international society? Is positive international law morally just? The questions are properly formulated. While Kant is often studied for insights about how states behave, the Kantian tradition has an essential normative component; it is concerned less with the science of international relations than with the justice of global arrangements.

In my view, there is a specific Kantian question about the organization of international society, a question Kantians would ask. That question is: given a commitment to human rights and democracy, what is the best arrangement of international society? And there is, I think, a specifically Kantian answer to that question: the just international society is the one formed by an alliance of separate free nations, united by their moral commitment to individual freedom, by their allegiance to the international rule of law, and by the mutual advantages derived from peaceful intercourse.[1]

Now one could reject the liberal principles grounded on Kant's general theory of justice (as communitarians do) or Kant's emphasis on reason and autonomy as the bases for democracy and human rights (as do utilitarians). Those objectors would be outside the Kantian tradition. Or one could be a Kantian in the first sense (that is, believe in some form of rights-based liberalism as the best organization of civil society) and ask the Kantian question, yet disagree with Kant on the answer to that question. And finally, one could be a full Kantian, agreeing with the defense of the liberal state *and* with Kant's answer to the international dilemma in "Perpetual Peace."

I think it is worthwhile for liberals to discuss the issue of the constitution of the international society from within the Kantian tradition. For it is quite obvious that if some people do not believe in the importance of autonomy and rationality or in the value of treating persons with dignity, there is no point in trying to convince them that the international society should achieve precisely what they don't believe in to begin with.

In that spirit, I will address several points raised by Professor Laberge in his chapter and underscore where our views differ.

The Subjects of International Justice: States or Individuals?

As Laberge rightly points out, whether states or individuals are the subjects of international justice is an essential question for any theory of international justice, let alone for one grounded on reason and autonomy. Laberge observes that it is hard to decide whether Kant understands the term "international society" to mean a society of states or of individuals. This choice between states or individuals is false, however, because it ignores distinctions among states—a distinction that Kant carefully preserved. Kant's thinking on this is subtle, innovative, and in my view essentially correct. For Kant, the international society is neither simply a global community of individuals nor simply a society of states. Roughly, the first view amounts to an extreme cosmopolitanism, the second to some form of realism, broadly construed. Kant was neither a universalist cosmopolitan nor a state-centered realist. Rather, the only society of nations that is both morally right and capable of securing an enduring peace is an alliance of democratic nations committed to both the domestic and international rule of law—hence the first definitive article requiring a republican constitution for all states, an element of the Kantian understanding of international order ignored or downplayed by realists. This is the international organization that is, in Kant's words, morally "pure," because it is the only one that simultaneously secures freedom and peace. It secures freedom because a liberal constitution, one that is objectively just, is required to be a member of the alliance. There is a collective commitment to

6. KANTIAN INTERNATIONAL LIBERALISM

human rights. And Kant's system of international law also secures peace because democracies do not go to war against each other.[2]

Laberge raises the problem of the relationship between Kant's *ius cosmopoliticum* and his *ius gentium.* As I interpret "Perpetual Peace," Kant's *ius cosmopoliticum* is consistent with his general view of a just international society. Cosmopolitan law is the right of individuals to conduct private transactions across national boundaries. Kant was concerned about the burden that such boundaries impose on individual preferences, and he wanted to emphasize, with his third definitive article, that even though the members of the alliance are sovereign states, statehood should not be a barrier to international commerce. On the contrary, because republics are internally free, they pose no significant obstacles to international trade. (Free trade follows from the principles that underlie a liberal democracy.) Cosmopolitan law is the set of principles and rules that governs the alliance itself: these are properly rights of states as long as those states remain democratic and representative: recall the paramount principle in the first article, the obligation of states to be representative and to respect human rights. As indicated above, cosmopolitan law refers instead to the possibilities for free trans-boundary relations among individuals.

Laberge is therefore correct when he observes that Kant was concerned both with men and with states. As he points out, an international society of individuals would be a superstate, which Kant opposes on the grounds that it would threaten liberty. Kant therefore holds that we ought to maintain separate states, provided they are free states: tyrants are excluded from the alliance. Laberge is also right to reject Bull's definition of the Kantian tradition. What Kant inherited from Hobbes was a belief in the natural disharmony of interests among individuals. For Kant, but not for Hobbes, *reason* leads naturally to freedom under the rule of law, to democracy, and to human rights. When the state is seen, not as an enemy of freedom, but as its promoter and protector, it is easy to conclude that we should not dismantle the state system.

Contrary to Laberge's suggestion, the Kantian tradition does not postulate a world republic as the ultimate goal. In "Perpetual Peace," Kant gives two reasons for maintaining separate states. The first is that global freedom is more likely to survive, whereas if the global republic turned into an evil empire there would be no place to turn, no refuge. In Kant's colorful prose, a world consisting of separate nations

> is rationally preferable to [its] being overrun by a superior power that melds them into a universal monarchy. For laws invariably lose their impact with the expansion of their domain of governance, and after it has uprooted the soul of good a soulless despotism finally degenerates into anarchy.[3]

The second reason to oppose a world state is that it makes sense to allow the dilution of political power, given a people's "community" preferences—their desire to associate with others that share the same culture, history, etc. Given the psychological fact that many people care about such things and that those preferences are not obviously irrational, local governments are more likely than a huge central bureaucracy to be responsive to different cultural traditions, within the limits imposed by human rights and democracy. So a liberal ought to support the alliance of separate democratic states as the foundation of international law, not because the world republic is too utopian (although Kant also believes this), but because it is the morally preferable arrangement on liberal grounds.

KANT'S THEORY OF DOMESTIC JUSTICE

Laberge's extended account of Kant's theory of justice is impressive—as far as it goes. In particular, I agree that it is imperative to reconstruct Kant's theory of domestic justice before tackling Kant's account of international justice. This is so because both are remarkably consistent: international law is founded upon an alliance of those states, and only those states, that are rationally justified on general moral grounds, that is, by the categorical imperative. Most of the commentary on "Perpetual Peace" has ignored this fact. Many commentators ignore the first definitive article and instead suggest a realist reading of Kant. But once one has read "Perpetual Peace" against the background of Kant's major writings on moral philosophy, a realist reading is no longer possible.

The main problem with Laberge's discussion of Kant's theory of justice is that he analyzes only the first version of the categorical imperative, the universalizability requirement. To be sure, this is essential for Kant's political philosophy, for it is the basis of no less than the coercive power of the liberal state. I therefore largely concur with Laberge's analysis. But one cannot draw strong political conclusions without introducing the second version of the categorical imperative: we should treat persons not only as means, but as ends in themselves. Kant believes this formulation to be logically derived from, or equivalent to, the first version, but I am not sure he is right about that. There are maxims that one could universalize in accordance with the first version but that would be immoral when measured by the second version. So both formulations are needed, and it matters little whether they are seen as separate or equivalent maxims. Kant's principle of morality, the categorical imperative, which in his political philosophy is reintroduced as the principle of freedom, consists both of the view that we should act according to a universalizable principle and that we should act so as to respect the inherent dignity of persons. Only the union of these two versions of the categorical imperative with the other two pillars of political justice, equality and independence, yields the republican constitution, the only one that is just.

Kant's theory of justice is not flawless, however. In my view, there are two important amendments that are more consistent with the Kantian tradition than what Kant actually says. The first is Kant's implausible and stubborn opposition to the right to revolution. The second is Kant's neglect of what Laberge calls *"fraternité"*—social and economic rights. Laberge rightly endorses the effort by distinguished scholars like Onora O'Neill to supply a modern liberal revision of Kant's excessively libertarian position.

In my view, this is easily done within Kant's general conception of morality. (Here, as elsewhere, this conception is more appealing than his sometimes bizarre views on specific issues like the death penalty, marriage, and women.) The second version of the categorical imperative, respect for persons, entails positive duties to fellow human beings. Social and economic rights must be secured if individuals are to flourish as autonomous persons. Respect for the dignity of persons requires, besides respecting their moral space, that we do our best to secure an adequate level of material well-being for every member of society. The republican constitution mandated by the first definitive article should therefore include some degree of economic redistribution. Without it, citizens cannot enjoy the benefits of freedom.

Kant's Theory of International Justice

Laberge's reading of the Kantian tradition in international relations, as summarized at the end of his chapter, is essentially as follows.

First, we should establish a world organization open to all states, republican or not, and an international law founded in it which prohibits intervention (but not interference). This is required by nonideal theory because of the existence of many different kinds of constitution (not just republican constitutions). At this stage, Laberge believes, nonintervention is required because otherwise states could not be persuaded to join in any organization that renounces war. This organization is the next-to-penultimate goal of the international society. Laberge suggests that this organization is not only required by the reality of world politics, but is morally defensible as the best way to the ultimate goal: a world republic.

Second, the penultimate goal of the nonideal theorist is a panrepublican alliance. Such an alliance is better than the world organization open to all states because it is more stable, given the affinity among democracies. As I read Laberge, the democratic alliance is formed for defensive purposes; wars to free the oppressed are excluded. The alliance of all states (including tyrannical states) and the panrepublican alliance might both be embryos of the world republic.

Third, as already indicated, the final goal is a world republic, a global democratic state.

While I applaud the general Kantian spirit that pervades Laberge's interpretation, I believe it fails to capture the richness of the Kantian tradition. Like many readers of Kant before him, he downplays Kant's first definitive article. A centerpiece of the tradition is Kant's visionary proposition that the only just international arrangement is an alliance of liberal democracies. This alliance, which excludes tyrannical states, might one day, one hopes, include all nations, but even then it would not be a superstate. This arrangement is both intrinsically just and the best from a prudential standpoint, because it is the only one that is capable of securing a lasting peace. Laberge's position is that of a Kantian in spirit who, seduced by the realist logic, succumbs to the temptation of finding some accommodation for dictators.

Laberge is drawn to this position by contrasting ideal versus nonideal theory. If individuals are going to choose the organization of global society, why have states? Rawls's answer to this dilemma is well known: states, not individuals, choose the principles of international law. I think this answer is mistaken, for reasons that I and others (especially Thomas Pogge) have explained at length, and which are even more powerful from a purely Kantian (and not just Rawlsian) perspective.[4] Individuals are the ultimate subjects and ends of morality and justice, and so whatever notion of international justice we propose, it has to be congruent with our basic principles of morality—the categorical imperative.

In ideal theory, Laberge suggests, individuals choose the constitution of an international society behind a veil of ignorance that conceals their nationality. They would therefore presumably choose a global Kantian-Rawlsian state. Once we lift the veil, however, states reappear, and with them the state of nature and war. So what Kant needs, Laberge suggests, is a nonideal theory, one that can account for the actual existence of separate states.

The line of reasoning followed by Laberge is, however, a realist trap. It runs as follows: Ideally, Kant is right that the best society of nations would be one that had only liberal democracies as members. But unfortunately, as Laberge puts it, "not all the constitutions of our states fit our principle of justice." There is a return to the state of nature, which the very scheme of "Perpetual Peace" wished to avoid. Therefore, Laberge thinks, we need to devise a principle that can be truly universal, truly international. And this principle, in his view, is that "states ought to govern their interactions in such a way that these interactions, at worst, do not make impossible, and, at best, favor the future coexistence of everyone's freedom with everyone's freedom agreed on in the ideal theory."

Such a view, of course, amounts to an almost unconditional surrender to realism—the only difference being that the global arrangements do not make individual freedom impossible. Yet the force of Kant's proposal in "Perpetual Peace" lies precisely in his requirement that the full members of international society be liberal states. Laberge proposes instead that the world be ordered in such a way that global freedom becomes impossible in the future. And the reason for this morally weakened international society is that in the real world we have states, some of them tyrannical. Indeed, Laberge's proposal is a regression from current international law, which imposes on states the duty to respect human rights, including the right to democratic representation.

Why does Laberge fall into the realist trap? I believe the answer is that he cannot find in Kant's scheme a way to deal with tyrannical states. Therefore, we seem to be back to the realist logic: in the international arena, states are essentially equivalent. All enjoy a right to sovereignty, and all should be basically respected, regardless of whether they are liberal or illiberal. It is true that Laberge adds the disclaimer that his reasons for respecting states, even tyrannical ones, have to do with the best chances to form a global republic in the end. Yet, in the meantime, his theory of international relations countenances despotism in a way that is at odds with the spirit of Kant's moral and political philosophy, and in two ways.

First, the "realist" international system, which includes all states, bestows legitimacy upon illegitimate governments, and this is an injustice on Kantian grounds. Laberge claims that his ultimate goal is the world republic and that establishing the federation of all states is justified because it is indirectly conducive to the world republic. But this would amount to a flagrant violation of the categorical imperative: by leaving persons at the mercy of dictators, we would be using them to prepare the grounds for a nebulous brighter utopia. In fairness to Laberge, Kant is often guilty of precisely this kind of inconsistency. On one hand, he is the champion of free will and human dignity; on the other, he is infatuated with the laws of history (or of nature), an infatuation that leads him to some very un-Kantian conclusions, endorsing situations or events where millions of people perish or suffer en route to a rosy future. Yet the Kantian tradition cannot have it both ways: if there is freedom of the will, there can be no laws of history pushing us around. We are rational autonomous beings who choose our future and we should be held responsible for our failures and successes, as well as for the way in which our behavior impinges on others.

Second, as recent research has shown, the "realist" world is inherently unstable and war-prone, precisely because of the difference in regimes. Democracies and autocracies do not coexist easily. Kantian principles require, therefore, that we do our best to move away from this intermediate stage and actively promote global democracy and human rights.

THE QUESTION OF UNIVERSALITY

A main reason why many good thinkers like F. H. Hinsley have fallen into the realist trap is the clinging allure of cultural relativism.[5] But Laberge is too good a Kant scholar to be tempted by relativism. He rightly points out that Kant is not a cultural relativist; the republican constitution is the only one that is just. Kant repeatedly warns against what he calls the "anthropological" approach, the temptation to believe that though different nations have different constitutions, they are morally equivalent. If the republican constitution is morally correct, then it is universally correct, because it is derived from universal traits of persons—their reason and autonomy. People have taken issue with this position, and it is certainly unfashionable in some academic circles. Yet moral objectivism is a centerpiece of the Kantian tradition. One simply cannot be an objectivist for domestic law and a relativist for international law.

But then why should we strive to form an alliance that, like the United Nations, treats all states as equally legitimate? Tyrannical regimes are illegitimate—it's that simple. They deserve no presumptive deference, and the only reasons to deal with them are prudential, not moral reasons (much as when the police deal with criminals who hold hostages). There is no moral value that is pursued by recognizing and accepting dictators in the United Nations. On the contrary, awarding them such deference is an indirect way to compound the oppression. (The recent example of South Africa is instructive: it was important that the international community not recognize the legitimacy of the racist regime.) So I find no moral reason, even in nonideal theory, to pursue Laberge's first step. Such a stage may, alas, be forced upon us by the circumstances—by the dictators' military or economic strength, for example—but in no sense can it be seen as responding to the demands of justice.

THE TWO LAYERS OF INTERNATIONAL LAW

While Laberge's solution is unsatisfactory, his intuition is right. We must find a way, within the Kantian tradition, to determine the principles that can govern a world in which liberal and illiberal states coexist. I suggest the following reading of Kant, based, with some amendments, on what he says in "Perpetual Peace."

The just international society is the global alliance of democracies (not a world state) described by the three definitive articles. This is the way to come out of the state of nature and of war. (I should add that the state of nature is not the worst possibility: the worst option is the global despotic superstate, the evil world empire.)

But the world liberal alliance cannot be achieved immediately. Its formation takes quite a long time. There are setbacks, and while one hopes that the liberal alliance will expand and consolidate, progress is often incremental: it took almost fifty years to end the Cold War. That is why Kant includes the preliminary articles. They are the ones that govern the intermediate stage in which the liberal alliance and illiberal states coexist. In other words, a just system of international law is the one obtaining only among liberal democracies. In contrast, relations between democracies on one hand, and autocracies on the other, are governed in part by the positivist logic so well defended by Terry Nardin in Chapter 1 above;[6] I say "in part" because on this intermediate state of seminature only the democracies are legitimate; the dictators are outlaws and must be dealt with as such. The relationship between liberal and illiberal states is, for the most part, a modus vivendi dictated by considerations of prudence. But not completely, because liberal states are bound by principles in which they believe, such as human rights principles, even when dealing with despots. This explains why the preliminary articles, with one important exception, consist of rules of *ius in bello*. (The exception is the nonintervention principle, which I consider misplaced for reasons give below.) These are the minimal rules of decency and prudence needed for even a minimally workable coexistence among potential enemies.

So the Kantian tradition, as I read it, postulates two layers of international law: a transitional layer defined by the preliminary articles and the final layer defined by the definitive articles. It might seem at first sight that my proposal does not differ from Laberge's, since he also proposes these stages en route to the world republic. Not so: not only do I disagree that the world republic is the ultimate goal, but on my reading only the liberal alliance defined by the definitive articles is morally justified. In the transitional or intermediate stage, again, only the liberal alliance has entered the stage of political legitimacy; only within the alliance do we find ourselves in the international rule of law. That is why it is imperative for the alliance to defend itself against illiberal nonmembers, against threats from the outside. It is not just that liberal states have the right of self-defense "comme tout le monde," as Laberge suggests, but rather they are the guardians of freedom and justice, and, consequently, of peace.

War and Intervention

Laberge insists that the first stage, the "society" of democracies and autocracies, must include the rule of (forcible) nonintervention. The reason is that "states will not renounce the use of force if other states are allowed to intervene by force in their domestic affairs." Similarly, for Laberge "a republicanizing war" to achieve peace—only a global republican alliance can maintain lasting peace—is unjustified.

This reading of Kant is undoubtedly supported by the inclusion of the principle of nonintervention as the fifth preliminary article. I therefore concede that Laberge's interpretation is a faithful reading of "Perpetual Peace." I just think both Kant and Laberge are mistaken. Recognition of a limited right of humanitarian intervention is a better Kantian view.

A liberal theory of international law must account for the place of force and war. For liberals (and Kantianism is the liberal moral theory par excellence), force may only be used in defense of persons, not of states as such. States may be defended when they are themselves legitimate in some sense, but not otherwise: the use of force to defend Nazi Germany cannot be justified. Because members of the liberal alliance are in compliance with the first definitive article, force may never be used to enforce international obligations. Only rational and peaceful methods of dispute settlement, such as negotiation and judicial or arbitral proceedings, are justified. Force will, however, sometimes have to be used against nonliberal regimes as a last resort in self-defense or in defense of human rights. Liberal democracies must seek peace and explore alternative ways to preserve it. But in extreme circumstances, force may the only means to defend the liberal alliance against dictators or to rescue their victims. The fifth preliminary article is therefore misplaced: nonintervention holds only among liberal republics.

One reason Laberge gives for holding that humanitarian intervention is unacceptable in the Kantian tradition is simply that Kant opposed revolution, and that he cannot be a revolutionary in foreign affairs and a reformist in domestic affairs. My reply to this is simply that Kant was wrong about the right to revolution. Many readers of Kant have pointed out that the right to resist tyranny follows from any liberal theory of the state, as Locke and Hume, among others, recognized.[7] Kant's views on revolution are unpersuasive. Since foreign intervention to protect human rights is an extension of the right to revolution, it becomes more plausible once Kant's opposition to revolution has been rejected.

I must add an important caveat here on the right to use force to defend human rights. That people are being oppressed by a tyrant does not mean that intervention is automatically justified. Because of the destruction caused by war, coercive intervention is reserved only for the most serious forms of human rights violations, when other means of redress have failed or proven useless. Furthermore, when benign intervention is likely to result in the disruption of the life in common in the target state (by destroying local institutions, for example), democracies must exercise restraint. The Kantian tradition mandates respect for a legitimate social contract even if the people so bound have the misfortune of being ruled by a tyrant—a ruler who, by definition, has achieved power by illegitimate means. And finally, the intervention has to be welcomed by the victims themselves.[8] So in the Kantian tradition the use of force is justified to defend the liberal state against outside threats and, in extreme situations, to rescue victims of brutal oppression or similar situations in illiberal states.[9]

CONCLUSION

Laberge's chapter is an impressive and erudite effort to combine the equally Kantian concerns of peace and justice, and I regard our disagreement as one about means, not about ends. (Laberge calls mine the "liberal" view, a title I proudly accept.) His own "progressive-conservative" view holds that "constitutional plurality" is "permissible as the price to pay on humanity's road to a world republic." But Kant's categorical imperative prohibits using persons in that way. The Kantian tradition makes individuals central. All law, including international law, is a vehicle for permitting the flourishing of free, autonomous human beings. This reading of the tradition is better, I think, than any that accords even temporary legitimacy to those tyrannical practices (and the *Realpolitik* associated with them) that Kant's monumental effort in moral and political philosophy was meant to dismantle.

NOTES

1. Laberge disagrees with this interpretation of Kant; see below.

2. See Michael W. Doyle, "Kant, Liberal Legacies, and Foreign Affairs," part 1, *Philosophy & Public Affairs* 12 (1983): 205. See also Fernando R. Tesón, "The Kantian Theory of International Law," *Columbia Law Review* 92 (1992): 53.

3. Immanuel Kant, "Perpetual Peace," in *Perpetual Peace and Other Essays*, trans. Ted Humphrey (Indianapolis: Hackett, 1983), 125.

4. See Fernando R. Tesón, *Humanitarian Intervention* (Dobbs Ferry, NY: Transnational Publishers, 1988), 58–71, and Thomas Pogge, *Realizing Rawls* (Ithaca, NY: Cornell University Press, 1989), 246–59.

5. F. H. Hinsley, *Power and the Pursuit of Peace* (Cambridge: Cambridge University Press, 1963).

6. See also Terry Nardin, *Law, Morality, and the Relations of States* (Princeton, NJ: Princeton University Press, 1983), part 2.

7. See Roger J. Sullivan, *Kant's Moral Theory* (Cambridge: Cambridge University Press, 1989), 244–45, and references therein.

8. On this, see Tesón, *Humanitarian Intervention*.

9. In a recent article, John Rawls sides with those who defend a right of humanitarian intervention for grave cases of human rights violations. See Rawls, "The Law of Peoples," *Critical Inquiry* 20 (1993): 36, 46, 59. A slightly different version of Rawls's article may be found in Stephen Shute and Susan Hurley, eds., *On Human Rights: The Oxford Amnesty Lectures 1993* (New York: Basic Books, 1993), 41–82. I examine Rawls's position in my article "The Rawlsian Theory of International Law," *Ethics and International Affairs* 10 (1995): 79–99.

International Society from a Contractarian Perspective

JOHN CHARVET

THE CONTRACTARIAN theory I present in this essay is my own version. It draws on both Hobbesian and Rawlsian elements. It is Rawlsian in using the idea of a contract to derive principles of justice, and Hobbesian in employing state-of-nature arguments to conclude that our obligation to interact with others on just terms is conditional on political association. I begin in the first part (the contract) by developing these two elements in abstraction from international considerations. The second part (a contractarian theory of international society) applies the theory to relations between states.

There is no reason in principle why the conclusion of the contractarian argument as applied to the world should not be a unitary world state. The grounds for the inappropriateness of a world state are pragmatic: the extreme improbability of being able to establish a responsible and just government for a citizen body composed of all humankind. Since for pragmatic reasons the contractarian argument for the state requires a multiplicity of states, a law-governed world will have to be conceived at least for the present and foreseeable future as a society of states, and a contractarian theory of international society will have to be understood as a contract between states. The second part sketches such a theory for states that are assumed to be domestically just in accordance with the principles of justice, as determined by the contractarian theory itself.

Finally, the third part (nonideal theory) considers the consequences of a nonideal international society in which some states do not accept those principles.

THE CONTRACT

The classical contract theorists of the seventeenth and eighteenth centuries were theorists of *political* obligation. They presupposed a standard of just interaction that was a system of natural law and natural rights and were concerned to show that a person had only a very weak obligation, or none at all, to follow this standard in his interactions with his fellows in the absence of the security and determinacy provided by a state. These theorists gave many the impression that they made political obligation depend on an actual contract. But it is perfectly possible, and only reasonable, to express their theories as hypothetical contracts concerning the terms of political association that would be reasonably accepted by persons in a state of nature, given their interests in just interaction on the basis of natural law.

Contemporary contract theorists appear to apply the idea of a contract to the terms of just interaction themselves. (Just terms of interaction are those that would be reasonably accepted by all in some suitably defined initial situation.) Such theorists are standardly distinguished into theorists of mutual advantage and theorists of impartiality.[1] The latter impose conditions on the contract, such as Rawls's veil of ignorance, which insure that the resulting agreement expresses some prior conception of the inherent moral standing of persons. The former seek to derive the moral constraints on the pursuit of self-interest from the self-interest itself. The contract theory that I shall sketch below cannot be identified with either of these positions. The weakness of the impartialists is that the contract turns out to be completely redundant and pointless once the underlying conception of the moral standing of persons is made explicit. The former's weakness consists in the total implausibility of pure mutual advantage constituting a sufficient motivation for our adherence to moral norms.

The sort of contractarian theory I espouse is one that seeks to give an account of the necessarily authoritative nature of moral norms, and which at the same time yields some conclusions as to their general content. By the "authority" of the moral norms I mean their character as overriding practical principles. To accept a moral norm is to undertake to conceive and pursue one's self-interest as part of a larger good, which includes that of other persons, and which is structured by the norm. The norm dictates how the good of others is to be taken into account by each individual in the formation of his own self-concern. It is a rule for the individual's pursuit of his good together with others as a common good. A contractarian theory of this authority holds that a valid moral norm is one that would be accepted by persons who are engaged in social interaction, under certain ideal conditions.

The adoption of this approach to moral theory involves rejecting moral realism and accepting the view that moral norms and their authority are a human invention. Yet obviously enough human beings did not self-consciously invent these norms and society at the same time. The authority of the norms around which human beings developed their social cooperation and their own capacities as self-conscious, reason-following beings was, at first, projected by them onto an external source in the form of gods, the one God, eternal and immutable ideas, and so on. So we are to think of the contractors as persons who have been formed in some society in accordance with its traditional norms, and who are thus already engaged in normative social cooperation. But as self-conscious, reason-following beings such persons are capable of reflecting on and calling in question both the authoritative claims and the substantive content of their traditional moral practices. We should think also that, in doing so, they reject any form of moral realism and adopt instead the view that the authority and content of their norms must derive from what can reasonably be agreed by the cooperators themselves.

Since the norms are to be understood as rules for each person to pursue his good together with others as a common good, or in other words collectively rather than individually, the contract supposes that social cooperation is an enterprise for mutual advantage. Given this pragmatically understood background to the ideal agreement, utilitarianism will seem an attractive theory. It would tell us to choose those norms that will have the best consequences from the point of view of the interests of the cooperators. I do, however, accept the criticism of utilitarianism by Rawls and many others that it allows the interests of some to be unfairly sacrificed for the greater utility of others, and I also allow their claim that the pursuit of the general good is acceptable only subject to the constraint of a strong equality principle, which utilitarianism even in its indirect form is unable to explain.[2] A strong equality principle in the context of a contractarian approach says that the contractors must be understood to enjoy an equal bargaining power. The postulate of the equality of the contractors constitutes the essentially ideal element in the contract. For we could think of the contractors reaching a nonideal agreement on the basis of their actual positions in the world. The agreement would then reflect their relative bargaining power as this is determined by the existing distribution of natural and social assets. But why should anyone accept such an agreement as authoritatively binding on his pursuit of his self-interest? It would at most consist in a modus vivendi to be overturned as soon as a person's relative power permitted. Hence it could not serve as the central element in a theory of the authoritative nature of moral norms.

It may well look as though the equality of the contractors is a necessary presupposition of contractarian theory itself. If this were so, Rawlsian contractarianism would collapse immediately. For the postulate of equal bargaining power would now depend on a prior commitment to the fundamentally equal value of persons, and this would justify an attribution to them of equal rights in respect of the treatment of their interests without regard to any agreement. We would in other words have access to the fundamental principles of justice without having to go through the procedure of an ideal contract. The contract could then at most serve the function it has in its classic form in theorists such as Locke for whom the basic principles of justice are given (by God), and the contract merely explains the possibility of a collective or political authority in regard to them.

If I am to substantiate my claims for contractarianism as a moral theory, then, I must be able to show how the equality principle is not in fact presupposed by the theory but derived from it. Now if we allow that the contract is necessarily constrained by the prior principle of the equal value of persons, we will be driven back into some realist conception of moral authority. For we will have to say that persons as such are inherently valuable and have rights, and I do not think that any sense can be made of such a claim unless we are to explain their value by reference to a fixed order that is independent of actual, living human beings and exists in the mind of God or in a noumenal world of timeless selves. No doubt this is a contentious claim, and I cannot but acknowledge the existence of many attempted justifications of the equality principle in secular form. None of them to my mind has any plausibility.

Assuming, then, that the contractors are necessarily antirealists (for otherwise they would be wasting their time), and recalling the social context of cooperation for mutual advantage in which they are deliberating, we can say that the contractors must accept the general position that the authority of the moral norms derives from their will as cooperators to pursue their good together under agreed rules. As we have seen, however, we cannot interpret the authority-creating agreement as made by persons enjoying whatever bargaining power they actually possess in their interactions. For such an agreement could not account for the authority of the norms. The contractors must therefore think of their agreement as made from a standpoint that abstracts from their particular characteristics and situation and as a result focuses only on their general nature and interests as cooperating agents.

What motivates the contractors' undertaking to deliberate from a general point of view? In the first place, they recognize the gains from cooperation, but, second, they desire to cooperate on moral terms—that is to say, on the basis of authoritative norms. Finally, they reject moral realism and recognize that the authority and content of the norms springs from their own wills. The first condition ensures the presence of a will to cooperate, while the third determines that the terms of cooperation have no authority other than their cooperative will. The second condition, however, requires that this will be their general will as agents rather than their particular wills. In this ideal agreement the contractors will be equally placed, since there is nothing that differentiates one from another. The idea of such an agreement will yield a strong equality principle, but does not presuppose it. What is presupposed is only the motivation to cooperate on moral terms, whatever these turn out to be through the contractual procedure. The meaning of the term "moral" at this point is merely its general *form* as authoritative higher-order norm for considerations of self-interest. The content of the moral norms is to be determined by what can be agreed under the specified conditions.

Yet one must still ask the question, why should they form the will to cooperate on moral terms? Is it simply a will that some persons have and others do not, but that no good reason can be given for possessing or acquiring such a will? The contractors, as socially formed beings on the basis of some authoritative norms, already have a moral character and hence the capacity to act morally. They are not inventing morality, and themselves as moral beings, from nothing. Nevertheless, morality as understood in this chapter could be an unnecessary social form, like the practice of shaking hands on meeting. I assume to the contrary that the practice of morality is advantageous from the point of view of stable social cooperation. It is an invention with an enormous payoff in utilitarian terms. For morality is the idea of interacting on terms that each person can accept, whatever his position under the cooperative scheme. Hence the rules of the social order are not vulnerable to the contingencies of power. But while this is a necessary condition for the rational formation of moral wills, it is obviously not a sufficient condition, for it cannot explain how individuals can rationally will the authoritative nature of moral norms. That is necessarily a commitment that takes them beyond the standpoint of self-interest. Yet one cannot say that it is an irrational leap in the dark. The point of making the commitment is clear for anyone to see. What the contractors commit themselves to is not to make themselves moral beings out of nothing, for they will already have received a moral education, but to take full responsibility on themselves for their moral being by recognizing that the moral norms have no ground other than their own wills, and at the same time *thereby* to accept that the foundation of their moral association must consist in their mutual respect as equals.

As I have presented the theory, it says that persons, who have reason to cooperate on moral terms, have reason to do so on the basis of collective adherence to a strong equality principle. The authority of the norms is a communal or collective one. It is grounded in the will of each to pursue his good in association with the others, where the terms of association consist in the authoritative norms. Does this mean that the terms apply only to specific persons who are committed to each other as members of an association, or to all persons everywhere insofar as they are involved in interactions? Of course, they can be relevant only to self-conscious, self-directing agents, and if such agents are necessarily social beings, the terms apply only to beings who have been formed in some society. But even if this means that in the first instance a person's rights and duties are relative only to the members of his society, it could still be the case that reflection directs them to universalize the moral rules. Universalization, however, would tell us that each person has reason to cooperate on just terms with any other provided that there are gains from moral cooperation, and provided that he can be assured of compliance by the other party. Obviously the gains from moral cooperation arise only in the long term, and this makes the assurance problem more acute. The assurance problem results from two facts. First, a person has an interest in committing himself to pursue his good in his interactions with others subject to the moral rules only if a sufficient number of those persons with whom he interacts will reciprocate so as to make his gains from just cooperation greater than his costs. Second, each person has a good self-interested reason not to comply with the moral rules even when the others do, since her gains from noncompliance, from a purely self-interested standpoint, will be greater still. So no scheme of moral cooperation is viable unless it provides for the effective enforcement of the rules against free riders.

This type of argument is familiar enough from classical contract theory and leads to the conclusion that a political society with some form of concrete collective authority is needed to make moral cooperation possible. One should note also another argument to be found in the classical contract litera-ture, which I shall call the argument from determinacy. Let us suppose that the equality principle as applied to general interests supports the claim that cooperation on just terms commits the cooperators to a mutual acknowledg-ment of their equal rights to life, liberty, and access to resources. Can we conclude from this that everyone as a potential moral cooperator is entitled to respect for his rights in a state of nature when this is understood purely in terms of the absence of any concrete collective or political authority, but not, of course, in terms of the absence of social interaction altogether? In such a world each individual would have authority to determine his rights and those of others. But these rights are not absolute rights. What a person is entitled to in respect of life, liberty, and resources can be determined only relative to the just claims of others. Whether some attack on me is to count as a violation of my rights by another or as a defense of his rights to liberty, and resources against my invasion, can be settled only by a joint determination of what belongs to each.[3] Once again this argument leads to the conclusion that moral life requires a political or collective form.

I am now in a position to move the argument forward to discuss the con-tractarian theory of international society, but before doing so it will be impor-tant for the sequel to say something more about the rights of individuals in the collective. The foundational principle of collective moral life, according to my contractarian theory, is the equal value of persons as free or self-direct-ing beings. Furthermore, this equal value translates into equal rights with regard to general human interests in life, liberty, and access to resources. But since these rights are to be determined collectively, their enjoyment, it might be thought, could be given a communist form. The members' rights would consist only in the right to participate (equally) in the collective determina-tion of each person's life, liberty, and resources. The anticommunist liberal interpretation requires individuals to have an area of negative freedom in which each chooses for himself how the content of the social order in this area is to be decided. It gives each person the right to decide on his own how his relations to the others are to be conducted. These rights are the classic liberal civil rights of property, association, movement, conscience, and opinion. I believe that the liberal interpretation is essentially correct, not because indi-viduals have absolute individual rights to negative freedom and property as ends in themselves, but because negative freedom and individual control over resources are necessary for the cultivation of personal autonomy. Further-more, the development of personal autonomy is needed if the members are to take full responsibility for their collective life by coming to an awareness that life is grounded in nothing other than their wills to pursue their good to-gether on the basis of authoritative norms of an antirealist nature. Each must alienate himself from his community by giving up his moral self-identification in terms of an unreflective acceptance of the authority of his society's norms, and must think of himself as an end for himself, in order to understand the

way in which his will, together with that of the others, is the foundation of
their collective moral life. Liberal society is the social form that generates in
its members the required individualism, and yet leads it back to a collective
expression as a form of social cooperation.

A Contractarian Theory of International Society

The above contract theory claims that moral life is possible, in the first instance at any rate, only through membership in a coercive association possessing some form of collective authority. In principle, this association could
comprehend the whole of humanity in a world state. But for obvious contingent reasons, moral life emerged in a multiplicity of separate associations and
is likely to continue to require them for some time. Hence if there is to be a
moral life encompassing all human beings, it must come about through relations between these associations. The participation of an individual in the
moral life of international society must then be through the mediation of his
membership in a particular association. In other words, we cannot affirm that
individuals are immediately members of a universal moral community of humankind by virtue of being ends in themselves or through the possession of
absolute natural or human rights. For such claims make no sense from an
antirealist perspective.

Could we not arrive at a conception of a universal moral community composed of all individual human beings through the application of the contractarian procedure to the developing interactions of members of different
states? As such interactions proliferate, individuals can consider together
what norms should be authoritative for them, and as they abstract from their
particular situations to a general point of view on their interests and powers,
they will reach agreement on a universal norm of equality and equal rights.
But this move is no advance on the argument of the first part of my chapter.
For the process of abstraction from their particular situation to the general
point of view must include a bracketing of their membership of particular
moral associations. They will then be faced with the assurance and the determinacy problems all over again, which can lead only to the reassertion of the
primacy of the particular associations in the moral life of an international
society. If there is to be such a moral life, in which individual persons interact
on moral terms, then the assurance and determinacy conditions for it will
have to be satisfied by relations between the states. The primary units of the
moral life of international society, to which the contractarian procedure must
apply, will be the states and not individuals.

Let us now consider the implications of the contractarian theory for relations between states. In the first place we do not have to suppose that states are
already engaged in a cooperative practice based on authoritative norms, as we
do in the case of individual persons. For persons as social beings must be
formed as norm-following beings through membership in some society be-

fore they can come to adopt the contractarian theory of norms. The contractarian theory does not require, as some thinkers seem to suppose, that persons be thought of as fully formed outside society, which they subsequently create through a contract.[4] But in respect of relations between states we are dealing with associated human beings who are already norm-following beings, so it would be perfectly possible for the representatives of states to seek self-consciously to make their interactions subject to authoritative norms. It must nevertheless be the case, for them to have a reason to do this, that cooperation on the basis of moral norms would be mutually advantageous. Each state would benefit, in terms of its interests in security and prosperity, if together they subordinated their pursuit of their good to the moral rules.

What if this condition is not met and some states could do better for themselves through a policy of expansion by coercive absorption of neighboring peoples and their territories? Prior to the emergence of an international society whose members are subject to norms of cooperation, there would be an international state of nature in which no state, on the contractarian theory, could be said to possess rights. The rights of states come into existence through international society, just as the rights of individuals arise through the collective life of a political association. So why shouldn't a powerful state use its power to protect itself by the further acquisition of power at the expense of other states? To reject such a policy one must have good reasons for thinking it to be prudentially risky. There can be no guarantee that in the struggle for power your state will eventually dominate the world rather than be destroyed; peaceful cooperation can better promote the prosperity of all. But more importantly, the states must be presumed by contractarian theory to be domestically just, so that their members will have fully developed their moral powers. As moral beings such citizens have committed themselves to cooperate with others on terms that all can agree to from a general point of view provided that the assurance and determinacy conditions are satisfied. Since states express the moral will of their members, they will be disposed to cooperate with other states on contractarian principles, and will not engage in an aggressive foreign policy unless there is no reasonable hope of forming a normatively based international society. Should they be compelled in self-defense to become expansionist themselves, they will have to extend their domestic moral life to the conquered peoples. We might think of such imperialism as a way of increasing the number of human beings and their interactions that are subject to a common moral order. Imperialism of this kind could indeed lead to a world state and a universal moral life. I shall, however, put this possibility aside and return to the idea that if there is to be a worldwide moral order it must be grounded in the mutual respect of states.

States, being greatly unequal, will no doubt find it in their interests to cooperate on terms that reflect their unequal bargaining power. This will be a modus vivendi and not a morally based cooperation. To achieve the latter, the states will have to abstract from their particular features and situations and consider cooperative terms only from the general point of view of their nature and interests as states. From this point of view they will necessarily endorse a principle that prescribes their fundamentally equal value. Since the states must be seen from the contractarian perspective as free beings in charge of their lives and interests, equality will mean their equal rights as such beings. But are such rights possible in an international society with no centralized state? The assurance and determinacy arguments claim that an authoritative system of rights and duties is possible only where there exists a collective authority to determine each right-holder's relative share and to contribute to the solution of the problem of mutual confidence. Collective authority need not take the form of a centralized state, however. I understand tribal society to be a form of political association whose members recognize the collective authority of the tribe as it is embodied in and expressed by chiefs, elders, and wise men. Tribal societies are usually stateless societies in which the enforcement of the members' rights is a matter of the self-help of individuals and families and their friends and allies. Even so, this anarchy is prevented from destroying the social order only by powerful cultural pressures that promote adherence to tribal customs and which include respect for the guidance and decisions of the elders.[5]

The mere absence of a state in international society is, then, not sufficient grounds to conclude that international moral life is not viable. For one thing, it certainly exists. International interaction between individuals and corporations from different states on the basis of mutual respect for rights takes place on a massive scale. So how do rights get determined in this society? They are determined through the combination of the domestic determination of individual rights in each state together with the mutual recognition by the states of their political sovereignty and territorial integrity. Each state thereby undertakes to respect the system of rights existing in the other states and to require its own members to interact with the members of other states on that basis. International society as a network of private relations is built up on the basis of the moral life created within each state together with the interstate peace that is made possible by the states' commitment to respect one another's rights to political sovereignty and territorial integrity.

International society as a society of states certainly acknowledges authoritative rules and practices as codified in international law, and has developed institutions that possess some degree of collective authority. But the most important of these institutions cannot be said to dominate the individual states very effectively, the more powerful of which retain considerable freedom to interpret the rules to suit themselves. Thus the UN forbids its members to settle their disputes by force,[6] but since the means of enforcing international law are in the hands of the states and the UN has neither a force of its own nor great moral authority, the ban has not prevented states from engaging in the traditional practice of self-help. This suggests that, despite the great growth of international transactions under law, the ethical life of international society is built on fragile foundations. Furthermore, the way in which rights are determined in it is far from satisfactory from a moral perspective. To understand this point we need to go back to the stage at which through the contractarian procedure the states recognize each other as equals and as entitled to equal rights. We have seen that the requirement of equality has in fact been met by treating the international status quo as the way of defining each state's initial entitlement under a system of equal rights. But this ensures that the distribution of entitlements will reflect the different and normally unequal situations of the different states without regard to the justice of those positions.

How should we conceive a better initial position? Obviously, in terms of an equal right on the part of states to security and resources (meaning a right, not to a state's existing level of resources, but to an equality of resources). The claim to equality must take into account the different size of population of different states, of course.

There is, however, a prior question about the identity of states. There is no equivalent in the case of states to the natural *personality* of human beings. (By this I mean only the basic features of an individual self-conscious psychophysical organism, which we call a human being.) Some people believe that the state equivalent of the individual organism is the nation, so that the basic equal claim of each state can be understood as the claim of each nation to be a state and to enjoy equal rights with other states. But nations are to a considerable extent inventions, and we cannot hope to be able to divide the world neatly into territorial spaces inhabited by natural social wholes. Is there, then, no alternative to endorsing the status quo in respect of the given personality of states? International law and practice does recognize conditions under which an existing state may lose its sovereignty over parts of its territory and people.[7] Yet once again these conditions appeal largely to *faits accomplis* in the form of successful rebellions against oppressive rule. What we need is a clear principle or set of principles for determining which collection of people are entitled to form themselves as states. While I do not think that we are at a complete loss what to say on this very important issue, I have no ready formula to appeal to, and rather than attempt to develop one here, I shall assume that we have a workable principle for the identity of states and shall concentrate on the question of their rights.

I have claimed that the contractarian theory as applied to states dictates the acceptance of their equal claim to the satisfaction of their basic interests, suitably interpreted to allow for differences in size. But this equality constitutes only a baseline below which none can justly fall, and, following Rawls, I take it to be irrational for persons or states not to agree to departures from equality that meet certain conditions.[8] What are these conditions? Obviously no one can reasonably be expected to accept an inequality that worsens her position, as this is established by an initially just distribution. I do not think, however, that Rawls's difference principle—which allows departures from the initial position only if they improve the situation of the least well off—is acceptable. The obvious alternative is the Pareto principle, which allows departures from the initial position that make at least one person better off and no one worse off. The Pareto principle should be modified in this context by the condition that an improvement in someone's welfare should be the result of his own labor.

The choice between the difference principle and the Pareto principle seems to depend on whether one believes that the distribution of natural assets between persons should be allowed to have an effect on the distribution of resources. The reasoning behind the difference principle is that the content of the moral rules should not be determined by factors that are arbitrary from a moral point of view. Indeed, I appear to have accepted this principle in my argument for understanding the contract as an ideal one made by persons from a general rather than a particular point of view. The argument against unequal bargaining power as the foundation of the contract, however, was that it was incompatible with the authoritative nature of the moral norms, since it made the validity of the norms for a person depend on particular and variable features of his self-interest.

This argument does not apply in the case of natural assets. For although the labor principle of just use of resources does permit persons to improve their positions relative to others, it does so only subject to the Pareto principle as applied to an egalitarian baseline. The labor principle, as presented here, is not a theory of primary, but of secondary, acquisition. It presupposes that one is already entitled to the resources one labors on. Its acceptance, then, does not call in question the regulative authority of the moral norms for the pursuit of self-interest. Of course, this argument is not in itself a reason to accept the labor principle; it merely tells us that the principle is not incompatible with the moral point of view. A positive reason for adopting it would involve the self-ownership view of human powers, together with the Hegelian-Marxist claim for the necessary externalization of such powers in things.[9] That persons are to be treated as owning their powers, in a way which sees the value of individual personality as embodied in those powers, is a view that can be rejected only at the cost of abandoning either all empirical relevance of moral theory or the notion of free personality. Once we accept that a person and his value are necessarily present in the exercise of his powers, we can see also that his powers are themselves necessarily embodied in things. A person becomes a potter only by making pots, a horseman by riding horses. So if a person's value is present in his powers, it must be present also in the interchange between himself and the world through which his activity changes the world. This, of course, does not mean that a person owns whatever he thereby changes. It means that if a person already owns the thing, and transforms it without worsening others' positions, then he is entitled to any added value he brings about.

I take these principles to be directly applicable to states. A just international society would be one in which the distribution of resources between states conforms to what would have occurred, if from an initial egalitarian baseline, all departures from equality satisfied the Pareto principle together with the labor principle of secondary acquisition. This treats states and their rights as analogous to persons and their rights, and the activity of states as the activity of their members. This is justified by the fact that on my contractarian theory persons have rights only as members of a political association (in short, a state), so that their moral life is lived through the life of states.

How is the egalitarian baseline to be defined? We might think of it in terms of an initial entitlement in a primitive state of the world before elaborate technologies transformed the relative value of different resources. For it seems that we should not include technology in the baseline, since it is the result of human invention, and one cannot have a just claim based on what others have done provided that the Pareto principle is not violated. But this would justify enormous inequalities between states, and would make the idea of their fundamental equal value a mockery. Furthermore, the actual history of the world has in no way conformed to this conception of a just development from an egalitarian baseline of continuously existing political associations. We need to think of the equality of persons and states in terms of what is necessary for the development of their essential powers. What these powers are will depend on the evolution of human and state personality. What is now necessary for a state to count as an autonomous power is certainly more demanding in terms of wealth and organization that what was necessary in fifth-century Greece. So if there is to be an international society whose members treat each other as moral equals, then they must acknowledge the claims of each to possess the means of being autonomous agents in the contemporary world.

Why should the more developed states recognize the significantly less developed to be equals at all? This commitment arises from their undertaking as moral beings to interact with others on moral terms, given the satisfaction of the assurance and determinacy conditions. Are these conditions in fact satisfied in international society? I have already commented on the assurance condition and indicated the extent to which it is only partially fulfilled. The determinacy condition states that a person is under obligation to respect the rights of others only if there is a collective authority capable of giving a determinate content to a system of rights and duties. The indeterminacy of liberty and property rights can be remedied to a certain extent by a collective understanding to accept the status quo in the form of the political sovereignty and territorial integrity of each state as the determining principle. But this is obviously unsatisfactory from the point of view of the disputable identity of states. It also needs to be modified by rules interpreting the egalitarian foundation of any scheme of justice, and a collective decision-making authority to determine the members' rights and duties in this regard is essential. Once again, the UN and other international agencies have some authority in these matters, but it is a weak authority and the members of international society do not follow their judgments. In the absence of an effective authority a state can have only a weak duty to promote the development of the most disadvantaged states. In my view, the aspiration to a more moralized international society must take the form of a desire to give greater weight to the collective authority of its institutions.

A fully just society of states, then, would have developed into something like a confederation with a strong collective authority that would adjudicate on questions of identity and distribution and authorize the use of force by its members. Such a federation would require its members to abide by common principles externally. But would it require them to adopt the same principles in their domestic organization? Would each state be expected to follow internally liberal-egalitarian principles broadly interpreted? Yes. From the contractarian point of view, states as moral entities are themselves based on an ideal agreement between their members through which they recognize each other's entitlement to determine for himself details of the social order. Thus an international federated society of states would commit itself to a mutual recognition of the liberal rights of one another's members. For each state would undertake to pursue its good together with the other states under authoritative norms, and the good of each state would itself be defined in contractarian terms as the good of its individual members pursued through authoritative norms that prescribe the acknowledgment of liberal individual rights. Such a society of states would permit the growth of an extensive international civil society with many and powerful transnational organizations. Nevertheless, on contractarian principles the moral status of such transnational organizations would be derived ultimately through the rights of their members as members of states participating in a just international society of states.

NONIDEAL THEORY

Of course, not all members of international society accept liberal principles for their domestic arrangements. Some are communist states, others Islamic states, and so on. A society composed of such states could not be a fully just one on contractarian principles. It could at most be partly just. The members would have to restrict their common authoritative norms to the mutual recognition of states' rights to political sovereignty and territorial integrity, and would have to treat domestic organizations as entirely beyond the purview of international society. Whatever is just according to the internal principles of each member would have to be acceptable from an international point of view.

Is such a conception of a partly just international society viable? Could the members acknowledge the authoritative nature of the international norms? It is certainly quite possible for different persons or states to cooperate on the basis of common authoritative norms while having different and incompatible theories as to the source of the authority of the norms. Thus, all may agree on broadly liberal egalitarian norms, even though some believe that the norms are commanded by God, others that they are grounded on the noumenal value of human beings as ends in themselves, derived from considerations of the general utility, or generated by an antirealist contractarianism. There is obviously no necessity for a viable, liberally just society to espouse the antirealist contractarian perspective. This overlapping consensus, however, would not be shared by communist and Islamic states. The legitimacy principle of these societies prescribes noncontractarian norms. Yet the international principle of mutual respect as equal sovereign states is an essentially liberal principle. It requires members of international society to treat each other as free and equal moral entities. Adherence to such a minimal conception of international society's liberal norms is of course no problem for states whose legitimizing principle commands a liberal order. If there is a problem for them, it is that the norms of international society are too limited in scope. But for the communist and Islamic states there is a serious problem of adherence. For what their legitimizing principles prescribe domestically as constituting just cooperation is incompatible with the liberal principles that they are required to follow internationally. In the international arena, they must accept the justice of an order based on the freedom and equality of each state, whereas their fundamental principles of domestic justice require in the one case the collective determination of resource use, and in the other a determination in accordance with the prescriptions of the Qur'an.

One way in which this incompatibility between the domestic and international principles of some members can be modeled is through Rawls's distinction in his later work between a purely political and a comprehensive liberalism.[10] On the former conception, the liberal principles of justice are to apply only to the public-political realm and not to persons' private lives. In private, persons may hold quite different beliefs about the good, beliefs that may even be incompatible with the liberal principles they endorse in the public sphere. So one could be a liberal in politics and a communist in one's private life. Of course, the basic institutions of society would have to be liberal ones, but within those liberal institutions persons may believe and live as they choose, even if their beliefs and lives are quite antiliberal. This distinction would fit the existing international society perfectly. The public-political realm governed by liberal norms prescribes the freedom and equality of the members, while domestically each state can run its affairs as it pleases, even on antiliberal principles.

The question to ask is not whether people and states can behave in this way. Obviously they can. Even a society governed by a comprehensive conception of liberalism necessarily allows its members to believe and act in their sphere of negative liberty as they please, provided they do not constitute a threat to liberal society. The question is then whether a person or state in adhering to public-political norms contrary to his or its "private" convictions can accept them as authoritatively binding moral norms, or only provisionally as a modus vivendi. Persons (or states) can, of course, subscribe to agreements that commit them to interact with others in ways that are wrong from the

point of view of their principles, because they are not in a sufficiently powerful position to insist on what they believe to be right. This would be a modus
vivendi, adopted in the interests of one's immediate peace and prosperity. A
modus vivendi does not involve a principled adherence to authoritative
norms. Nevertheless, what begins as a convenient arrangement can turn into
an authoritative principle simply through a change in the reasons persons
accept for their adherence to it. Given a liberal modus vivendi, the change to
liberal moral norms requires the acceptance of liberal reasons for following
them. The question the later Rawls poses is whether the acceptance of liberal
reasons can be limited to the public-political realm and can be compatible
with the acceptance by the same persons of antiliberal reasons in the private
sphere. How could such a dichotomy be coherent unless the two realms of
public and private, or international and domestic, were entirely independent
of each other? But this is evidently not the case. For public-political norms are
authoritative for what is permissible in the private or domestic sphere. They
determine what one may or may not legitimately do in those spheres. To
accept them is to undertake to organize one's private or domestic life on the
basis of respect for the higher-order principles. One cannot say, then, that the
two realms can exist side-by-side on different principles as if they were independent of each other. If we see persons as unified beings, aspiring to coherence in their thought and action, we must suppose that they seek to develop
coherent and comprehensive conceptions of authoritative norms for their
lives, in a way that excludes the strategy proposed for pluralist societies by
Rawls's political liberalism.

The point of the Rawlsian strategy is to accommodate diverse conceptions
of values within a common system when no agreement on values can reasonably be expected. One might hold that, since no reasonable agreement on
comprehensive theories of the good can be obtained, every one has a reason
to accept liberal principles for public-political life, and to leave private life for
each person's subjective decision on the good. This would be a more coherent
position than Rawls's political liberalism, since it argues from a skepticism
about the good to neutral public principles of justice. Thus it requires everyone to have the same attitude to "private" values, namely that because it is
reasonable to be skeptical about the objectivity of value, private values would
be seen as subjective in nature. While this would permit individuals to make
subjective decisions about the good for their lives, it is doubtful whether it
could sensibly accommodate whole collectivities making collective subjective
decisions, which are then imposed on the members. Furthermore, it suffers
from a degree of incoherence also in that, despite its claim that values are
subjective, it requires the liberal neutralist values of the public-political realm
to be authoritative for everyone, and not a matter of subjective decision. If we
accept that coherence is our aim, then this cannot be achieved short of a
comprehensive liberal theory, one that covers both a person's "private" reasons and his public reasons in a single scheme.

CONCLUSION

In my view, the best contractarian theory of just association, as applied to the question of world order, will yield the idea of a society of states whose members acknowledge the authority of common moral principles and legal rules that express their mutual respect, and the mutual respect of each other's citizens, as equals. This is, of course, the idea of an ideally just international society. In a less than ideal world, members are obligated to subordinate their self-interest to the rules of international society only to the extent that the assurance and determinacy conditions of moral association are fulfilled. Since these conditions are not very satisfactorily met in the existing world, members should aspire to develop the authority of the central institutions of the confederation of states—namely the UN and its agencies, and the International Court of Justice—although not by building up effective coercive powers in their hands. That would almost certainly produce a tyrannical world government. But it must be admitted that there can be no hope that the moral authority of world institutions will increase without a parallel advance in moral consensus among the member states.

Since the UN is officially committed through its declarations and conventions on human rights to principles of justice, which can be broadly called liberal, and which can be endorsed from a contractarian point of view, and since a good part of the world is in varying degrees more deeply pledged to the same principles, we should not despair of such a consensus eventually emerging. Little can be expected, however, unless the richer liberal states cooperate more effectively in satisfying the redistributive implications of those principles.

The contractarian theory sketched in this chapter may look remarkably similar to Kant's political theory. This is hardly surprising since Kant's theory is a contractarian one that, like mine, stresses the conditionality of our obligation to be just and which is similarly applied to the problem of relations between states. The major difference is, of course, that mine is a theory of the conditionality of *moral* as well as political obligation, and hence a theory of the unity of moral and political life; whereas Kant's moral theory, in affirming the unconditionality of morality, is deeply at odds with his political theory.

This difference is traceable to a fundamentally different conception of the authority of moral norms. As I see it, contractarianism has nothing to contribute as a moral theory unless it adopts an antirealist perspective on moral value. I believe, however, that the Kantian conception of the moral person is unavoidably realist and for that reason highly implausible. Cosmopolitan and natural law moral theories seem to me to be equally committed to a realist conception of the source of moral authority. Although they may be used to support conceptions of domestic and international justice comparable to those of contractarian theory, they will therefore suffer from the same tensions between unconditionality and conditionality that pervade Kantianism. In other words, there can be and probably is an overlapping consensus on broadly liberal principles between these theories and contractarianism, combined with radically divergent metaphysical commitments.

Legal positivism has no such problem because it defines the authority of the norms of a legal system in terms of the members' acceptance of the system. For the nonpositivists, the authority of the legal system rests ultimately on its conformity with moral principles, and hence nonpositivists need an account of the source of the authority of those principles. The positivist aspires to provide a wholly self-contained theory of legal authority, but this aspiration cannot be satisfied. For it can be reasonable for each participant in a rule-governed system to acknowledge the authority of the rules solely on the basis of their acceptance by the others only if the various rules available for an authoritative choice all satisfy some basic condition of justice, so that the choice itself is to that extent morally indifferent. Positivism cannot explain that basic condition, since there is no ideal element in its notion of general acceptance. Once we introduce such an element into the idea of what can be generally accepted by the participants in a practice, and at the same time guard against the reification of that element, we get the contractarian theory sketched in this chapter.

Notes

1. Will Kymlicka, "The Social Contract Tradition," in Peter Singer, ed., *A Companion to Ethics* (Oxford: Blackwell, 1991), 186–96.

2. John Rawls, *A Theory of Justice* (Cambridge, MA: Harvard University Press, 1971), 27. The others are so many that there is no point in citing them. However, I find the account of utilitarianism's inadequacy in respect of equality by Will Kymlicka in his *Contemporary Political Philosophy* (Oxford: Oxford University Press, 1990), 31–44, to be particularly clear.

3. Classic formulations of this argument are to be found in Thomas Hobbes, *Leviathan* (Oxford: Basil Blackwell, 1955), 110; Jean-Jacques Rousseau, *The Social Contract* (London: Penguin, 1968), 66; Immanuel Kant, *The Metaphysical Elements of Justice* (Indianapolis: Library of Liberal Arts, 1965), 76.

4. Kant expresses the essential point as follows: "The state of nature is not . . . to be contrasted to living in society; . . . rather, it is to be contrasted to civil society, where society stands under distributive justice." Kant, *Metaphysical Elements*, 70. Charles Taylor's "Atomism," in his *Philosophy and the Human Sciences: Philosophical Papers, Volume 2* (Cambridge: Cambridge University Press, 1985), is an influential contemporary expression of this misunderstanding.

5. My view of tribal society is taken largely from Marshall Sahlins, *Tribesmen* (Englewood Cliffs, NJ: Prentice-Hall, 1968).

6. UN Charter, Chapter One, Articles 2(3), 2(4), and Chapter Seven, Article 33.

7. Brownlie says this of the principle, adopted by the UN, of self-determination of peoples: "The principle appears to have corollaries which may include the following:

(1) If force be used to seize territory and the object is the implementation of the principle, then title may accrue by general acquiescence and recognition more readily than in other cases of unlawful seizure of territory; (2) The principle may compensate for a partial lack of certain desiderata in the field of statehood and recognition; (3) intervention against a liberation movement may be unlawful and assistance to the movement may be lawful. . . ." Ian Brownlie, *Principles of Public International Law*, 4th ed. (Oxford: Oxford University Press, 1990), 597–98.

8. Rawls, *Theory of Justice*, 62, gives the most general formula for justified inequalities, namely that "all social values . . . are to be distributed equally unless an unequal distribution of any, or all, of these values is to everyone's advantage."

9. Hegel's formula goes thus: "The person must give himself an external sphere of freedom in order to have being as Idea." *Elements of the Philosophy of Right*, ed. Allen W. Wood (Cambridge: Cambridge University Press, 1991), §41. I take this to mean that a necessary stage in our self-understanding as self-determining beings involves our being able to control parts of the world through the exercise of our will. We could have no grasp of our powers of willing if our willing consisted merely in inner volitional acts with no externality. Our free will has to be apprehended through its presence in the external world.

10. John Rawls, *Political Liberalism* (New York: Columbia University Press, 1993), Lecture 1.

Contractarian Thought and the Constitution of International Society

CHRIS BROWN

IN THE preceding chapter, John Charvet makes a strong case for the relevance to international society of a reworked contractarianism.[1] His use of the notion of contract differs from that of most of his classical and modern predecessors, and it is these differences that make his chapter so interesting and of such potential importance to theorists of international relations. In what follows, the differences between Charvet's contract theory and that of mainstream contractarian writers will be elucidated to highlight what would be gained, and what would be lost, by adopting his reworking of the basic metaphor; in the process, the wider relevance of the idea of contract for the constitution of international society will be examined. The first part of the chapter will focus on the nature of the contract itself; the longer, second part will examine the implications of this and other varieties of contractarian thought for international relations.

CHARVET'S CONTRACT

The basic model offered by Charvet runs as follows: (1) Society is based on mutual advantage, but mutually advantageous social cooperation requires the presence of moral norms, that is, norms that are accepted as overriding the demands of self-interest if and when they conflict with the latter. (2) In the first instance, these norms will be understood in a "realist" manner, that is, as deriving their authority from "an intrinsic moral order susceptible to authoritative representation,"[2] and stable, morally grounded social cooperation is possible on this basis. (3) There comes a point in the development of society, however, when reflective persons will come to appreciate that the authoritative nature of the norms necessary for social cooperation, and the content of the norms themselves, cannot be understood in this way; instead they must be seen as the product of human invention. (4) At this point, the idea of a contract becomes relevant; it becomes clear that authoritative norms can only be those which would be willed by persons contracting together for the purpose of creating or endorsing norms under certain ideal conditions. (5) The point of these ideal conditions is to abstract from the actual bargaining power possessed by persons: Charvet specifies these conditions as the product of a rational will to cooperate on moral terms; in their search for the general will, contractors are obliged to treat each other as equals.[3] (6) This willed postulate of "the equal value of persons as free or self-directing beings" will generate the "classic liberal civil rights of property, association, movement, conscience, and opinion,"[4] and, in order that these rights can be exercised, the collective political authority of the state. (7) Charvetian contractors do not produce principles of "distributive justice" as this term is conventionally understood,[5] but the placeholder for such a notion can be constructed from comments appearing later in the argument: in essence, the initial position involves equal access to assets and resources, but there is no bar to the development of such resources by one's own labor save the Paretian requirement that no one be made worse off by one's own attempt to become better off; in the outcome, inequality in the possession of natural assets or resources is not regarded as problematic. Inevitably, this summary does not do justice to the richness and complexity of Charvet's argument, but it does cover most of the main points.

It may not be entirely clear what an orthodox contractarian position would be nowadays, but it is clear that Charvet's theory is not one. Both classic theorists of the social contract, and contemporary contractarian thinkers, would find in this position some points of contact, but rather more grounds for disagreement. As Charvet acknowledges, for many classical writers, it would be points (2) to (4) that would present difficulties—that is, the idea that the move to contract is a product of the realization that moral realism no longer works, and that norms must be invented. It is unwise for nonspecialists to be firm about these matters, but the current majority view in Hobbes and Locke studies seems to be that both these writers, though in different ways, employ natural law thinking, that is to say, neither moving beyond moral realism, nor innovating as to the content of law.[6] Instead, they focus on the circumstances under which political authority is established, assuming the absence of government (and, in Hobbes's case, society) in the "state of nature" that exists prior to the contract. It is not clear whether Kant's categorical imperative can be considered a "realist" notion (a case could be made for or against this proposition), but it is reasonably clear that Kant does *not* see his version of the social contract as giving authority and content to moral norms. Some of Charvet's terminology is drawn from Rousseau but even here there are significant differences (which will be discussed later); all in all, the structure of the argument is much closer to that of Hegel and the English Idealists than it is to anyone else, and they are not usually thought of as contract theorists.[7] On the other hand, for most contemporary contractarians, points (2) and (3) would be less problematic—not necessary to their arguments, but not ruled out by them either—but the treatment, or lack of treatment, of distributive justice would seem somewhat strange. One way or another, Charvet's contract seems not to relate closely to any of its predecessors.

This is, of course, more or less entirely to the good. Reworking a metaphor that, while still powerful, is becoming stale is a worthwhile project, and

Charvet's reworking of the contract metaphor has some clear advantages over most of its immediate alternatives. His notion that contractors are already part of a functioning scheme of cooperation helps to cope with those "communitarian" critiques of liberal contract theory which focus on its alleged need to work with impossibly presocial contractors.[8] As will be argued later, his approach to international relations theory is particularly useful, revitalizing what has become a rather stale debate. In one significant respect, however, this progress has been achieved at a high price, namely, the undermining of a good part of the *radical* impulse of much, although certainly not all, contractarian theory.

The central point here is that Charvet's contractors are presumed to live in a society in which cooperation already takes place on the basis of mutual advantage, buttressed by traditional moral norms, but which is experiencing a crisis in the realm of ideas, the collapse of moral realism. The notion of a contract solves this crisis by providing a different, more plausible, support to the morals which promote cooperation, namely, the general will of the cooperators. But what of the *content* of the norms of cooperation under the old regime? What if existing moral norms buttress injustice, mutual advantage works only for the privileged, and society is corrupted in its essentials? At least some versions of classical contract theory envisage such a situation and employ the language of contract to legitimize the idea of a new beginning. Rousseau, for example (a very good example, since Charvet uses so much of his terminology), is clear that society corrupts, and that this corruption is about the greed and possessive individualism that go with the inequality that the institution of private property has set in train. Rousseau's social contract is about freeing people from these chains as well as the chains of political and moral tyranny.

This is not to say that Rousseau has the answer; as Charvet notes, there are good reasons why the undermining of private property would be a bad thing, and, in any event, Rousseau rather unhelpfully believes his contract could not be entered into by those who have been corrupted by existing societies. The point is that Rousseau's contract can be used to some effect in radical discourse. The same might be said of Locke's theory; even if the current wisdom is that Locke himself was far from being a revolutionary, or even a radical, his ideas, or a version of them, inspired many people who could be so described.

Could Charvet's account of the contract be employed to similar radical effect? In principle, yes. He is clear that all the arrangements of a society are to be seen as subject to critique; the end of moral realism potentially leaves all questions open. But since cooperation is already taking place on the basis of mutual advantage, it is difficult to see why, in practice, the mutually advantaged cooperators would wish to wipe the slate clean and forge a new beginning. The point is that those who might have an interest in such a radical procedure are those for whom the existing circumstances are *not* mutually advantageous, and they are, by definition, excluded from his version of the contract. This is a substantive and not a technical point. For most modern contract theorists, determining the criteria which allow one to become a contractor poses some problems. Even those writers who are content to produce theories of "justice as mutual advantage," to use Brian Barry's terminology,[9] are obliged to come up with some kind of solution to the problems posed by the presence in the real world of persons who would not be members of schemes of social cooperation formed in this way but whose interests may be *prima facie* reasons for taking them into account, such as future generations, foreigners, the handicapped.

On Charvet's theory these problems simply disappear, because the scope of the cooperative scheme is already a given: the contractors are persons who have been "[formed] in some society in accordance with its traditional norms and *who are thus already engaged in normative social cooperation.*"[10] The contract is not to be seen as a foundational document setting out the terms under which contractors will come together, but as a device to relegitimize an existing scheme of cooperation, which is thus not obliged to justify its membership restrictions to anyone else. In the international context, this may be a helpful feature of Charvet's contract, but in domestic terms, a price is paid, namely, the loss of at least part of the radical impulse behind more traditional contract thinking.

CONTRACTARIANISM AND INTERNATIONAL SOCIETY

In this section of the chapter, some of the ways in which conventional contract thinking has looked at international relations and international society will be examined, before Charvet's revision of the tradition is investigated.[11] In the tradition, three stages can be delineated and analyzed. In the first, with the contract of Hobbes and Locke, analogies drawn from characteristics of the "state of nature" are applied to international relations; in the second, the constitutional implications of the domestic contract in Rousseau and Kant are worked through in terms of international society. In the third and last, the fallout from Rawls's notion of two contracts—a domestic contract that involves distributive justice, and an international contract that is purely procedural—is investigated.

Hobbes draws a specific analogy between states in their relations with one another and men in the state of nature, with the inevitable result that international relations is characterized as a permanent state of war with no possibility of there being an "international society" in the sense of a norm-governed set of international relationships. The only good news is that although states are in a posture of war with one another, Hobbes believes, rather optimistically, that the normal miseries of the state of nature can be avoided because behind frontier fortifications sovereigns can protect, and uphold the industry of, their subjects.[12] Locke is nowhere as specific, but it seems reasonable to assume that he also would leave states in a state of nature in their relations with one another, with this crucial difference: in his state of nature, society *is* possible, albeit with suboptimal levels of cooperation in the absence of government. Here a theory of international society might be derived—indeed has been by Martin Wight,[13] but not a *contractarian* theory. The Lockean point is that even in the absence of contract, society (including an international one) is possible.

Neither Hobbes nor Locke had any great interest in international relations, unlike their eighteenth-century contractarian successors, Rousseau and Kant, both of whom contributed to the literature on projects for universal peace produced by their era. Rousseau was skeptical of the value of these projects; a scheme for the compulsory arbitration of Europe's disputes would be good in principle, but its establishment would be accompanied by such disruption that "it would perhaps do more harm in a moment than it would guard against for ages."[14] In *The Social Contract*, Rousseau's inspiration gives out at the point at which an extended discussion of international relations should appear,[15] but other writings suggest that he regarded international relations as posing such serious problems that one should have as few of them as possible; see, for example, his espousal of autarky as a strategy for Corsica in his constitutional project for that island.[16] Again, no contractarian theory of international society is attempted.

Kant, on the other hand, *does* produce such a theory. Disturbed by the destructiveness of war, and wholly unconvinced by the Hobbesian point that rulers can protect their subjects from its consequences, and indeed that the excessive power of rulers *is* precisely one of the evil consequences of war, he makes bringing the relations of states under the rule of law a central aim of his social theory. The cornerstone of this theory is the requirement of morality that states of a "republican" form be established, republican in this context signifying the rule of law and the separation of powers, and this establishment is clearly under threat while war remains a possibility.

The solution to this problem, outlined in "Perpetual Peace," involves the temporary coexistence of two kinds of international society.[17] One such society, governed by the six Preliminary Articles of a Perpetual Peace, covers all states and is based on the presumption that conflicts of interest will occur and that war is a possibility; the rules of this society are close to those of twentieth- but not eighteenth-century international law and are designed to regulate conflict and ameliorate its effects. The second society, characterized by the Definitive Articles of a Perpetual Peace, has as its members only republican states and is based on the renunciation of war and the establishment of "the *civil right* of individuals within a nation . . . [the] *international right* of states in their relationships with one another . . . [and] *cosmopolitan right*, in so far as individuals and states . . . may be regarded as citizens of a universal state of mankind."[18]

The first of these international societies is based on prohibitions, stated in the Preliminary Articles, which are not established by contract; they are simply posited as a civilized code for imperfect times. But the Definitive Articles *do* involve a contract. The second article states that "The Right of Nations shall be based on a Federation of Free States,"[19] and it is clear that what is involved here is a treaty obligation, hence, in effect, a second contract to go along with the original contract that, on Kant's reasoning, is required to establish a republic in the first place. This contract is minimal, however; it establishes a "particular kind of league, which we might call a *pacific federation (foedus pacificum),*"[20] which differs from the normal peace treaty in ending all wars and not simply one war, but which does *not* establish a governing federation. In this limited contract, war is abolished but the continued freedom of state is assured.[21] This position is interesting because the structure, although not always the content, of Kant's argument prefigures several themes of twentieth-century contractarian thinking on international relations, in particular Rawls's idea of two contracts and Charvet's sketch of the different kinds of international society that are generated by the initial establishment of liberal states by contract.

In *A Theory of Justice*, Rawls takes a society to be "a cooperative venture for mutual advantage" and reasons that the principles of justice such cooperators would choose under ideal conditions would involve not only equal political rights but also a "difference principle" that arranges social and economic inequalities to the greatest benefit of the least advantaged.[22] Rawls assumes that the societies for which these principles are designed are essentially self-sufficient entities that will need to determine further principles of justice in their relations with one another. In the original formulation this was to be achieved through a meeting of representatives again choosing under ideal conditions, but this thought-experiment is not necessary to the argument and has since been more or less dropped. In *A Theory of Justice*, Rawls argues that the principles this second contract will produce are the classic principles of international law: equality of states, self-determination, nonaggression, self-defense, *pacta sunt servanda*, and so on.[23]

The contrast with Kant is interesting; Rawls's principles are those that Kant thinks are appropriate to international relations in general (the Preliminary Articles), while just (that is, republican) societies are expected to contract to engage with each other at a deeper level to create perpetual peace. Rawls moves some way in Kant's direction in his recent Oxford Amnesty Lecture, "The Law of Peoples."[24] Here the law of peoples applicable to relations between liberal states is taken to include principles supportive of fundamental freedoms and basic human rights as well as the procedural requirements identified at the end of the last paragraph. Moreover, these principles are taken to be applicable also to well-ordered "hierarchical" societies. War is only legitimate in self-defense and so, in principle, would not take place between these societies. In this respect, Rawls approaches Kant's position quite closely. As with his formulation in *A Theory of Justice*, and following Kant, however, his notion of the law of peoples does not involve principles of distributive justice; there are still two contracts: one, domestic, with the difference principle, the other, international, without it.[25]

Rawls's "two-contracts" position has been widely seen as unsatisfactory. Some who wish to retain his basic categories have argued that he was mistaken to have assumed that societies are essentially self-contained, and that while this may once have been a viable position, it is no longer so in an era of "complex interdependence." The principle that inequalities are acceptable only when they are to the benefit of the least advantaged ought therefore to be applied on a world scale, with, of course, very radical results. This was the position of Charles Beitz in *Political Theory and International Relations* and is that of Thomas Pogge in *Realizing Rawls*.[26]

But as Beitz later acknowledged, and as critics of Rawls like Brian Barry had argued all along, this will not do, because the world taken as a whole cannot plausibly be seen as a "cooperative venture for mutual advantage."[27] But if the difference principle cannot be extended in this way, then it would seem that if we are to be Rawlsian, his initial distinction must stand, which would imply that the most serious and damaging examples of social and economic inequality with which we are familiar cannot be brought within the purview of a theory of justice. This view, as Barry has consistently argued, is simply perverse. A theory of justice that cannot offer principles to cope with international inequalities, indeed cannot even recognize such inequalities as unjust, is not worth the name. Moreover, this inadequacy stems directly from a key element of Rawls's theory, namely, the fact that his contractors are those engaged in a mutually advantageous social venture.

To summarize, theorists like Kant who produced a contractarian theory of international society have generally done so on the basis that the contracting parties are states acting as collective persons, not individual human beings, and that the rules they establish do not include principles of distributive justice. From the perspective of the most influential school of modern contractarians, a worldwide contract that *did* establish such principles could only emerge if the link of justice to mutual advantage were abandoned, that is to say if all the inhabitants of the world were taken to be parties to the contract as individuals. At this point, Charvet's position comes back into the picture, via his argument that this link cannot be broken without undermining the strength of the contract metaphor. He states that it is the mutual advantageousness of cooperation that makes it rational for cooperators to will the transformation of society from traditional to contractual; thus, mutual advantage, broadly conceived, is a necessary but not sufficient condition for the adoption of moral norms. If this is a correct reading, the possibility of a contractarian account of international distributive justice, as the term is usually employed, is eliminated, although in his model the same modified Paretian type of justified inequality may be applied internationally as well as domestically.

Arguably, this is a constructive move. While it may be desirable for there to be a large-scale worldwide redistribution of income and wealth, always presupposing this could be done effectively, this is not a conclusion that can be reached by any variety of contractarian thought that attempts to take the root metaphor of a contract seriously and apply it to international society. Much depends here on the weight given to "seriously"; the point is that in any use of contract that takes the metaphor seriously, the contractors have to be brought into a cooperative relationship with one another, and given the current level of development of world society, it is difficult to see how this could be accomplished. Charvet performs a valuable task by redirecting attention away from the unpromising line of inquiry represented by the contest between Rawls on the one hand and the Rawlsians Beitz and Pogge on the other. Moreover, the value of his work is not simply negative. His own approach to the problem of international inequality has far more of a radical purchase on the problem *internationally* than it does domestically.

This point requires elaboration. The principles he espouses—initial equality of access, development with one's own labor subject to the criteria of not worsening the position of others—are the same domestically as internationally. Unless the labor requirement is defined in an extremely restrictive way, these principles could, and would, lead to a very high level of inequality with, arguably, undesirable consequences; even if notions of "relative deprivation" are excluded, and there is no reason why they should be, the purely political consequences of great economic inequality would be, indeed are, considerable. It could be argued that simply in the interests of preserving political freedom, checks on excessive economic inequality are required, but, in Charvet's account, the original contractors could refuse to agree to this because such restrictions would go beyond what is required by a rational will to cooperate on moral terms. If this interpretation is right, the consequences domestically are undesirable; however, internationally these same principles have a different impact—far more radical, less generous to the status quo.

There are two reasons for this, the first of which is a "second-best" argument that relates back to the issue of mutual advantage. In brief, though domestically it may be possible to push to an acknowledgement of obligations to fellow citizens that go beyond what can simply emerge out of the gains from cooperation, the same possibility may not exist internationally. On a world scale, if, as seems inevitable for now, the members of international society are *states*, principles that emerge out of mutual advantage like those espoused by Charvet are, probably, the best that can be achieved. Moreover, second, in purely consequentialist terms, Charvet's principles would have far greater effect internationally than domestically. The resource transfers that would be required to allow all states to act as autonomous agents in the modern world would be considerable: the international equivalent of the various educational and welfare services provided, though at inadequate levels, in Western liberal democracies. At present in most such countries, transfers connected with these activities take up perhaps 30 to 40 percent of the GNP; given that the same countries congratulate themselves if they come close to transferring 1 percent of the GNP in the form of international aid, the impact of a require-

ment on the part of rich and powerful states that they should give substance to the moral equality they recognize in the poor and weak would be
considerable.

Moreover, there is another respect in which Charvet's general approach
has positive advantages at the international level, and this is in raising the issue
of the different kinds of relationships that are appropriate between members
of international society that are differently constituted—that is, the relationship between states that are internally just, but in different ways from each
other, but also between societies that are just and those that are unjust in their
internal structures. This is an important issue that played the central role in
Kant's thinking, but which modern international contractarians like Beitz and
Pogge seem to be less interested in.

Charvet is, surely, right to regard this neglect as unfortunate. His chain of
reasoning goes as follows: in order that states can give substance to the moral
equality they recognize in each other, they need to create rules and decision-
making procedures, and for these to be effective, institutions of considerable
authority are required. In effect, a kind of federalism appears in international
society (but without transforming the latter into a world state). But such a
federalism requires agreement on the part of its members not just on common
external principles, but on common internal ones. In effect, what is required,
on Charvet's account, is a federated society of *liberal* states.[28] This is so partly
because only such a society would allow for the emergence of an international
civil society and the mutual recognition of the rights of the individual citizens
of each state, but also because differently constituted states would be unable
to agree on morally substantive *external* principles. Thus, for example, Islamic
states would wish to conduct their external relations in terms of their religious
principles, as well, of course, as structuring their domestic societies on
Qur'anic as opposed to liberal lines. Such is the situation of a society that is in
some sense just but not liberal; presumably there will be other societies that
will be in every sense unjust and principles will be needed to govern relations
between them and the just societies.

Charvet examines one possibility here, which is to think in terms of a partly
just international society in which norms of an authoritative nature governing
such matters as nonaggression, self-defense, and *pacta sunt servanda* exist, but
where the domestic arrangements of states are allowed to vary. This is close
to Kant's Preliminary Articles, Rawls's account of the second contract in *A
Theory of Justice*, and, most of all, to Nardin's notion of international society
as an Oakeshottian practical association.[29] Such a partly just international society could, if the notion is viable, coexist with a fully just federated society of
liberal states (which again puts these ideas in contact with Kant).

As Charvet recognizes, however, there is a problem here. For even a partly
just international society to work, its members have to acknowledge that its
norms are authoritative, and there are some societies that are organized on
lines that would preclude such an acknowledgement. For instance, again, an
Islamic state might take the view that while its own domestic structures should

be inviolate, being constructed on lines mandated by God, those of non-Islamic states deserve no such protection, especially when these latter structures allow individuals to "slander" Islam in the name of liberal freedoms.

Charvet briefly explores the possibility that such an argument could be met by an international application of the distinction Rawls makes between a political and a comprehensive liberalism, between justice political and justice metaphysical.[30] From this vantage point, nonliberal societies might come to accept that their nonliberalism or antiliberalism is a matter for their "private lives" (that is, internal structures) while allowing the authoritative practices of international society to govern their "public life" (international relations). It is difficult to be optimistic that antiliberals will actually think this way. The very distinction between political and metaphysical is the product of liberal thought, so it is hard to imagine that Islamic or other religiously based societies would adopt the disassociation between private and public that this model requires for unless pressure is bought to bear on them. Norms such as nonintervention and a clear distinction between domestic and international jurisdiction are a product of modern, Western, secular thought; in an important sense, they *are* metaphysically grounded, part of a comprehensive scheme, and there seems little point in pretending that this is not so.

Even the remote chance of a contract based on mutual noninterference, however, seems more plausible than the solution to the problem offered by Rawls in "The Law of Peoples." Here he assumes that between liberal states, and well-ordered hierarchical states a law of peoples could emerge which would cover not simply the procedures of practical association, but also fundamental freedoms and certain basic human rights. This is possible because these hierarchical states are assumed to be based on a legal system committed to the common good: a system of consultation; rights to subsistence, liberty, and property; a degree of freedom of conscience, and the right to emigrate.[31] It seems very much as if Rawls is solving a problem here by defining it out of existence; a well-ordered society of this kind would indeed have no great difficulty relating to liberal states, because it would actually *be*, in most respects, a liberal state, though without formal representative institutions and, perhaps, with a state religion. It is reasonably clear that very few, if any, actual hierarchical states are "well ordered" to this extent.

Charvet raises an important issue here without providing a satisfactory answer. Perhaps there is no answer. Perhaps international *society* is a description that applies only to relations between states that are similarly constituted on broadly liberal lines, that is to say that it is only between such societies that normatively grounded relations are possible. In this view, relations between such states and others—even those based on some principles of justice—could only be governed by expediency, interest, and power, and even the minimal comfort provided by the sort of legal code endorsed by Kant in the preliminary articles, and Nardin as the rules of practical association, would be "tainted with contingency" and by no means authoritative. This is a sobering conclusion, but it is possible to argue that the number of broadly liberal states

142   CHRIS BROWN

has increased and is increasing. Here at least there are grounds to expect an
expansion in the scope of a fully just international society, whether or not it
is constituted through a contract.

NOTES

1. This chapter has been partly shaped by discussions with other contributors to
this book and, in particular, with John Charvet, who would not, however, accept a
number of the interpretations of his work presented here.

2. This is Connolly's formulation of what is required by what he terms "the Augustinian Imperative." See William E. Connolly, *The Augustinian Imperative: A Reflection on the Politics of Morality* (Newbury Park, CA: Sage, 1993).

3. This is, perhaps, much to the same effect as Scanlon's notion of "rules [that] no
one could reasonably reject as a basis for informed, unforced general agreement."
Thomas M. Scanlon, "Contractualism and Utilitarianism," in Amartya Sen and Bernard Williams, eds., *Utilitarianism and Beyond* (Cambridge: Cambridge University
Press, 1982), 110.

4. John Charvet, Chapter 7 above.

5. This is because the contractors have nothing to redistribute, that is, the social
product does not depend on the outcome of their deliberations.

6. For a recent, very radical, statement of this thesis, see John Milbank, *Theology and
Social Theory* (Oxford: Blackwell, 1990), ch. 1.

7. The English Idealists (especially Bosanquet and Green) did tend to obscure the
differences between Rousseau and Hegel, and so do come close to endorsing a variety
of contractarianism.

8. Charvet here refers to Charles Taylor's thinking, but as significant if not more
so has been Michael Sandel's *Liberalism and the Limits of Justice* (Cambridge: Cambridge University Press, 1982). See also the excellent discussion in Daniel Bell, *Communitarianism and Its Critics* (Oxford: Oxford University Press, 1993).

9. See Brian Barry, *Theories of Justice*, vol. 1 of *A Treatise on Social Justice* (Hemel
Hempstead: Harvester Wheatsheaf, 1989), part 3.

10. Charvet, Chapter 7 above (emphasis added).

11. For another review of the tradition, see David R. Mapel, "The Contractarian
Tradition and International Ethics," in Terry Nardin and David R. Mapel, eds., *Traditions of International Ethics* (Cambridge: Cambridge University Press, 1992).

12. Thomas Hobbes, *Leviathan* (Oxford: Basil Blackwell, 1946).

13. See Martin Wight, *International Theory: The Three Traditions* (Leicester: Leicester University Press, 1991), 38–40, where Wight sees Locke as one of the sources of
"rationalist" theories.

14. Jean-Jacques Rousseau, "Judgment on Saint-Pierre's Project for Perpetual
Peace," in *The Theory of International Relations*, ed. M. G. Forsyth, H.M.A. Keens-
Soper, and P. Savigear (London: George Allen and Unwin, 1970).

15. See Jean-Jacques Rousseau, "The Social Contract," in Frederick Watkins,
trans. and ed., *Rousseau: Political Writings* (Edinburgh: Nelson, 1953), bk. 4, ch. 9.

16. Because "with any movement of trade and commerce it is impossible to prevent
destructive vices from creeping into a nation." Rousseau, "Social Contract," 309.

17. See Immanuel Kant, "Perpetual Peace: A Philosophical Sketch," in Kant, *Political Writings*, 2nd enlarged ed. (Cambridge: Cambridge University Press, 1991), 93–130.

18. Kant, *Political Writings*, 98n (Kant's emphasis).

19. Kant, *Political Writings*, 102; in the original, "Das Völkerrecht soll auf einen Föderalism freier Staten gegründet sein," *Zum ewigen Frieden* (Stuttgart: Reclam, 1984).

20. Kant, *Political Writings*, 104 (Kant's emphasis).

21. This is one of the reasons why Hegel is certain that Kant's scheme would not work; the agreement would always be "tainted with contingency." G.F.W. Hegel, *Elements of the Philosophy of Right* (Cambridge: Cambridge University Press, 1991), §333. Pierre Laberge argues convincingly in Chapter 5 above that Kant sees this as a second-best arrangement, justifiable only because a world republic is not achievable.

22. John Rawls, *A Theory of Justice* (Cambridge, MA: Harvard University Press, 1971). Of course, no one-sentence summary can do justice to the complexity of the argument, much less to the later reformulations, collected and amplified in his *Political Liberalism* (New York: Columbia University Press, 1993).

23. See Rawls, *Theory of Justice*, 378, for the most succinct summary of his position.

24. John Rawls, "The Law of Peoples," in Stephen Shute and Susan Hurley, eds., *On Human Rights: The Oxford Amnesty Lectures 1993* (New York: Basic Books, 1993).

25. At this point the analogy with Kant breaks down because neither of Kant's contracts involves distributive justice in the late-twentieth-century sense of the term.

26. Charles R. Beitz, *Political Theory and International Relations* (Princeton, NJ: Princeton University Press, 1979), and Thomas W. Pogge, *Realizing Rawls* (Ithaca, NY: Cornell university Press, 1989).

27. For Beitz's change of argument (although not of conclusion) see Charles R. Beitz, "Cosmopolitan Ideals and National Sentiment," *Journal of Philosophy* 80 (1983): 591–600. For Barry's position see, for example, "Humanity and Justice in Global Perspective," in J. Roland Pennock and John W. Chapman, eds., *Ethics, Economics, and the Law*, Nomos 24 (New York: New York University Press, 1982), reprinted in his *Democracy, Power and Justice* (Oxford: Oxford University Press, 1989), 434–63.

28. Liberal here should be very broadly defined to include, for example, social democratic as well as liberal capitalist societies. What is crucial is that the rule of law, civil rights, and private property are guaranteed.

29. Terry Nardin, *Law, Morality, and the Relations of States* (Princeton, NJ: Princeton University Press, 1983).

30. See Rawls, *Political Liberalism*.

31. Rawls, "The Law of Peoples," 61–64.

CHAPTER 9

International Society from a Cosmopolitan Perspective

BRIAN BARRY

The Cosmopolitan Idea

Now that the Ethikon enterprise has been going for some time, we can begin to reap the rewards of continuity. Instead of offering my own definition of cosmopolitanism, I shall therefore take over the definition put forward by Charles Beitz in an earlier Ethikon book, *Political Restructuring in Europe*. According to Beitz, the two essential elements defining a cosmopolitan view are that it is inclusive and nonperspectival. "If local viewpoints can be said to be partial, then a cosmopolitan viewpoint is impartial."[1] What I am concerned with here is what Beitz calls "moral cosmopolitanism," of which he says that "it applies to the whole world the maxim that answers to questions about what we should do, or what institutions we should establish, should be based on an impartial consideration of the claims of each person who would be affected by our choices."[2]

Beitz distinguishes this moral cosmopolitanism from what he calls "institutional cosmopolitanism." It is important to recognize that moral cosmopolitanism leaves open the question of the ideal constitution of international society. Institutional cosmopolitanism is one answer to that question, or more precisely a family of answers. Thus, institutional cosmopolitanism "pertains to the way political institutions should be set up—to the political constitution of the world, so to speak. . . . Although the details may vary, the distinctive common feature is some ideal of world political organization in which states and state-like units have significantly diminished authority in comparison with the status quo and supranational institutions have more."[3]

As Beitz says, "there is no necessary link between moral and institutional cosmopolitanism."[4] Thus, one may be a moral cosmopolitan without believing that its precepts would best be satisfied by institutions of the kind commended by institutional cosmopolitanism. At the level of domestic politics, it is quite consistent to start from a utilitarian position and then argue for a minimum state. Similarly, there is no inconsistency in counting the interests of everyone in the world equally and concluding that those interests will tend to be best advanced by a state-centered system with only weak international authority. Whether or not this is thought to be so will depend on what one takes the main interests of human beings to be and on the way in which one thinks the world works.

Conversely, one may support the policy conclusions embodied in institutional cosmopolitanism on a basis other than that of moral cosmopolitanism. Beitz himself says that "it is hard to think of anyone who has defended institutional cosmopolitanism on other than cosmopolitan moral grounds."[5] But it is easy to see that the case for a strengthening of international authority vis-à-vis states can plausibly be derived from Hobbesian premises under contemporary conditions. Warfare between countries now has a potential for almost unlimited destruction, and only concerted action can address global problems such as ozone depletion, the "greenhouse effect," and pollution of the oceans. I believe, therefore, that universal self-interest would support a shift toward institutional cosmopolitanism, as Beitz defines it. In addition, I believe that moral cosmopolitanism leads to the endorsement of international redistribution of a kind that Hobbesian premises do not appear to underwrite. My reasons for thinking this will appear later.

The general point I have made about moral cosmopolitanism is also made in this book for all the other approaches surveyed. That is to say, there is no automatic move from the ethical premises to any particular conclusion about the ideal world constitution. Where moral cosmopolitanism shows itself to be more distinctive is in its denial that membership of a society is of deep moral significance when the claims that people can legitimately make on one another are assessed. This differentiates it sharply from, for example, the kind of contractarian view advanced in this book by John Charvet, within which the bounds of society are also the bounds of justice.[6]

I should explain what I mean by saying that membership of a society does not have *deep* moral significance. We can in a variety of ways acquire obligations that we owe to some people and not to others. There is no reason for doubting that the members of a politically constituted society can acquire obligations to one another that they do not owe to others. What moral cosmopolitanism insists on, however, is that it should be possible to justify this special treatment on grounds that can in principle be accepted by those excluded. A standard way of doing this is, of course, to point out that those who are excluded can and do acquire special obligations to members of their own societies in exactly the same way. The point has been put well by Thomas Hill, Jr., in the following way:

> All the impartiality thesis says is that, if and when one raises questions regarding fundamental moral standards, the court of appeal that one addresses is a court in which no particular individual, group, or country has *special* standing. Before that court, declaring "I like it," "It serves *my* country," and the like, is not decisive; principles must be defensible to anyone looking at the matter apart from his or her special attachments, from a larger, human perspective.[7]

Some Cosmopolitan Principles

At the heart of moral cosmopolitanism is the idea that human beings are in some fundamental sense equal. All claims are to be weighed in the same balance. But how is this balancing to be carried out? An answer that naturally presents itself is that we reduce all claims to interests and then resolve conflicts of interest by saying that the outcome that most satisfies interests (the one in which the greatest sum of interest satisfaction obtains) is the best. If "interests" are given a subjective interpretation this is the utilitarian prescription. It is objectionable on two grounds. First, it is not true that all claims can be expressed in a single currency: claims are irreducibly heterogeneous in their nature. And, second, the formula is indifferent to issues of distribution. Nobody has any good reason for accepting that he or she should do very badly merely because this is the most effective means of maximizing some aggregate good, however defined.

Rather than canvassing a number of alternatives, let me simply present what seems to me the best way of giving content to the idea of impartial treatment that underlies moral cosmopolitanism. Following an idea put forward by T. M. Scanlon, I propose that we should ask of any rule or principle whether or not it could reasonably be rejected by somebody who was motivated by "the desire to find principles which others similarly motivated could not reasonably reject."[8] We thus posit a hypothetical negotiating situation marked by equality (since everybody stands on an equal footing and is equipped with a veto to protect interests that cannot reasonably be denied) and freedom (since nobody can coerce anybody else into accepting an agreement by the exercise of superior power). Principles of justice are those principles that would emerge from a process taking this form.

We may envisage a variety of different sets of people making choices in such a hypothetical situation. By far the most effort has gone into the case in which the choice is made by people who are members of the same politically organized society. But for the present purpose I want to focus on the case in which the choice is made by all the people in the world, since it is quite possible to imagine a world in which each country is internally just but the system as a whole is extremely unjust. On the criterion of justice proposed here, this would be so if the rules governing relations between countries could reasonably be rejected by some people.

It seems clear that the premise of fundamental human equality applies without regard to time as well as without regard to place. There is no good moral reason for saying that the interests of people who will live in the future should be given less (or more) weight than the interests of those alive now simply because they come later in time. I do not, however, believe that it is useful to extend the idea of a hypothetical choosing situation to encompass relations between generations, mainly because asking how we would negotiate with people as yet unborn (especially those in the distant future) creates gratuitous problems. The point here is that, where the parties are contemporaries, the problem posed is closely related to a kind of which we have experience. Indeed, we can hope to learn from actual cases of agreement (relatively consensual policies in countries, or payment schemes in large organizations, for example), making adjustments to compensate for deviations from equal power relations. It does not follow, however, that we are without recourse to anything except a direct appeal to the idea of fundamental equality in regard to future generations. We can take the principles that would be agreed upon by contemporaries and ask if there is any reason why they should not be extrapolated to relations between different generations, perhaps being appropriately modified to cope with the special features of those relations. My belief is that this procedure will provide all we need in the way of guidance beyond the idea of fundamental equality itself.

Following Rawls, I shall take justice to be the highest-order organizing concept within political philosophy.[9] The following are, I wish to maintain, four principles of justice. I shall say a little (but only a little) in defense of each as I go along. A point to be made about all of them together is that they meet the two objections to utilitarianism: their subject-matter is heterogeneous and they are sensitive to questions of distribution.

First principle: the presumption of equality. All inequalities of rights, opportunities, and resources have to be justifiable in ways that cannot reasonably be rejected by those who get least.

This principle does not immediately generate specific conclusions. But it is important in directing attention toward those who have the best prima facie reasons for rejecting some proposal. It emphasizes that any inequality must make sense to them. As it stands, it may appear a very weak principle, and it is undeniably lacking in content. In spite of this, what impresses me is how many relations of inequality at all levels cannot meet its demands. These relations are maintained by unequal power relationships, or (not quite the same thing) by inertia, forming part of a pattern which it would not be advantageous to anyone acting alone to disturb. Thus, those disadvantaged by an inequality may well choose to act in ways that sustain it, even though they would reject it in a hypothetical ideal-choice situation.

There is a temptation (succumbed to by Rawls in some contexts) to drive the principle of the presumption of equality toward closure by specifying that the *only* justification for an inequality is that the minimum is as high as is feasible. I do not accept this because it would be inconsistent with the second principle. For this, as will be seen, has the implication that those who do worst from an inequality may under certain conditions accept reasonably that those who do better deserve to do better.

At the same time, I wish to ensure that the idea of the priority of the worst-off retains some critical force. I therefore add an *anti-aggregation* rider: aggregate gains by "winners" do not constitute a justification to "losers." This simply makes explicit the point that, from the perspective of the losers, the argument that there will be a net gain is not a sufficient ground for withdrawing a veto.

Second principle: personal responsibility and compensation. It is prima facie acceptable for people to fare differently if the difference arises from a voluntary choice on their part; conversely, victims of misfortunes that they could not have prevented have a prima facie valid claim for compensation or redress.

The first clause embodies the basic idea that human agency must be respected. It is an essential aspect of a fully human life that one's decisions should have some impact on the world, and that can happen only if what they do makes a difference to what actually happens. There is a great deal of evidence, both from surveys of opinion and from studies of freely accepted inequalities, to support the notion that the first clause would emerge from a hypothetical choice situation. What the formulation leaves open is, of course, the conditions under which a choice counts as being voluntary. The clause about personal responsibility sets the terms of the debate, however, and, I believe, imposes definite limits on the range of reasonable disagreement.[10]

The second clause is the obverse of the first. It may be said to embody what Richard Arneson has described as "the intuition that when people's lives go badly through no fault or voluntary choice of their own, it is morally incumbent on others to offer aid to the disadvantaged so long as the cost of providing aid is not excessive."[11] I should, however, wish to approach the proviso at the end of this statement with some care. What makes the cost "excessive"? Not, I think, simply that the cost is high: if the loss is great, the cost is liable to be high, but that does not affect the force of the claim. The valid form of the proviso is, I suggest, that the obligation is weakened or in extreme cases extinguished altogether if the cost of providing the aid is greatly disproportional to the benefit gained by the recipient(s).

We may combine the two parts of this principle to obtain a somewhat more precise version of the doctrine of compensation. Suppose that people fare badly not as a result of their voluntary choices but as a result of unpreventable misfortune. Then, we may say, they can legitimately demand that (1) where "nature" is the cause, the more fortunate should contribute to a scheme of compensation; and (2) where the voluntary act of some person (or persons) is the cause, redress should be looked for in the first instance from that source.

Third principle: priority of vital interests. In the absence of some compelling consideration to the contrary, the vital interests of each person should be protected in preference to the nonvital interests of anyone. Vital interests include security from physical harm, nutrition adequate for the maintenance of health, clean drinking water and sanitary arrangements, clothing and shelter appropriate to the climate, medical care, and education to a level sufficient to function effectively within one's society.

It should be observed that this principle expresses priorities not in terms of persons (as the first principle did) but in terms of types of claim. The idea underlying it is that there are certain minimum requirements of living a good life that can be acknowledged to be such by almost everyone, whatever his or her own particular conception of the good may be.[12] If the second principle is related to the idea of desert, this third principle is related to that of need. Thus, the second and third principles capture what are the commonly accepted bases for moral claims. The first principle is concerned with a third basis—the allocation of rights.

Fourth principle: mutual advantage. Whenever it would be to the prospective advantage of everyone to depart from the application of the above principles (compared with the results of applying them), it is permissible to do so. Where more than one arrangement has this property, the one to be preferred is that which maximizes the gain of those who gain least from the departure.

This principle is one of collective rationality: it endorses Pareto improvements over the baseline set by the operation of the other three principles. The second half of it provides a way of choosing between potential Pareto improvements and incorporates the idea of "the priority of the worst off." It should be observed, however, that the identity of the "worst off" here is not the same as it was in the anti-aggregation proviso. Here the worst off are defined in relation to the baseline created by applying the other principles. Those who stand to gain least by applying the fourth one may not be those who were the worst off from the application of the other three.

Read carelessly, the fourth principle may look as if it renders the others nugatory and simply gets us back to utilitarianism. It is important to recognize that this is not so. The other three principles retain their integrity. They can be supplemented by the fourth principle but they cannot be displaced by it. For those who like the vocabulary, we may say that the first three principles jointly have lexicographic priority over the fourth. This, of course, leaves us without a formula for resolving conflicts among the first three principles, but who said that ethical problems should be easy?

Justice Denied

The principles of justice I have put forward are intended to function as guides to debate: they should be capable of specifying kinds of argument that can be accepted as valid while ruling out other considerations that might be put forward. This structuring of moral discourse is what I believe principles should do. Clearly, for the full development of a theory of justice we would need to see how the principles put forward here work together to produce some conclusions about the kinds of institution they underwrite. In the space at my disposal, I have no hope of doing that. What I shall focus on, in keeping with the topic of this chapter, are the largest-scale global implications, extended into the distant future.

The most striking feature of the world as it exists at present, if we line it up against the principles of justice, is the extent to which the third principle is violated. Probably half the total world population lacks the material conditions that are necessary for the satisfaction of their vital interests. Even in Latin America, which is on the average considerably wealthier than Africa, the Indian subcontinent, and China, half the total population was estimated by a United Nations agency to have "unmet basic needs" in 1986.[13] These conditions coexist—in contravention of the principle of the priority of vital interests—with over a quarter of the world's population living at material standards vastly in excess of anything required to meet their basic needs.

A second observation is that there is no tendency toward an equalization of average incomes between rich and poor countries. On the contrary, the richest countries are continuing to increase their affluence (if slowly), while many poor countries have actually become poorer in the past decade, especially as a result of debt repayments. (On balance, poor countries now make net transfers to rich ones.) Moreover, within poor countries, the burden of the "adjustment" imposed by the IMF and the World Bank falls mainly on the poor, who are hit by increased unemployment and the disappearance of basic public services.

It is, of course, conceivable that the prima facie injustice arising from the wholesale violation of the third principle is nullified by the application of one or more of the other principles. There are two candidates: the second and the fourth. Under the second, it might be argued that the plight of those whose vital interests are not being met is entirely their own fault. This is immensely implausible. Insofar as natural resources make some countries better off than others, this is clearly a matter of pure good fortune. The inhabitants of the wealthier countries can claim some credit for maintaining their economic capital, social capital (institutions that work to provide a framework for prosperity), and human capital (a well-educated workforce). But even then much is inherited from previous generations. Within poor countries it is pure fantasy to suppose that the children of landless laborers in the country or dwellers in *favelas* or shanty-towns round the cities could all by sheer personal effort raise themselves in one generation to a position in which their vital interests would be fulfilled.

The other weapon of the apologists for the justice of the status quo is the fourth principle: any attempt to improve the lot of the worst off by redistributive measures, it is sometimes claimed, would have such an inhibiting effect on the efforts of the better off that in the end everybody would be worse off than they would be under a policy of leaving the outcome to market forces. Looking at the inequalities in many poor countries and in the world as a whole, this would be hard to believe, even if indefinite increases in global production were feasible. But they are not, and this has profound implications for the fourth principle. Recall that in the previous section I said that the interests of those who live in the future must be given as much weight as the interests of those who live in the present. This means (under principle two) that we cannot justly leave them worse off than we are, since this would not reflect a voluntary choice on their part. It also implies (under principle three) that we cannot give our own pursuit of our goals priority over their vital interests.

There is, manifestly, a range of views about what this would entail. But the general form of the question is clear: unless it blows itself up or destroys its environment, there is no reason why the human race should not continue to inhabit the globe for hundreds of thousands of years to come (as against about ten thousand since the beginnings of civilization). We cannot know how people in the future will live or what inventions and discoveries they will make. But we know that they will need an inhabitable planet, with such amenities as an ozone layer, land that is neither desert nor eroded, relative freedom from air and water pollution, and a diversity of species. This requires that the current generation should not leave its successors with conditions that are worse in these respects, or if this is impossible that the current generation at least moves as far toward "substainability" as is feasible. What is crucial is that the capacity of the planet to regenerate depleted natural resources and render toxic wastes harmless (metals such as mercury, lead, and cadmium, and nuclear waste, for example) is strictly limited. Some people say that we need not worry about any of this because people in the future *may* come up with some "technological fix" that will solve all the problems. This, however, is scarcely consistent with taking seriously the interests of future generations, since if we acted on the optimistic assumption and it turned out to be wrong the consequences would be catastrophic.[14]

There is apparently little disagreement among those who accept this general diagnosis that current production levels globally are unsustainable. The only question is how far they would have to be reduced to become sustainable. A widely held view is that the world left the path of sustainability in the early 1950s. To the extent that processes of production are modified to use fewer natural resources and create less pollution, we can avoid the conclusion that production levels must go back to those prevalent in the early 1950s, but they would still have to be reduced substantially. Even if sustainability entails only freezing total production, this is enough to demand a fundamental reorientation of virtually all thinking in the last fifty years (and most of that in the preceding hundred) about distributive justice. For a common theme running through the work of thinkers on both the left and the right of the political spectrum has been that production is not a zero-sum game. What unites these thinkers is the "productivist" premise that "a rising tide lifts all boats." Inequalities of income are therefore of no moment in themselves. Only simple-minded people, according to the conventional wisdom, believe that the poor are poor because the rich are rich; on the contrary, the poor are as well off as they are only because the rich are rich. Inequality increases the size of the cake, so that even those with the smallest slices get more.

If we drop the presupposition of an indefinitely expandable cake, the older idea that the poor are poor because the rich are rich comes into its own again. Let us suppose that we are at the sustainable maximum, and that it would be possible to stay at this maximum while shifting income from rich to poor.

Then it does become true that anyone with a large slice of the cake is directly responsible for somebody else having a small one. Internationally it means that poor countries can expand production (within the limits of global sustainability) only if the rich countries cut back to make room.

This would be true even if sustainability demanded only that total production level out at its current volume. Now suppose (as seems to me more plausible) that long-run sustainability entails a substantial overall reduction in what is produced. Then further implications can be derived. Thus, the rationale (widely acted on in all western European countries in the past decade) for cutting high marginal rates of taxation—that the incentive effect of letting high earners keep more increases economic growth—has to go into reverse. Since, however, the evidence suggests that reducing marginal tax rates from their previous levels has had negligible effects on effort, it seems likely that post-tax earnings could be almost equalized before production fell by a substantial amount. The limits on equalization would perhaps lie rather in those imposed by the second principle, which permits the consequences of voluntary choice to be reflected in outcomes. People who are particularly keen to make more money should be able to do so by working at a job within their capabilities involving longer or less convenient hours or more unpleasant conditions than other jobs open to people with their capabilities. It should be observed, however, that the second principle does not legitimize inequalities that do not result from choice, and I believe that it would not therefore underwrite the vast majority of existing earned income inequalities. The only ones it would support would be of an essentially compensatory nature.

A parallel argument may be made about transfers from one country to another. Even if unlimited expansion of production were feasible, it would be grossly implausible to maintain that even a low level of transfer from rich to poor countries would hamper production in the rich countries so much that in the long run everyone would lose. There seems to me no real case for thinking that production in rich countries would necessarily be reduced at all by some modest level of transfer. Even if it were, poor countries would still be better off with transfers. For unless some of the increased wealth of the rich countries is deliberately channeled to poor countries, there does not appear to be any mechanism that automatically results in the increased wealth of the rich countries creating more in the poor ones. There is certainly one force moving in the other direction, which is that technological progress tends to make the rich countries less and less dependent on the raw materials (jute and sisal, for example) that are the export staples of some poor countries.

Now suppose that global production will have to be reduced if pollution and resource depletion are not to place an unfair burden on future generations. In this case, any inhibiting effect on production of the extra taxation imposed on rich countries by international redistribution becomes a positive advantage. Assuming that aggregate global output needs to come down substantially, I should be very surprised if that goal could be accomplished solely through the drag on production in the rich countries imposed by international transfers. Governments in rich countries would still have to introduce deliberate measures to curb the propensity of their economies to produce more than is compatible with long-run sustainability.

MORAL COSMOPOLITANISM AND INTERNATIONAL REDISTRIBUTION

Moral cosmopolitanism is, in essence, an individualistic doctrine in that it focuses on how individuals fare. This does not mean that it slights the importance of families, communities, and countries. But it treats their value as derivative: they are of value to exactly the extent that they contribute to the welfare of individuals (both those within the group and those outside it, weighting their interests equally).

This moral individualism, taken together with the considerations advanced in the previous section, leads to a radical conclusion. The demands of cosmopolitanism would, I suggest, be best satisfied in a world in which rich people wherever they lived would be taxed for the benefit of poor people wherever they lived. On the revenue-raising side, the model would be that of the United States, where the federal government imposes a federal income tax, leaving the states to raise whatever taxes (including income taxes) they like. The expenditure side is rather more messy. I believe that a large proportion of the payout would have to be to individuals, either in the form of a universal unconditional basic income or an income dependent on status (youth, age, sickness and disability, unemployment). But it would clearly be advantageous for some of the resources to go to the improvement of communal facilities in areas where the most deprived people are concentrated.

As I have already said, the units within the federation (states in the US, countries within a world federation) would be able to raise their own taxes in addition and spend them as they wished. Nevertheless, it is clear that any such system would constitute a considerable derogation of state sovereignty. (It may be recalled that in the US the introduction of a federal income tax required a constitutional amendment.) It seems to me that the least one can say is that any such scheme would be unimaginable unless it had been preceded by a long period in which transfers of a systematic kind between countries had become a well-established practice. On this alternative understanding, "international redistribution" means redistribution among countries. This immediately raises problems, since an unconditional transfer to a poor country may not benefit any poor people within that country. If, for example, the money having been raised by a broad-based tax in a relatively wealthy country goes straight into the Swiss bank accounts of the ruling elite, the net result will be predominantly a shift of resources from those in the middle to the very wealthy. Any system open to such abuse would fail to generate support from the contributors, and reasonably enough.

I do not wish to slight the importance of these problems. They are, however, best regarded as falling within the scope of a more general issue. This can be stated as follows: given a world that is made up of states, what is the morally permissible range of diversity among them? I shall postpone the discussion of this question of diversity until the next section. In the rest of this one, I shall leave on one side the question of the way in which the money is to be spent within countries and focus on the mechanism of transfer between countries.

We are looking for an alternative to a system in which an international authority levies taxes directly on individuals. The simplest alternative is to assess countries for contributions according to their gross national product at some standard rate (for example, one percent) provided their average income per head is above some level (roughly, that of the OECD countries). One percent is an amount that would scarcely be noticed, but it is vastly in excess of the amounts currently transferred and would make a large difference. I do not doubt that moral cosmopolitanism calls for more, but the point is that even that amount would represent a real transformation in the level of international transfers.

A scheme in which the levy is proportional to GNP, above some cutoff point of average income, is the simplest, as I have said. It would, obviously, be possible to make it more fancy by introducing an element of progressivity, so that (within the set of contributors) richer countries paid a larger amount in proportion to their GNP. There is no need to pursue such refinements here. The essential feature common to all is that each state would be assessed by some international authority according to some schedule and it would then be up to the state to determine how the money was to be raised—whether by direct or indirect taxes, for example. An example of such a system that is effective is the system prevailing within the European Union whereby constituent countries have to provide a sum each year, part of which is disbursed (as "solidarity" funds) to the poorer regions.

The case for taking something like income per head as the basis of assessment is twofold. The first is that if you want to raise money you had better go where the money is. In terms of classical taxation theory, the criterion is "ability to pay." In terms of the principles of justice set out earlier, it is that a rich country can afford to collect the money demanded without jeopardizing the vital interests of anybody in it. (Of course, this says only that it has the ability to do so. It may actually raise the money in a way that is detrimental to the interests of the worst-off members of the society. This is the obverse of the problem that the proceeds may go to the rich in the recipient society.) There is a second argument as well, and this is that income per head is a proxy for the use of natural resources and the degradation of the global environment. It is not, it must be admitted, precise: the United States, for example, is much more profligate in the resources it expends for a given unit of production than other countries at a roughly similar economic level. Nevertheless, there is enough of a correlation to add support to the case derived from ability to pay.

This argument, however, suggests an alternative way of raising money for an international redistributive authority: a system of user fees (as an alternative to a rationing scheme that would create windfall gains) and taxes on the infliction of global environmental damage. The object here would be two-fold. In part it would be driven by considerations of equity: those who make use of inherently limited facilities should pay, and those who impose burdens on the rest of the world should compensate for the damage they cause. But it would also work to modify behavior by providing an incentive to economize on scarce resources, and to reduce pollution.

Some recently proposed ideas are a surcharge on air tickets, a charge on ocean maritime transport, a special fee for maritime dumping of waste, parking fees for geostationary satellites, charges for the use of the electromagnetic spectrum, and charges for fishing rights in certain areas.[15] A more ambitious extension would include a "carbon tax" on emissions contributing to global warming, and a tax on the production of the CFCs that deplete the ozone layer. The author of this proposal does not discuss how the charges would actually be collected. Ideally, they would be gathered directly from the users or polluters. Only this would ensure that the cost entered into their calculations. It appears to me, however, that many charges would, as a practical matter, have to be levied against governments. The alternative would require an international corps of collectors of fees and taxes that would constitute the same infringement of sovereignty as a corps of international income tax inspectors. The result of assessing governments is that it would be possible for a country to pay its "carbon tax" by, in turn, assessing taxpayers at large rather than by imposing, say, a levy on the burning of coal and petroleum. There is, however, no way in which such slippage can be prevented. What can at least be said is that the system of fees and taxes would put some pressure on governments to reduce their liability.

It is worth noticing that this kind of indirect taxation has a different status vis-à-vis the taxation of individual incomes from a levy based on GNP per head. Both of the rationales for taxing national income would be better served by taxing individual income: ability to pay would be more sensitively captured by taxing individuals, and individual income acts as a proxy for resource use wherever the person with the income lives. The fees and taxes I have just been proposing, however, would be desirable regardless of the way in which the direct tax element might be collected. How much it could be expected to raise would depend entirely on the rates set and the scope of the tax net. Adding a "carbon tax" could make it substantial. I believe, though, that direct taxation based on "ability to pay" is inevitably going to be required. For the indirect taxes would fall on poor countries as well as rich ones. No doubt by the nature of the case rich countries will pay the bulk, but poor countries pursuing "dirty" industrialization (for example China) will also have to pay. So they should: the whole point is to attach a realistic cost to their conduct. But the scheme as a whole can be acceptable only if there is also an element of straight transfer from rich to poor countries.

It may well be said that it is slightly absurd for me to pass over the idea of an international tax-collecting corps on the ground that it is politically infeasible when everything else I am advocating is politically infeasible. Let me begin a response by saying that it still makes good sense to say that one proposal is much *more* politically infeasible than another, even if both seem a long way off adoption. Turning to the question of feasibility head on, I suggest that we should divide it into two. What is commonly seen as the major problem is that of coercing recalcitrant states to play their part. I think the seriousness of this problem can be exaggerated. The European Union collects from its member states because that is the price of staying in, and there are perceived to be advantages in not being excluded. There is no suggestion that troops would be sent to storm the treasury of a nonpaying member. Similarly, the World Trade Organization has the authority to rule on violations, and has at its disposal the sanctions of expulsion or, short of that, denial of certain advantages available to adherents. Generalizing from this, the relatively wealthy countries (the only ones that concern us in this context) belong to a whole network of international agreements, and if the assessed contribution to the fund for international redistribution were the price for remaining a member in good standing, it would be worth paying.

The real problem is not so much coercing backsliders as setting up the scheme in the first place. I do not underestimate the scale of this problem, but I want to emphasize that the kind of political will required to create such a scheme will have to stem from moral motivation. Hobbesian reasoning, as I suggested at the beginning of this chapter, will go quite a way, but it will not underwrite international redistribution. Attempts are, of course, made regularly to argue that it is in the self-interest of rich countries to transfer resources to poor ones. I have the strong impression, however, that those who make such arguments are themselves led to the conclusion by cosmopolitan moral considerations. It is therefore hardly surprising that their arguments fail to convince. All I can suggest here, then, is that, unless the moral case is made, we can be sure nothing good will happen. The more the case is made, the better the chance.

The Limits of Diversity

I take it as axiomatic that, in comparison with many other approaches (especially those of a communitarian cast), moral cosmopolitanism tends toward an endorsement of universally applicable standards. (In this it is not, however, differentiated from the Kantian or natural law approaches, as they are presented in this book. Indeed, they might quite perspicuously be thought of as alternative ways of working through the moral cosmopolitan project, making use of alternative mediating premises.) Although I do not have the space to argue it here, I believe that the hypothetical contractarian approach taken here will underwrite the familiar list of basic human rights.[16] Anybody whose human rights are violated—say, by being denied freedom of speech or freedom of religious worship—has a legitimate complaint, according to moral cosmopolitanism, regardless of the opinions of others in the society. Even if there is something approaching a consensus on the legitimacy of executing religious deviants, that is still a proposition that the nonbeliever in the society's orthodoxy can reasonably reject.

It follows from this that morality is socially constituted only to a limited extent. The principles of justice are valid for all societies. This is far less a straitjacket than it might appear. As I have already pointed out, the principles require interpretation, and there is a good deal of room for interpreting them differently. It should also be emphasized that there is a very wide range of possible institutional embodiments of the principles of justice. In particular, the significance of individualism in the specification of the moral cosmopolitan position should not be misunderstood. What it insists is that every institution be judged by its impact on individual human beings. It rules out appeals to the destiny of a class, race, or nation that are not reducible to claims about the rights, interests, and welfare of individuals. But it is not committed to the idea that these are best advanced in a society that imposes very weak social obligations, another sense of "individualism" that is logically quite distinct. Thus, it is quite consistent with cosmopolitan principles of justice that people may find their greatest fulfillment within a dense network of family and community obligations.

At the same time, however, a cautionary note must be sounded. Enthusiasts for "multiculturalism" have a tendency to sentimentalize traditional arrangements that are grossly oppressive and exploitative when looked at close up.[17] The ultimate test is that nobody affected could reasonably reject the arrangement: the principles of justice are advanced as guidelines to give some structure to that judgment. Unfortunately, the norms constituting extended families and wider (but still small-scale) communities all too often create inequalities (characteristically but not exclusively in relations between the sexes) that could reasonably be rejected by those whose position is the worst under them.

Moral cosmopolitanism would be satisfied if the high level of interdependence and cooperation were retained but its terms reformed so as to be acceptable to all. Where there seems to be no prospect of this happening, however, those who subscribe to the moral cosmopolitan doctrine will typically welcome a weakening of the existing social bonds, and the opening up of an "exit" option for those who wish to get out from under the oppressive set-up. From the point of view of the worst-off, this may well backfire. For the "exit" option is most attractive to those who have most to gain by leaving, and those may well be the stronger rather than the weaker members of the group. The lot of the worst-off may thus even deteriorate as the obligations of the better-off are relaxed or evaded altogether. Nevertheless, the belief that moral cosmopolitanism endorses individualism in this sense is no doubt sustained by the tendency of those who despair of reform to welcome and encourage the dissolution of traditional institutions.

A common move among the multiculturalists is to suggest that social institutions may rest on consensus, even if outsiders might consider them to be radically unjust. It is then argued that it is nobody else's business if there is general acceptance among those actually concerned. In all such cases, however, the quality of the consent given by those who do poorly must be suspect. Often, it does not exist in any form: the exploited and oppressed know perfectly well that they are being treated badly, and the consensus that is blandly asserted to obtain is actually to be found only among the more articulate and powerful members of the group. Even when acceptance is genuine, it is invalidated if the person giving it is too ill-educated or restricted in access to relevant information about alternative forms of organization to be able to make an informed judgment. We must also distinguish acceptance from resignation: if there is no realistic prospect of improvement, it is less psychically costly to put aside any thoughts of justice or injustice and concentrate on survival.

There is nothing in our hypothetical construction, however, to rule out the theoretical possibility that a social arrangement failing to satisfy the principles of justice might be freely accepted as just by all the participants. Suppose, for example, that they all subscribe to a religious system according to which different hereditary groups have higher or lower spiritual status, and that this has strongly inegalitarian implications for the distribution of rights, opportunities, and resources in this world. (The Hindu Varna system is the obvious model here.) On the basis of this, let us stipulate that they all freely accept a social system that violates the principles of justice. What follows?

What does not follow is that the set-up is just. It could still reasonably be rejected (even though it happens not to be), because anybody could reasonably reject basing an inegalitarian social system on a set of religious beliefs. For these beliefs could themselves reasonably be rejected. (It does not follow that they could not reasonably be accepted.) The case for saying that it is just has to rest, it seems to me, on the maxim *Volenti iniuria non fit*. But this maxim is rejected by all municipal legal systems: there are rights to bodily integrity and liberty that cannot validly be surrendered by the consent of the party concerned. We need not, however, draw from this the conclusion that unjust inequalities that are accepted as just by the parties should, if possible, be suppressed. Whether something is unjust is one question; what, if anything, should be done about it by outsiders is another. It can be argued that if people choose freely to live in unjust conditions of powerlessness and material degradation in furtherance of their religious beliefs, then their own view of their greater good should be respected. I have to say that I regard the whole question as purely conjectural, however, since I do not believe that the problem will ever present itself in this way. In any society that meets the information condition, I predict that there will always be found some people who reject the religious system that legitimizes unjust inequalities.

Intranational Injustice and International Redistribution

My primary focus in this chapter is on the distribution of income, and I want in this final section to return to it. Here, the range of legitimate variation is inherently limited, since the principles of justice bear directly on the distribution of income. The great majority of existing countries have a degree of inequality greatly in excess of that which could reasonably be justified under the principles of justice set out here. How does this affect the case for international redistribution, whether conceived as transfers from rich to poor individuals (regardless of location) or as transfers from rich to poor countries?

The answer is perhaps surprising. Take first a scheme in which an international authority collected income taxes from relatively wealthy individuals and gave money to relatively poor individuals. (Some proportion of the money might go to such things as schools and hospitals or water and sewerage systems designed to benefit poor people collectively.) The contributors to the scheme could afford to take a quite relaxed attitude to the distribution of income within recipient countries both before and after the transfers had been made. So long as governments in the recipient countries did not use their taxing powers to take away the benefits gained by the poor, it could be said that at any rate the scheme was working in that resources were being transferred from rich to poor individuals.

Now think about a scheme in which the governments of relatively rich countries transfer resources in some systematic way to the governments of relatively poor countries. Here the distribution of income within the recipient countries becomes a matter of legitimate concern. There are two reasons for this. The first is that the whole notion of the transferred resources going to the poor is now less than transparent. The only way of determining that the results of whatever the government does can be said to constitute a transfer of the money to the poor is to ask if the poor have collectively benefited to the extent of the money provided. This requires close attention to the actual distribution of income and a comparison between it and what the distribution might be hypothesized to have been in its absence.

The second point is rather more subtle. We can best approach it by observing that the individualistic scheme treats national boundaries as having no significance (for this purpose, anyway). In contrast to this, any scheme that makes countries the units of redistribution immediately throws an emphasis on the internal distribution of income. Suppose that the distribution of income in a poor country is extremely unjust (as it actually is in virtually all cases). What implications, if any, does this have for the obligations of those in rich countries to pay taxes in order to provide the resources for transfers to be made to poor countries?

I have already mentioned one case: that in which not only is the distribution of internally generated income unjust but also any additional income from outside would be appropriated by the ruling elite. Here there can be no morally compelling reason for making transfers. There is, instead, a case for international intervention to displace the government and, if necessary, place the country under international trusteeship until more adequate institutions can be created. This intervention will have to be military rather than taking the form of economic sanctions. For (as the examples of Haiti and Iraq illustrate) a government can ensure that the worst burden of economic sanctions falls upon the poorest, and there is no reason to suppose that a government that had already proved itself indifferent to the suffering of its poorest citizens would be motivated to reform by the prospect of their plight becoming even worse as a result of economic sanctions.

The wisdom of military intervention can be challenged, and recent United Nations efforts (in the Horn of Africa, for example) are scarcely encouraging. I cannot here enter into that argument. I assert only the principle that cosmopolitan morality cannot object to intervention under the circumstances I have outlined except on grounds of inefficacy or counterproductiveness. For whatever can be said in favor of state autonomy as a contribution to the well-being of the citizens holds only contingently. Any government which is little more than a gang of looters (as in much of sub-Saharan Africa) forfeits any respect for its independence. If it can be toppled without making things worse, that has to be a (relatively) just outcome.

Bypassing cases in which the poor gain some from international transfers but less than by the amount of the transfers, let us consider now a case in which all the benefit of the transfers goes to those who should justly receive it. It might be suggested that this still does not create an obligation to make the transfer. To put the case in its strongest form, suppose that many people in the country are failing to have their vital needs met, but that there is an economically (though not politically) feasible internal redistribution of income that would enable everybody's vital needs to be met. (This is, in the nature of the case, going to be true only if the average income per capita of countries entitled to be recipients is set quite high. Brazil might then be a candidate.) It could be said then that justice begins at home: why should people elsewhere make sacrifices that would not be called for if the rich in the poor country were to behave justly?

We are here, as so often in matters of justice, confronted with the problem of the second best. If some people are not doing their bit, does that mean that others do not have to step in? If they do not, the vital needs of the poor in poor countries will continue to go unmet. If they act, vital needs will be met and the cost will be spread over hundreds of millions of people. It seems an inescapable conclusion that justice will be advanced by making the transfer. This is especially clear in the (normal) case in which even a just internal distribution would leave a need for international transfers. It would surely be unconscionable to use the lack of internal redistribution as an excuse for not acting. This is not to say that efforts should not be made to provide the government of the recipient country with strong incentives to do its bit for its poorer citizens. It would be reasonable to deny the country any development aid, for example, and this might well have some effect on the willingness of the better-off members of society to accept a measure of internal redistribution.

The obligation on rich countries to transfer resources to internally unjust poor countries might under certain conditions be challenged in another way. Imagine a country in which everyone accepts the unjust internal inequality. Can the victims of this injustice reasonably demand that their material position be improved by transfers from outside the country if they have no complaint against it themselves? This is obviously a variant of the argument from consent whose strength and scope I assessed in the previous section.

The best case would be a democracy in which a majority persistently voted for parties that did little or nothing when in government to make the distribution of income more just. The electoral success in India since independence of either the Congress Party or parties economically to its right might be advanced as a case in point, given that neither has done anything significant to tackle the maldistribution of wealth and income that the new state inherited. The argument is weak, however, even in this most favorable case. Suppose we were to accept that majority support for the status quo implied majority acceptance of the justice of status quo, a majority is far from the consensus that the argument needs. But there is no reason to make that deduction. As Gunnar Myrdal observed many years ago, India is a "soft state," marked by lack of administrative effectiveness, and in particular the cooptation of officials by the wealthy and powerful in each locality.[18] An attitude of passive resignation on the part of the poor in the face of the failure and subversion of tax and land reform legislation is therefore scarcely to be wondered at. It cannot plausibly be deduced from passivity that they accept the moral legitimacy of the status quo.

This reply, of course, brings us back to the question of the efficacy of international transfers. If the administration of a state is so liable to derailment by powerful interests that its internal efforts at reform are hijacked, what are the prospects of external funds going to the poor rather than being misappropriated? I can only repeat in conclusion that there is no case from cosmopolitan justice for making transfers unless they do get to the people for whom they are intended. But in a second-best world, that does not provide any reason for not making transfers in the remaining cases. The outcome is more just if that is done than it would otherwise be. Needless to say, it is a question of immense practical importance how great a limitation on the scope of international redistribution this proviso imposes. But the answer to that question does not affect the validity of the idea that transfers should be made where they are called for by the principles of justice and will be efficacious in making the situation more just.

NOTES

1. Charles R. Beitz, "Cosmopolitan Liberalism and the States System," in Chris Brown, ed., *Political Restructuring in Europe: Ethical Perspectives* (London: Routledge, 1994), 123–36, quotation at 124.

2. Beitz, "Cosmopolitan Liberalism," 124–25. Thomas Pogge, in the same volume, claims that all cosmopolitan positions are marked by three features: individual human beings are what ultimately matter; they matter equally; and nobody is exempted by distance or lack of a shared community from potential demands arising out of the counting of everybody equally. Thomas W. Pogge, "Cosmopolitanism and Sovereignty," in *Political Restructuring in Europe*, 89–112 at 89. There is no conflict between this and the Beitz formulation in the text, on the definitions of impartiality and equal concern that I give here.

3. Beitz, "Cosmopolitan Liberalism," 124.

4. Beitz, "Cosmopolitan Liberalism," 125.

5. Beitz, "Cosmopolitan Liberalism," 126.

6. John Charvet, Chapter 7 above.

7. Thomas E. Hill, Jr., "The Importance of Autonomy," in Eva Kittay and Diane Meyers, eds., *Women and Moral Theory* (Totowa, NJ: Rowman and Allanheld, 1987), 132.

8. T. M. Scanlon, "Contractualism and Utilitarianism," in Amartya Sen and Bernard Williams, eds., *Utilitarianism and Beyond* (Cambridge: Cambridge University Press, 1982), 103–28, quotation at 116, n. 2. For an elaborated exposition of this idea, see my *Justice as Impartiality*, Vol. 2 of *A Treatise on Social Justice* (Oxford: Oxford University Press, 1995), esp. 67–72.

9. John Rawls, *A Theory of Justice* (Cambridge, MA: Harvard University Press, 1971).

10. This conclusion is arrived at in an article whose general line I endorse: Arthur Ripstein, "Equality, Luck, and Responsibility," *Philosophy & Public Affairs* 23 (1994): 3–23.

11. Richard Arneson, "Property Rights in Persons," *Social Philosophy and Policy* 9 (1992): 201–30, at 209.

12. See T. M. Scanlon, "Preference and Urgency," *Journal of Philosophy* 72 (1975): 655–69.

13. Eduardo S. Bustelo, "Social Policies in Times of Cholera," paper presented to the IPSA World Congress, Buenos Aires, August 1991, 25, table 3.

14. See Stein Hansen, "Entropy Implications for Global Development," Centre for the Study of Global Governance, London School of Economics, 1993.

15. I. G. Patel, "Global Economic Governance: Some Thoughts on Our Current Discontents," Centre for the Study of Global Governance, London School of Economics, 1994.

16. For an argument to this purpose, I must refer readers to my *Justice as Impartiality*, especially ch. 4.

17. For a representative example, see Bhikhu Parekh, "The Cultural Particularity of Liberal Democracy," in David Held, ed., *Prospects for Democracy*, published as a special issue of *Political Studies* 40 (1992).

18. Gunnar Myrdal, "The 'Soft State' in Underdeveloped Countries," in P. Streeten, ed., *Unfashionable Economics: Essays in Honour of Lord Balogh* (London: Weidenfeld and Nicolson, 1970), 227–43; cited and discussed (and its contemporary relevance affirmed) in Adrian Leftwich, "States of Underdevelopment," *Journal of Theoretical Politics* 6 (1994): 55–73.

CHAPTER 10

The Limits of Cosmopolitan Justice

DAVID MILLER

ANYONE WHO takes in hand a table of cross-national socioeconomic indicators such as those issued periodically by bodies like the World Bank is likely to feel at once that the present constitution of international society is radically unjust.[1] The vast disparities in per capita GNP, life expectancy, infant mortality rates, education levels, and so forth between different countries, coupled with the prosaic observation that the rich countries now have the technical capacity to transfer large quantities of resources to the poorer countries, seem to point inexorably to the conclusion that the making of such transfers is morally obligatory. How can we tolerate such relative deprivation when correcting it appears simply to require the political determination to do so on the part of the affluent nations? This moral response has been articulated with both force and subtlety in Brian Barry's paper, whose purpose is to show that moral cosmopolitanism entails an international scheme of redistribution whereby individuals in rich countries would be taxed, individually or collectively, to provide extra income for the world's poor.

It is difficult to dissent from this picture of international society and its ethical condition without giving the impression that one is morally indifferent to the fate of those millions of people in today's world whose lives are marked by suffering, starvation and disease. It is difficult also to avoid the impression that one's dissent is motivated by a selfish concern to maintain the high standard of living to which most of us in the rich nations have become accustomed. The moral cards are thus loaded very heavily in favor of a picture like Barry's. To say this is not to make an argument against that picture. It may be that our first response, when presented with comparative tables of social indicators—"these disparities are unfair and intolerable"—is the right one. Certainly our final response, after we have thought more carefully about the issues involved, ought to find room for it. Panglossian complacency about international society is not sustainable. But has Barry drawn the correct conclusions from a cosmopolitan stance in international affairs? More fundamentally, what does moral cosmopolitanism mean in the first place?

MORAL COSMOPOLITANISM: STRONG AND WEAK

Like Barry, I think that moral cosmopolitanism has been well defined by Charles Beitz.[2] But I do not think that the part of Beitz's account that Barry has fastened upon—which identifies cosmopolitanism with the adoption of an impartial viewpoint, or "impartial consideration of the claims of each person who would be affected by our choices"—is the most illuminating aspect. Beitz gets to the heart of the matter when he says of moral cosmopolitanism that "its crux is the idea that each person is equally a subject of moral concern, or alternatively, that in the justification of choices one must take the prospects of everyone affected equally into account."[3] In other words, when we have to decide how to act, or which institutions to establish, we should weigh the claims of each affected person equally, no matter where they live, which society they belong to, or how they are connected to us. This may sound as though it is equivalent to being impartial, but I should argue that impartiality has to do with the even-handed application of rules—rules which may themselves require us to treat different categories of people differently.[4] It is therefore possible to act impartially without giving equal weight to the claims of everyone affected by your actions in cases where the rule you are following requires you to discriminate. And the rule itself may be impartial when there are good moral reasons for discriminating in this way. So impartiality per se cannot be used as a benchmark to distinguish cosmopolitan moral outlooks from their rivals.

Weighing the claims of each affected person equally, by contrast, *is* a distinctive feature of cosmopolitanism. As Beitz points out, this implies in particular that boundaries between states and other communities have no deep moral significance. In choosing between courses of action and between institutions, I cannot give greater weight to the claims and concerns of my compatriots, say, than to outsiders. Barry, in his gloss on this, remarks that

> we can in a variety of ways acquire obligations that we owe to some people and not to others. There is no reason for doubting that the members of a politically constituted society can acquire obligations to one another that they do not owe to others.[5]

All that is required is that the special obligations should be justifiable on universal grounds, that is, by appeal to principles that do not themselves have restricted scope. In this way, it seems, moral cosmopolitanism can accommodate the particular loyalties and obligations we feel to our fellow-countrymen and others with whom we have special ties.

I am far from convinced, however, that this accommodation can be achieved so easily. Consider a simple case by way of analogy. Suppose I am made responsible for the hundred students who are attending a summer school, on the basis that I treat them equally and show them equal concern— so that for instance if some of the students run into difficulties, the amount of time and effort I will devote to each will depend only on how serious their problem is, and I will completely disregard factors such as their religion or nationality. Can I consistently with this acquire special obligations to some but not others? In one sense I clearly can: for instance, I can promise one group of students to take them on an extra outing, or I can enter into some task-sharing arrangement with another group. The question, however, is whether acquiring additional obligations in this way is permissible given my brief, and it seems that it is not. If I take on obligations to some which (because of time constraints, say) I cannot take on to all, I am no longer treating the whole group equally.

Suppose we change the example a bit, and imagine that the summer school now has five responsible supervisors. Then it seems perfectly consistent with equal treatment overall to divide the hundred students into five groups of twenty, and make each supervisor responsible for one group. Here special obligations to a particular group appear compatible with "cosmopolitanism" toward the school as a whole. But note two important qualifications to this argument. We must assume that each of the five supervisors is equally able to deal with the problems of those put in his or her charge, and we must also assume that the problems that arise will be randomly distributed among the groups—for instance, that among the groups there isn't one that includes a concentration of students with language difficulties. These qualifications are quite stringent, and show just how difficult it is to justify special obligations from a cosmopolitan standpoint. In particular, the idea that obligations similar to those normally acknowledged to compatriots can be vindicated from a cosmopolitan perspective ignores the vast differences both in capacities and in needs between different national communities.

Moral cosmopolitanism seems then to be a demanding doctrine, insofar as it requires equal consideration not merely of a restricted group but of human beings at large when ethical decisions are being made. But at this point we must begin to draw some distinctions. How demanding the doctrine is must depend on the content of the moral principles that we adopt, not merely their scope. We could, for instance, as Barry points out, adopt utilitarianism as our cosmopolitan morality, in which case we are committed to considering what effect each action we might take, or each institutional change we might make, would have on the welfare of every single human being. At the other extreme, we might adopt a libertarian morality where all that is required of us in our dealings with others is not to infringe their rights to life, liberty, and property. Adopting a cosmopolitan perspective does not in itself settle this question of content: to that extent, the idea of their being *a* cosmopolitan perspective on international society may be misleading. I shall discuss Barry's own principles shortly. But first I want to conclude this section be drawing a distinction between strong and weak versions of cosmopolitanism.

According to the strong version, the cosmopolitan perspective just *is* the moral point of view. All moral principles must be justified by showing that they give equal weight to the claims of everyone, which means that they must either be directly universal in their scope, or if they apply only to a select group of people they must be secondary principles whose ultimate foundation is universal. The weak version, by contrast, holds only that morality is cosmopolitan in part: there are some valid principles of equal consideration with a universal scope, even though there may also be independent, nonderivative principles with a more restricted scope. According to weak cosmopolitanism, then, we may owe certain kinds of treatment to all other human beings regardless of any relationship in which we stand to them, while there are other kinds of treatment that we owe only to those to whom we are related in certain ways, with neither sort of obligation being derivative of the other.

Weak cosmopolitanism seems to me quite plausible, and strong cosmopolitanism quite implausible. Weak cosmopolitanism draws its strength from considerations such as the following: suppose I find myself by chance in the company of a person with whom I have no connections and nothing in common beyond our shared humanity, but who is in some distress that I can relieve. We may think I have an obligation to do so, which can only stem from our common humanity; in other words this is a kind of concern that I owe equally to everybody. On the other hand, to suppose that all our obligations are ultimately of this kind is to deny that our particular identities as members of communities, groups, and associations of various kinds have intrinsic ethical relevance, and this is what makes strong cosmopolitanism hard to accept.

It is not clear to me whether Barry subscribes to a weak or a strong version of cosmopolitanism. His opening remarks suggest a strong version, but it may be significant that in his critique of present-day global injustice he appeals to a principle that might well feature in a weak version of cosmopolitanism—the principle that protecting everyone's vital interests should take priority over the nonvital interests of anyone in particular. Since protecting vital interests does not exhaust our moral concern for others, we may want to combine a cosmopolitan commitment to the priority of vital interests with more localized principles to govern the distribution of nonessential resources and benefits. In the following section I shall suggest that some of the other principles of justice Barry cites are best understood as having such a restricted scope.

Principles of Justice

Barry presents four principles of justice which he claims can be vindicated by applying a criterion due originally to Scanlon, which I shall call the "reasonable rejection" test.[6] According to this, a moral principle is valid if it could not reasonably be rejected by somebody motivated by the desire to find principles which others similarly motivated could not reasonably reject. This is not the place to explore Scanlon's test in detail, but I wish to draw attention to one particular feature of Barry's use of it. This is the special weight he assigns to the views of those who would fare worst if the principle of justice under consideration were to be applied.

There are two quite different kinds of reasons one might have for rejecting a proposed principle, and correspondingly two different ways of interpreting Scanlon's test. The first sort of reason is principled: one holds another principle that conflicts with the principle under discussion. If for instance we are considering a principle of liberty that includes a woman's right to choose whether or nor to abort a foetus she is carrying, then someone who on theological grounds holds that all life is sacred may have grounds for rejecting that principle. This is so regardless of how he or she would fare personally if the principle were applied. A different sort of reason is that one would lose out materially or in some related way if the principle were to be applied. On the first interpretation, the test rules out principles to which some people can reasonably take exception on moral grounds; on the second interpretation it rules out principles that would leave some people badly off, provided that they can point out alternatives whose consequences would not be equally bad or worse for others.[7]

Scanlon's test looks quite different under the two interpretations. In the first case we envisage a discussion in which conflicting moral claims are put forward, the idea being that it may be unreasonable for some people to persist in advancing their claims when they see that others can reasonably reject what they are proposing.[8] In the second case we envisage something closer to a negotiation in which people are looking for the principles under which they would fare best, but are willing to listen to the objections of the prospective losers. Here a different sense of reasonableness is involved, one in which, for instance, you are being unreasonable if you demand that someone else should accept a worse situation than anyone need endure under some feasible alternative arrangement.

In appropriating Scanlon's test for his own ends, Barry seems to me to shift between the two interpretations. In general, he treats the test as a means of filtering our moral reasons that someone committed to reaching agreement on reasonable terms could not continue to insist on. But in order to give the resulting principles the egalitarian content that he wants them to have, he has to employ the second interpretation. To see this, consider the first principle: "all inequalities of rights, opportunities, and resources have to be justifiable in ways that cannot reasonably be rejected *by those who get least*."[9] Why does Barry single out those who gain least from an inequality when applying the reasonable rejection test? On the first interpretation those who lose materially from the application of a principle have no special standing; the injunction to search for terms of agreement applies in the same way to everyone, regardless of their material situation. To tip the scales so that gaining the consent of the losers becomes critical we have to shift to the second interpretation, which makes the reasonableness of someone's rejection of a proposed arrangement depend on how they would fare under it. But Barry is unwilling to travel all the way down that road, for it seems to lead directly to the Rawlsian difference principle, which holds that inequalities of rights, opportunities, and resources are justifiable only when they serve to make the worst-off group as well off as possible—to set the minimum level of benefits as high as it can be set. Barry rejects the difference principle on the grounds that it conflicts with his second principle of personal responsibility. This holds that an inequality in people's circumstances may be justifiable if it arises from a voluntary choice on their part, which implies that raising the position of the worst-off may not be required if their present situation reflects the choices they have made (for instance, not to take paid employment in circumstances where they have the capacity to do so). But the principle of personal responsibility could only pass Scanlon's test on the first, moral interpretation of that test. Although there is no certain guarantee that it would universally be agreed upon, it is at least plausible to suggest that it would emerge when people examined the moral convictions that they were prepared to defend in public; whereas it would certainly not emerge from a negotiation between material gainers and losers.

So, to sum up, Barry's first principle, which sets out a presumption of equality, draws on one version of the reasonable rejection test, while his second principle, which vindicates inequalities arising from voluntary choice, draws on a different version. Why does this matter? It matters because Barry's ambivalence makes the argument for a global form of egalitarianism seem far easier to make than it actually is. The logic runs as follows. We begin with moral cosmopolitanism as defined above. Then we say that principles of justice, which occupy the primary position in our moral outlook, are those that would emerge from a Scanlonian choosing situation. Then by manipulating the Scanlonian test, we derive a principle of equality that requires material inequalities to be justifiable to those who gain least. Admittedly this is qualified by the principle of responsibility. But the upshot is that the present pattern of global inequality is unjust and unacceptable *unless* it can be shown to work to the advantage of those who have fewest resources, or the better off can justify it by appeal to the principle of voluntary choice—defenses which, on the face of it, seem fairly implausible.

Suppose instead we were to stick consistently to the first interpretation of the reasonable rejection test: we would then have to work much harder to justify any substantive form of global egalitarianism. Let me at this point introduce a distinction between comparative and noncomparative principles of justice.[10] Comparative principles are those that assess the justice of a mode of treatment or of a resulting distribution by comparing how each member of the relevant group fares when compared with everyone else. If I say, "It's unfair that teachers are paid less than bank clerks," I am invoking a comparative principle of justice, for instance one specifying that the wages different people receive should be proportional to how difficult and demanding their jobs are. (The comparison may not always be explicit: I may say, simply, "It's unfair that teachers are paid so little"—here I am tacitly drawing a comparison between teachers' pay and the pay received by other occupational groups who, by implication, are no more deserving than the teachers.) Noncomparative principles, by contrast, assert that certain forms of treatment are inherently just or unjust regardless of what is happening to others. We are perhaps most likely to invoke noncomparative principles of justice when discussing punishments or other forms of harm. When I say "It is unjust for people to be executed for theft," my meaning is that to execute people on this basis (or perhaps on any basis) is intrinsically wrong, regardless of how other people are being treated. In other words, my judgment is not that executing people for theft is out of line with the punishments currently being handed out for other crimes, but that there is some intrinsic lack of fit between this punishment and this crime, or perhaps some intrinsic wrongness in deliberately executing people in any circumstances.

Applying this distinction between comparative and noncomparative principles of justice, we can see, for instance, that principles of equality are always comparative principles, whereas principles of human rights are noncomparative. A principle of equality requires that each member of the relevant group should enjoy equal benefits of some kind, so what each member can justly claim will depend on what the other members are going to get. Principles of human rights, by contrast, identify forms of treatment that everyone is owed, regardless of what is happening to others. If I say that each person has a right to a fair trial, or not to be tortured, I mean that he or she is owed this whether or not other people are currently enjoying these rights: the fact that others in the society in question are being tortured or denied fair trials does not weaken or alter the force of my claim.

The question we must ask is whether the principles of justice that apply globally are comparative or noncomparative principles. If we look at the four principles sketched by Barry, we find that principles of both kinds are represented. The first principle, requiring equality in distribution unless inequality can be justified to those who get least, is plainly comparative. The second principle, likewise, which says that it is acceptable for people to fare differently if this results from voluntary choice, whereas conversely people who fare badly through no fault of their own should be compensated, requires us to look comparatively at how different people are faring and to see whether the differences arise from voluntary choice or from unpreventable misfortune The third principle, requiring the protection of vital interests, is by contrast noncomparative. It tells us that we have a duty of justice to secure for everyone conditions such as security from physical harm, adequate nutrition, and so forth, and that this duty should take priority over other possible ways of using our resources.[11] The fourth principle is once again comparative insofar as it tells us to support those Pareto-improvements which maximize the gain of those who gain least from departing from an initially just distribution.

Barry's principles were designed to lay out an interpretation of social justice; they were not intended to apply specifically to international justice. He evidently thinks that no special issues are raised when one shifts from a domestic to an international setting. The scope of the principles is enlarged, but the principles themselves remain the same. This is in sharp contrast to John Rawls who, also using the idea of a hypothetical choosing situation to generate principles of distributive justice, explicitly confines them within the boundaries of "a self-contained national community."[12] After working out the principles of domestic justice, Rawls says, we can proceed to reconstruct the choosing situation with the parties in it now acting as representatives of different societies in order to work out "the law of peoples." Inspection of the content of Rawls's proposed "law of peoples" quickly reveals that its principles are not principles of distributive justice, and have little overlap with the two principles that Rawls has defended as principles of domestic justice.[13]

Without endorsing the details of Rawls's theory, I think he is right to suggest that the principles of social justice that apply within societies cannot be extended in any straightforward way to the international level. Specifically, I want to argue that *comparative* principles of justice operate only within national boundaries, while noncomparative principles may also operate across them.[14] This argument assumes that in order for comparative judgments of justice to have force, they must apply to persons who are connected together in some way, for instance by belonging to the same community or association. Once a common membership is established, it makes sense to ask whether individual members are enjoying their fair share of advantages (or carrying their fair share of burdens) in comparison to other members. In the absence of such a common membership, on the other hand, only noncomparative questions of justice arise. In an encounter with a stranger from another community, there are certain things that I may not do—I may not injure him or steal his property—and certain things that I must do—if he is ill or in pain I must do what I can to help him—but it makes no sense for either of us to try to apply comparative principles—for instance to insist on equality in some respect.[15] More generally, whatever obligations of international justice there are—obligations between people belonging to different national communities—cannot be expressed in terms of comparative principles. So it seems that Barry is wrong to suppose that the four principles he jointly proposes are germane to a discussion of justice in the constitution of international society, whatever merits they may have as principles of domestic justice.

I have claimed in this section of the paper that Barry exploits an ambiguity in Scanlon's reasonable rejection test to derive principles of international justice with an unwarranted egalitarian component. If, instead, one were to ask what people representing different national societies might agree to when asked simply to appeal to reasons that others could not reasonably reject, noncomparative principles of justice would be likely to emerge, given that the participants could not reasonably consider themselves as forming a single community or association. Nothing I have said is meant to cast doubt on the very idea of international justice. The issue is the form that principles of international justice should take. The claim made in this section is that Barry's principles do not have the right form.

Protecting Vital Interests

Although the argument of the preceding section, if valid, discredits Barry's general theory of cosmopolitan justice, it does less immediate damage to the practical recommendations he makes in the later sections of the paper. For these recommendations are very largely derived by applying principle three, the priority of vital interests, which as I suggested earlier is a noncomparative principle of justice. Barry's presentation of his case obscures this at times by couching the issue in terms of rich and poor countries and individuals, as though justice here was concerned with the relative shares of income and resources going to people in different places. But the gravamen of his charge against existing international society is that it contains many people who fall seriously below the resource threshold at which their vital interests would be secured, while on the other hand the industrialized West is profligate with its resources. It is a claim about absolute deprivation against a background of affluence, not a claim about relative deprivation.

This distinction between relative and absolute deprivation should affect our reading of the tables of development indicators. Picking examples at random, we find that Germany has a per capita GNP of $25,000, while Kenya has a per capita GNP of only $250. How, we are inclined to ask, can this hundred-fold inequality in average living standards possibly be just?[16] But if our concern is with absolute deprivation, the question we should be asking is whether the vital interests of Kenyans are currently being protected, and if not what responsibilities Germans and others bear toward them.

Here we must look beyond a snapshot picture of income distribution within and between countries to get at the causes of the distribution, or, more specifically, the reasons why some countries are unable to protect their citizens' vital interests. We need in particular to consider two issues that are largely ignored in Barry's analysis, namely population growth and the effects of different economic and political systems on rates of economic growth.

Barry's neglect of the population issue is surprising given that environmental questions figure heavily in the later stages of his argument. He maintains that global economic sustainability requires that rich countries should cut back on existing levels of production, and he therefore sets aside the claim that "a rising tide lifts all boats," that is, that living standards in the poorer countries will rise spontaneously as global levels of production increase, without the need for redistributive policies. If the cake has to shrink in size rather than increase, he claims, redistribution becomes imperative. But we cannot decide what level of production is actually sustainable without considering the size of the population; obviously, the fewer people there are, the less resources are needed to maintain any given standard of living. So if, following Barry, we think that we have a duty to our successors not to leave them worse-endowed with environmental and other resources than we are, the question of population size becomes crucial. To put the matter starkly, it would not matter if the next generation had only half as many resources as the present generation has available to it so long as there were only half as many of them as there are of us. We do not have a duty to generate collectively any particular number of offspring; our duty is only to ensure that those we generate have adequate resources to live rich and fulfilling lives. And indeed, if it were possible to halve the size of the next generation without imposing morally unacceptable costs on the present generation, then on environmental grounds it would surely be desirable to do so.

This bears on the question of redistribution in the following way. Barry applies the principle of vital interests statically: he asks what institutional arrangements would most effectively provide poor individuals with a minimum income adequate to cover their basic needs. He does not consider whether the arrangements he favors may not have bad incentive effects, such that their dynamic effect is to increase the number of people whose primary incomes fall below the minimum. As a quick glance at the relevant tables will readily confirm, poor countries generally have rates of population growth several times higher than rich countries. Do the citizens of rich countries have obligations of justice to aid not only those existing people in poor countries who fail the vital-needs test, but as many others as may be brought into existence through procreation?

The extreme position on this issue is the neo-Malthusian claim that unless population levels can be kept within the limits set by the earth's productive capacity by deliberately chosen human policy, natural forces such as starvation will do the job instead. Keeping an expanding population in poor countries alive by means of food aid will in the long term simply reduce the rich countries to the same level of poverty.[17] Thus rich countries are justified, on long-term humanitarian grounds, in cutting aid to countries with rising populations and also in preventing immigration from those countries. A more moderate view recognizes the need to limit population expansion, but not the existence of a rigid ceiling, and so favors policies that link aid to measures to control numbers. Thus Onora O'Neill, who cannot possibly be accused of hard-hearted Malthusianism, argues in favor of institutional and cultural changes that would control population growth by noncoercive means, while recognizing that in the last resort there may be no alternative to coercion:

> If [noncoercive] policies fail, and just productive and redistributive measures too cannot meet needs, direct coercion of procreative decisions would not be unjust. Such emergencies would arise only when recklessly fertile people persist in having children whose needs could not be met, by their parents or by others, either by increasing or by reallocating resources. Such procreators act on a maxim that cannot be widely shared without exacerbating needs and so increasing injustice. Preventing such reckless procreation would coerce less than would failing to prevent it.[18]

This seems to me a sane and balanced view to take on the issue of rising population and basic needs. In Barry's chapter, by contrast, the population issue is completely ignored. Barry's proposal is for an international tax regime in which "rich people wherever they lived would be taxed for the benefit of poor people wherever they lived." The benefits would primarily be allocated "either in the form of a universal unconditional basic income or an income dependent on status (youth, age, sickness and disability, unemployment)."[19]

The existing incentives leading people in poor countries to have large families are well known; this scheme adds to them by endowing each additional child with an income provided through the tax system (even if the income was made status-dependent, presumably children would simply receive it at a lower rate than adults). There are no disincentives in the scheme: nothing that would deter would-be parents from procreating at a rate that causes rapid population increases of the sort that we are currently witnessing.

It is sometimes argued in reply to these concerns that as living standards approach those currently enjoyed in the developed world, populations will stabilize of their own accord. Let us suppose that the premise behind this argument is true: that increased living standards are accompanied by cultural changes that make small families the social norm. It does not follow that income redistribution will produce this happy outcome, because rapid population growth may mean that we never get to the point where the cultural change begins to cut in. If we could instantly bring it about that people in the poorest countries enjoyed incomes at, say, the bottom end of the Western European scale, then perhaps over a couple of generations we might see families shrinking to two or three children per unit. But this proposal is wildly implausible, and certainly not the scenario that Barry has in mind when he speaks of protecting vital interests and meeting basic needs. (Figures here must be very crude, but on the basis of his judgments about particular countries, I guess that he would regard a per capita annual income of some $1,000—$2,000 as an acceptable minimum, whereas the Western European scale *begins* at around $10,000).

Let me turn now to the second respect in which Barry's proposals for cosmopolitan justice seem to be indefensibly static. A striking feature of the global economy over the last couple of decades has been the marked difference in rates of economic growth between countries whose starting point has been similarly low. Countries such as Indonesia and Thailand have achieved annual growth rates of 6 percent or more, while in many African and some South American states, growth rates have either been close to zero or negative. Plainly any society whose economy grows consistently at around 6 percent is going to cross Barry's threshold in a relatively short time (how quickly will also depend on the distribution of income within the society: here there is a rough correlation between level of economic development and degree of income equality within the society, but again big variations between countries).

This suggests that Barry is wrong when he identifies, as the key issue in a scheme of cosmopolitan justice, how to create an international tax system that ensures that the rich contribute their proper share and the poor get the income that they need. Seeing the question as one of income redistribution, on the model of a domestic tax system, gives us the wrong picture. Instead, we should be asking what can be done to get as many countries as possible on the track followed by Indonesia and Thailand. This is not the place for an extensive discourse on the conditions for economic growth (nor am I competent to supply one), but three main conditions can be identified without provoking much controversy: political stability (in particular the absence of violent intergroup conflicts), an appropriate economic framework (in particular a set of background institutions that enables a market economy to develop), and a culture of economic achievement (a Protestant ethic or its functional equivalent). Now clearly none of these features can be instantly implanted in a society that lacks them; but it may be possible by external policies to foster, over time, the first two conditions at least—for instance, by making development aid conditional on governments' following sound economic policies, by penalizing governments that discriminate against ethnic minorities, and so forth.

There is, in fact, a great deal that could be done, by both governments and individuals in the developed world, to create incentives for people in the poor countries that will lead, in due course, to economic growth. Aid can take the form of investment in technology of a scale that is appropriate to the people who are going to use it; stable trading links can be established so that the producers of a particular commodity or artefact know that there is a market for it in the developed world, and at a price that is sufficiently steady to make investment in new technology worthwhile. Thinking about development aid seems to me to have moved in this general direction in recent years, and away from the idea that the solution to world poverty is to send food and other consumption goods directly to the poor (leaving aside here the relatively rare case of famines whose immediate causes are natural disasters like drought or flooding).[20] If we adopted Barry's proposals we would be taking a step backwards in our approach to this vital issue.

CULTURAL DIVERSITY AND PRINCIPLES OF JUSTICE

My argument in the previous section accepted as a premise that people in rich countries had an obligation to ensure that the vital interests of people in poor countries were protected; but I challenged Barry's thesis that the right way to discharge this obligation was through an international tax regime, and argued instead for a more dynamic approach that sought to create incentives for population stability and economic development in the poor countries. I have not yet, however, asked how the holding of conflicting principles of justice in different countries might affect the obligation itself—particularly in the case where people in society S hold and act on principles of justice which entail that certain of their vital interests, as defined by us, are not protected. Barry addresses this question when he asks, in the section headed "The Limits of Diversity," about societies that adopt principles of justice which contrast sharply with our own. In Barry's view, even if the members of society S genuinely accept and live by principles that conflict with those that he favors, this does not show that S is just. Accordingly, though Barry does not take this point very far, outsiders ought in principle to be prepared to intervene in S to make it conform to *correct* principles of justice, such as the four that Barry lists.

The argument here proceeds through several steps. Barry claims first that moral cosmopolitanism, in its Scanlonian formulation, "will underwrite the familiar list of basic human rights."[21] There is no reason to dissent from this claim; indeed I would argue that what is valid in the cosmopolitan perspective is best captured precisely by such a list of rights. That is to say, if we reflect on what we owe other human beings considered merely as such, apart from all the particular relationships in which we stand to them, the best answer is going to be "respect for their basic human rights," including here rights to subsistence as well as rights to bodily integrity, freedom of movement, etc. But there is a very big jump indeed from this premise to Barry's next claim, which is that "the principles of justice are valid for all societies," assuming that he means by "principles of justice" not merely the list of basic rights, but all those procedural principles and principles of distribution that we apply from day to day in allocating resources, opportunities, honors, jobs and so forth. For here any comparative study will reveal a great deal of variation, both historically and between contemporary societies, in how justice is understood, and it is going to be difficult to defend the claim that there is a single set of principles, derived in Scanlonian fashion, that has cross-cultural validity.[22]

Barry seeks to soften the stark assertion cited in the last paragraph by saying that "there is a very wide range of possible institutional embodiments of the principles of justice" and also that "it is quite consistent with cosmopolitan principles of justice that people may find their greatest fulfillment within a dense network of family and community obligations."[23] I do not think, however, that he can make these concessions so easily. Take a principle like the following: "medical care should be distributed on the basis of need." It is true that there are different institutional ways of implementing this principle: there may be a national health service funded by the state, or people may voluntarily form Friendly Societies for the purpose of getting medical care which all have as their operative principle. But institutional variation must have its limits if the principle has any substance; for instance, it clearly rules out any system in which medical care is bought and sold through a market in medical services. Yet many societies have treated medical care in this way.

Barry's gesture of reconciliation toward communitarians is also problematic. For to find one's fulfillment in a dense network of family and community obligations, it is necessary precisely to regard these as *obligations*, that is as special duties and responsibilities to some—members of one's own family or community—and not to others. However, as I argued earlier, it is not clear how, from a strong cosmopolitan perspective, one may be justified in taking on such special obligations, in violation of the requirement to show equal moral concern for everyone, regardless of who they are or where they live. One possible tack here would be to say that the cosmopolitan perspective supplies us with our principles of justice, whereas the additional obligations that we may legitimately acquire to particular groups are not of this kind. But this is surely not plausible. We not only regard the demands that family and community make on us as demands of justice, but we feel the intense conflicts that may arise between our different commitments—between, say our loyalties to family and to country—precisely as conflicts over what justice requires us to do.

After making these concessions, Barry goes back on to the offensive and challenges the claim that there can be a genuine social consensus on local principles of justice that conflict with the egalitarian principles he favors. He argues that apparent consent of this sort will be invalidated "if the person giving it is too ill-educated or restricted in access to relevant information about alternative forms of organization to be able to make an informed judgment."[24] Although I agree that we need to distinguish genuine acceptance of principles of justice that differ from ours from forced or manipulated acceptance, Barry's condition is going to be hard to apply in a number of real cases. Consider, for instance, an Amazonian Indian belonging to a tribe that has so far had little contact with the outside world, but regulates itself by principles that all the members appear to accept. How could such a person be put in a position where he could make an informed choice between different forms of social organization, saying in effect, "Yes, I've had a good look at Western liberal societies, compared them with some religious oligarchies and single-party states, but I still think that the tribal ways are best"? Anyone who has access to the conceptual categories and forms of knowledge needed to make such a judgment is necessarily going to reject the tribal principles. Now we might hold that having such capacities is intrinsically desirable, believing with John Stuart Mill that "it is the privilege and proper condition of a human being, arrived at the maturity of his faculties, to use and interpret experience in his own way. It is for him to find out what part of recorded experience is properly applicable to his own circumstances and character."[25] But this would involve a substantive commitment to an ideal of reflective individuality; it cannot be derived simply from the claim that people must genuinely endorse the principles of justice that they live by.

A similar point can be made against Barry's argument that an inegalitarian social system built on religious foundations such as the Hindu Varna system cannot be just even if there is genuinely free acceptance of its principles. His reason for saying this is that the religious beliefs in question could reasonably be rejected even if, as it happens, nobody in the society does reject them. But here we cannot avoid asking whether there are beliefs that, as a general matter, could *not* reasonably be rejected. Perhaps there are some: the truths of mathematics, for example, and some basic empirical propositions such as that water boils at 100° C. We might be able to add to this list some very basic moral propositions, for instance that it is wrong to disable someone without good cause. But if we consider most of the basic tenets of a liberal egalitarian ethical system such as Barry's—for instance the claim that men and women are entitled to equal treatment in a variety of fields—I cannot see why these could not reasonably be rejected by someone who held, say, a religious worldview which saw unequal treatment as flowing naturally from the structure of a hierarchically ordered universe. What it is reasonable for someone to reject depends on what other beliefs they hold, and how deeply they hold them. Here I think Barry was right when in an earlier article he argued that liberal political principles cannot be defended without first imbibing a large dose of religious skepticism.[26] But it is not a requirement of reasonableness as such that one should be a religious skeptic. Once again a substantive, and contestable, commitment has been introduced into what appears to be a procedural requirement, namely that valid principles of justice must pass a reasonable rejection test.

What follows once we recognize that it may be reasonable for others, depending on their worldviews, to reject liberal egalitarian principles of justice? Not that our own allegiance to these principles should be in any way be weakened—these after all are *our* principles, the ones that most faithfully reflect our own deepest worldview and the social practices that embody it. But it may legitimately affect the way we understand our obligations to members of societies whose principles are different from ours. So long as these societies respect their members' basic human rights, our main obligation is to promote the conditions under which they can live up to their own principles of social justice—an obligation we discharge in most cases by not interfering with and not exploiting these societies, but which may in some cases require positive aid to rebuild a society that has been torn apart by ethnic conflict or outside intervention by third parties. It should not concern us that some members of these societies lack opportunities that they would have under a liberal egalitarian regime. If someone sincerely holds principles that restrict their opportunities, no injustice is done to them: we do not consider Eric Liddell a victim of injustice because his religious conscience forbade him to compete in the 100 meters heats at the 1924 Olympics, held on a Sunday.[27] In a similar way, if a social group or an entire political community embraces a culture or supports social practices whose effect is that they achieve less or have fewer options than might otherwise have been the case, they do not have a claim to redress against outsiders. Of course "sincerely" matters here: people who are manipulated into holding principles that then restrict their opportunities represent a different case, one in which intervention is more likely to be justified. As will be clear from the argument of this section, however, I do not share Barry's faith that the principles of justice that can be sincerely held are all variants of liberal egalitarianism.

CONCLUSION

I began this chapter by taking note of the very large inequalities between countries in capacities and resources that are such a striking feature of the contemporary world. Moral cosmopolitans, I argued, have a natural impulse to try to narrow this inequality by redistributive mechanisms of one kind or another. My case has been that this impulse is misdirected, if its aim is to bring about a form of global equality that mirrors equality of the kind that is frequently pursued *within* political communities, particularly those of a liberal or social democratic complexion. Contra Barry, there is nothing unjust about international inequalities as such. Such inequalities are a natural feature of a world in which more-or-less independent political communities pursue the aims and purposes of their members, including local conceptions of distributive justice.

What *should* concern even weak cosmopolitans, however, are societies which cannot guarantee their members' fundamental rights—societies which fail to protect basic freedoms of expression and association, or which cannot provide adequate food, education or medical care. The existence of such societies triggers our general obligation to support and aid other human beings regardless of political or cultural boundaries. It does not follow that the correct response is to set up an international tax regime of the kind advocated in Barry's paper. Besides being driven by a misplaced concern for global equality, this is insensitive to the issue of the causes of deprivation, and the connected issue of where responsibility lies for combating it. We have to adopt a more dynamic approach, I have argued, in particular by adopting policies that discourage population expansion and foster the conditions for endogenous economic growth within poor countries. What we should be aiming for, as (weak) cosmopolitans, is a diverse world in which independent political communities can pursue different projects and different conceptions of justice, but in which each community has the (cultural[28] and material) means to protect its members' human rights.[29]

NOTES

1. For instance, *World Development Report 1996: From Plan to Market* (New York: Oxford University Press, 1996).

2. Charles R. Beitz, "Cosmopolitan Liberalism and the States System," in Chris Brown, ed., *Political Restructuring in Europe: Ethical Perspectives* (London: Routledge, 1994).

3. Beitz, "Cosmopolitan Liberalism," 124.

4. On this point see further David Miller, *On Nationality* (Oxford: Clarendon Press, 1995), 53–55.

5. Barry, Chapter 9 above, under "The Cosmopolitan Idea."

6. The original source is T. M. Scanlon, "Contractualism and Utilitarianism," in Amartya Sen and Bernard Williams, eds., *Utilitarianism and Beyond* (Cambridge: Cambridge University Press, 1982). Scanlon has subsequently indicated that he regards his contractualist theory as providing a philosophical account of moral rightness and wrongness, rather than as offering a normative criterion that can be used to assess the validity of prospective moral principles: see T. M. Scanlon, "The Aims and Authority of Moral Theory," *Oxford Journal of Legal Studies*, 12 (1992):1–23. When I refer to "Scanlon's test" or "the reasonable rejection test," therefore, I mean

the test as understood by Barry, rather than Scanlon's own contractualist theory of morality.

7. Scanlon himself seems to me to invoke each of these contrasting interpretations at different points in his original description of the test.

8. I ought at this point to come clean and say that I have never been able to understand how the reasonable rejection test can play an independent role in ethical argument, since it relies crucially on being able to distinguish *reasonable* rejection of a proposal from *unreasonable* rejection—so that everything depends on what is to count as reasonable, which in this context inevitably brings into play substantive moral commitments. In other words there is no neutral or merely formal idea of reasonableness to which appeal can be made. I intend, however, to set these doubts aside for the time being in order to focus on Barry's use of the Scanlonian test to generate principles of international justice.

9. Barry, Chapter 9 above, under "Some Cosmopolitan Principles" (my italics).

10. Here I follow Joel Feinberg, "Noncomparative Justice," *Philosophical Review*, 83 (1974): 297–338.

11. At first glance Barry's third principle might also seem to be a comparative principle insofar as it tells us to regard as unfair a situation in which the non-vital interests of some people are promoted in preference to the vital interests of others. But I believe that the crucial unfairness here consists in *failing to protect some vital interests in circumstances where it is in our power to do so*—the significance of there being others whose non-vital interests are being promoted is that it shows that there are available resources which might instead be used to help those in need. Compare here Derek Parfit's analysis of the distinction between egalitarian and prioritarian principles in *Equality or Priority?* (Lindley Lecture, University of Kansas, 1995).

12. John Rawls, *A Theory of Justice* (Cambridge, Mass.: Harvard University Press, 1971), 457.

13. See John Rawls, "The Law of Peoples," in Stephen Shute and Susan Hurley, eds., *On Human Rights* (New York: Basic Books, 1993).

14. I do not mean that such principles operate only at the national level; they also apply within smaller groups and associations inside national communities. Nor do I wish to exclude the possibility of there being certain transnational contexts in which comparative principles may apply. The international community of scientists is sufficiently well-formed for us to say that it is unfair that Professor Smith, an American, received a Nobel prize for Chemistry while Professor Malenkov, a Russian, was passed over. I do, however, want to deny that there presently exists an overall "world community" within which comparative principles of justice apply. On nations as the privileged locus for implementing comparative principles of justice, see Miller, *On Nationality*, chs. 2–4.

15. In making this argument, I follow the lead of Charles Taylor, "The Nature and Scope of Distributive Justice," in his *Philosophy and the Human Sciences: Philosophical Papers*, vol. 2 (Cambridge: Cambridge University Press, 1985), and Michael Walzer, *Spheres of Justice* (New York: Basic Books, 1983), ch. 2.

16. The disparity in living standards is in fact likely to be smaller than the disparity in per capita GNP, but this complication need not detain us here; no one could reasonably deny that Germans are, on average, far better off than Kenyans on any relevant measure of living standards.

17. This position is defended in Garrett Hardin, *Living Within Limits* (New York: Oxford University Press, 1993).

18. Onora O'Neill, *Faces of Hunger* (London: Allen and Unwin, 1986), 158.

19. Barry, Chapter 9 above, under "Moral Cosmopolitanism and International Redistribution."

20. See, for instance, *Our Global Neighborhood: The Report of the Commission on Global Governance* (New York: Oxford University Press, 1995), ch. 4.

21. Barry, Chapter 9 above, under "The Limits of Diversity."

22. This is certainly not a claim that Scanlon himself would wish to defend, as he makes clear in "The Aims and Authority of Moral Theory."

23. Barry, Chapter 9 above, under "The Limits of Diversity."

24. Ibid.

25. J. S. Mill, *On Liberty*, in *Utilitarianism; On Liberty; Considerations on Representative Government*, ed. H. B. Acton (London: Dent, 1972), 116.

26. Brian Barry, "How Not to Defend Liberal Institutions," in his *Liberty and Justice: Essays in Political Theory* (Oxford: Clarendon Press, 1991). Barry's argument there concerns the legal prohibition of behavior which from a religious perspective would be regarded as sinful, but a parallel argument, I am suggesting, can be made about religious justifications of inequality.

27. To make the example watertight we should assume that there was no alternative to holding the races on a Sunday.

28. I refer to cultural means to take account of those few societies whose predominant culture is such that there is little prospect of human rights being protected domestically—for instance, the culture of warlordism which appears to have taken hold of Somalia around the time of the US-led intervention of 1992. It is, however, very difficult to know how to respond effectively to the plight of people immersed in cultures such as this.

29. I am very grateful to David Mapel for his helpful comments on the first draft of this chapter.

PART TWO

Theological Commentaries

Jewish Theology and International Society

DAVID NOVAK

THEOLOGY AND CONTEMPORARY POLITICAL DISCOURSE

Before one can intelligently present a theological perspective on any matter of contemporary political discourse, he or she must first indicate how any theology, which stems from the perspective of a singularly constituted faith community, can possibly contribute to discussing any normative issue defined largely by those who do not share this faith or any faith. I think the answer to this question depends on how one views the role of religious tradition or traditions (the distinction will soon become evident) in post-Enlightenment secular societies. Here there seem to be four possibilities.

One, any religious tradition could be regarded as a historically limited, hopelessly particularistic, point of view, based on the irrational acceptance of an authority. In terms of the topic of this volume, dealing as it does with "international" society, it would seem that reason and not revelation is what we should be seeking since the universalism of reason is more appropriate to what pertains *between* particular nations. We can assume a universal operation of reason, whereas such an assumption about any revelation cannot be made. That would mean that discussion here of teachings from any of these traditions is at best superfluous and at worst dangerously distracting. This is the most predominant "secularist" view at work in secular societies. It is a common enough view among many intellectuals today to warrant mentioning it at the outset since it is one that any religious public intellectual, that is, any public intellectual whose religious commitments are integral to his or her intellectual opinions, must be prepared to counter.

Two, it can be maintained that the division between universal reason and particular traditions, which fundamentally becomes the division between reason and revelation, is one of degree rather than one of kind. In other words, religious traditions can be seen as cultural matrices out of which reason slowly develops. If this is the case, then these traditions can be taken as historical sources that cannot be ignored because all rational attempts, in the case at hand the rational attempt to constitute an international society, are themselves historically located and do not, therefore, spring up *de novo*. In this recognition of the cultural factor in reason itself, the religious character of traditional cultures (the very word "culture" comes from *cultus*) cannot be ignored.[1] This could be seen as a "conservative" Enlightenment position, "secular" but not strictly "secularist" like the more radical position mentioned previously. The question is, however, whether the religious themselves should be contributing to this secondary, supporting role for their own traditions. After all, adherents of living religious traditions are, by definition, living in the present not the past. Their respective traditions must be more than footnotes.

Three, one could reject the Enlightenment altogether, opting for the medievals over the moderns, and return to a position that regards *a* (one's own, of course) theology to be once again "queen of the sciences." Adherents of this view could show that the preference for reason over revelation has been that reason seemed to unify people whereas revelation divided them. That is, there are always *many* revelations without there being a universally valid transcendental criterion by which to judge critically which is true and which is false. During the seventeenth century, with its interminable "wars of religion" that seemed perpetually to threaten peace, such an aversion to all revelations seemed to be politically wise. However, our historical experience since that time has shown us that secular points of view, ideologies claiming to be rational not revealed, present just as many incommensurable political options, and that they have been every bit as divisive and bellicose as those of the religious traditions. Furthermore, as Alasdair MacIntyre more than anyone else has brilliantly shown of late, even the viewpoints of "universal" reason themselves come out of quite particularistic traditions.[2] With the historical evidence now being at least equal, so to speak, the adherent of a theology can now claim that he or she has the advantage of providing the certitude of a faith that cannot be matched by mere human knowledge.

Nevertheless, just *which* faith perspective is to be adopted as authoritative cannot be established by simply arguing that a *general* faith perspective is preferable to secularist alternatives. For authority is always the function of a *particular* authority; and just as there is no rationality in general but only rationalities, so is there no faith in general (what the French would call "la religion même") but only faiths. Adherence to any faith perspective seems necessarily to presuppose some sort of actual conversion or personal confirmation. To assume that one is argued into faith as one is argued into an intellectual opinion is to confuse faith with philosophy, which does a great injustice to both.

Finally, a theologian can present what he or she thinks is the most coherent view of international society coming from his or her religious tradition, and then see which aspects of the various secular political philosophies presented in this volume are compatible with that vision and which are not. This hopefully has the effect of showing that traditions based on revelation can and should take seriously philosophical points of view dealing with issues facing all people who live in the world. Religious traditions like those represented in this volume—Judaism, Christianity, and Islam—themselves have constituted more general horizons of concern and are thus not only concerned with their own singular communities. In other words, although not *of* the world, they are still *in* it and *for* it.[3]

This is different from the previous approach, which could be termed "triumphalist," because it does not attempt to convince anybody who is not already convinced of its superiority. It is more an attempt to interact *with* someone else than to act *upon* someone else. If the various philosophical viewpoints can do the same thing with the teachings of religious traditions—each accepting the fact that the others will not and should not be dismissed or conquered—then a volume like this can be an occasion for true dialogue, a model of mutuality that itself is appropriate in seeking some sort of international society. In other words, just as the religious can and should acknowledge the rightful presence of the secular in public discourse, so the secular should be able to do likewise as regards the religious. Without that, however, we are only left with subservience on one side and dominance on the other. Transcending this impasse is itself a necessary precondition for any international society that is not based on force exerted by any one group over all the others. For, after all, any attempt to reorder international society must counter the claim that the most powerful efforts in this direction, especially in this century, have been made by totalitarian regimes.

WHERE TO LOCATE THE JEWISH VISION OF INTERNATIONAL SOCIETY

It has been the opinion of many modern Jewish thinkers that the place to locate a Jewish vision of international society is in Jewish eschatology, particularly in the messianic doctrine of Judaism. This is a result of the Jewish entrance into a larger political world that has come about because of the emancipation of the Jews from the medieval ghetto. For although so much of the actual teaching of Judaism, past and present, seems to be specifically constituted for the Jews alone, the messianic doctrine about the future clearly involves all humankind, whose members are minimally the subjects of any international society. A number of modern Jewish thinkers have been quite proud to point out that Judaism seems to have introduced the notion of genuine futurity into the world. This Hebraic idea is seen as having a vision of the ultimate union of all humankind that is unlike any comparable idea from any other culture about humankind and its ultimate unity.[4]

The link between the Jewish past and present and the universal future, in this modern Jewish view anyway, seems to be the idea of progress. Greatly encouraged by what appear to be secular acknowledgments of this Hebraic idea, most prominently by Hegel and Marx, it is assumed that the ongoing upward development of Judaism, especially its social ethics, sets a trajectory that can be followed by all humankind in its quest for a universal order of justice and peace.[5] Although many Jews who have been involved with progressivist, let alone utopian, social and political movements have simultaneously divorced themselves from their Jewish backgrounds, regarding their old Judaism as an impediment to their universalist dreams, other Jews have assumed that these new involvements themselves are an authentic part of Judaism.

Although it is not to be denied that there are aspects of Jewish messianic doctrine that do lend themselves to this type of modernist appropriation, a very good case can be made that the preponderance of Jewish teaching of this doctrine is in truth antiprogressivist.[6] For what most of the modern Jewish progressives seem to miss altogether is that most of Jewish eschatology is decidedly apocalyptic. The progressivist constitution of the relation of the past, present, and future is fundamentally different from the way Jewish apocalypticism constitutes that relation. As such, the question of the constitution of international society coming out of these two competing visions is as fundamentally different as they themselves are.

In the progressivist view, the past contributes to the present, which in turn contributes to the future. Thus the present can judge the past as to how much it has contributed to the present that is valuable for it, and then the present determines where its activities are to be directed for their final and valuable consummation. The present determines both its background and its foreground. The future is the directed extension of the present; it is its project.

Jewish apocalypticism, conversely, can be seen as rejecting this progressivist view for two reasons. One, progressivist messianism seems to overlook the mysterious role of divine judgment, assuming that once the world has been created it is totally turned over to the authority of humans. Two, it seems to overlook the tentativeness of all human judgments, and how so much of what humans project into the future is evil and destructive precisely because of its totalizing arrogance.[7] Certainly, the events of the twentieth century alone have convinced many thoughtful persons of the pretentious dangers of progressivist messianism, even if few of them have been able to embrace the positive alternative of apocalypticism itself and the faith it presupposes.

Whereas for the progressivist faith, the present determines both the past behind it and the future before it, for apocalypticism, the future is not an extension or project of the present. Instead, the future invades the present precisely because it is the judgment on all that has transpired and is still transpiring, and it is a judgment, a final judgment, coming from a totally transcendent perspective. The faith that this messianic culmination of history stands over all of human efforts in the past and the present means that these efforts must regard themselves as partial, tentative efforts to comply with God's ultimate plan for the world he has created.

This apocalyptic messianism in turn requires a more major emphasis of the present necessity of revelation for those who are waiting for God's kingdom to finally come. For if humans cannot by their own efforts predict, much less realize, the universal realm of justice and peace for which they long, then they need direction from God in the present to teach them how to live so that their lives will be consistent with that kingdom, and how they can live with hope for it. Indeed, the very human effort to constitute a sufficient human society here and now and by progressive projection into the future is essentially at loggerheads with the notion that the present needs revealed direction here and now and a hidden horizon of future redemption in order to be worthy of the kingship of God. For this reason, then, Jewish eschatology, even in its most political aspect which is its messianism, cannot be invoked to equate any human effort at international society with its intended redemption. It can only function as a negative limit on the suggestion that the establishment of any such international society can itself be the solution to the human predicament in this world. That predicament seems to me to be that humans are still not fully at home in this world as evidenced by their essential restlessness, however much at ease they might be in certain specific areas of their existence.

Nevertheless, this does not mean that the Jewish tradition has nothing to say about international society. The only provision seems to be that this society recognize the present pluralism of the human condition, especially in its political manifestations, and that it be recognized as both necessary and tentatively desirable short of the true culmination of this world by the apocalyptic act of God and God alone.

Because of this, it seems that the best place to look for Jewish sources to contribute to this vision is in the Jewish doctrine of creation, especially as it intersects with the Jewish doctrine of revelation. For Jewish tradition has been quite adamant that although the Torah is the word of God, its function in the world is determined by human criteria of judgment.[8] Now human criteria of judgment are both singular and general. The singular criteria of judgment are those concerns in the interpretation of the Torah that come from the unique history of the Jewish people. However, there are other criteria of judgment that are more general because they are concerned with the situation of the Jewish people in relation to other human communities. These criteria are taken to be more natural than historical in the sense that they are seen as dealing with aspects of the human condition itself that are permanent and ubiquitous in any humanly significant situation. This is the realm of what the ancient rabbis called *sidrei bere'sheet*, "the orders of creation," that is, the nature of the world created by God.[9] In the traditional Jewish concern with this order, one can find much of interest to those concerned with international society, but which does not attempt to usurp the essential mystery of the final and complete redemption of humankind and the world. This should lead one to distinguish between the desirability of a more closely interrelated world society and the undesirability of an overarching and all-powerful world state. There is certainly an essential difference between an *inter*national society and a *super*national state. The latter would seem necessarily to entail the sin of the builders of the Tower of Babel, who according to rabbinic interpretation, subordinated the rights of all humans to their end of universal power, and attempted to wage war against God himself.[10]

It is now appropriate to begin to examine some of the issues raised by the various philosophical positions that are usually invoked when there is discursive speculation about the international order. Unlike the religious doctrines of revelation and redemption, which are the domain of religious tradition per se and thus whose questions must be originally theological, the doctrine of creation is about the world in general. As such, its questions must be originally philosophical. That is, it is concerned with the realm of ordinary human experience and wisdom which, even for many religious believers, is something that is constituted prior to revelation in and for the present and redemption in and for the future. Creation is the past inasmuch as it represents that which is *already there* for all humans to understand and appropriate as best they can. And regarding essential questions of human polity, among which the question of international society is certainly paramount, even theologians can assume with full integrity that the various options are best presented by political philosophy. That is, when one understands the word "philosophy" to designate the most profound and systematic effort to understand the most basic structures of the world in which humans are now consigned to live and work.

THE PRIMACY OF LAW

The first point that anyone committed to the Jewish tradition would have to make in terms of suggestions for the proper ordering of world society is the primacy of law in any ordering of human life, either locally, nationally, or internationally. Indeed, the worst thing that can be said about anyone, according to the rabbis, is that he or she assumes "there is no law (*leyt din*) and there is no judge."[11]

Because of the primacy of law in the Jewish tradition, many Jewish scholars are partial to what might loosely be called legal positivism.[12] This is because so much of Judaism developed without a state of its own, but always with a law of its own. Therefore for Judaism especially, the rare discussions of anything resembling what we today might mean by international society must often take place in a decidedly legal context.

In his chapter, Terry Nardin explicitly mentions the Jewish concept of Noahide law, which contains those norms that Judaism sees as binding on all human beings and which are to be enforced by all human societies. For many this is the opening for Jews to speak to the normative issues facing the world outside its own particular community, that is, from a formal definition of law per se.

The "Seven Commandments of the Noahides" is a term that appears regularly in Rabbinic literature.[13] It designates seven basic laws (actually, seven groupings of laws) that the Rabbis assumed are binding on all human beings (who, after the Flood, are the descendants of Noah). These laws pertain to three areas of human relationships: those with other humans, those with God, and those with other sentient beings. They are: (1) the requirement to appoint judges, that is, establish a regular system of adjudication; (2) the prohibition of blasphemy; (3) the prohibition of idolatry; (4) the prohibition of incest, homosexuality, adultery, and bestiality; (5) the prohibition of murder (including abortion[14]); (6) the prohibition of robbery; (7) the prohibition of tearing a limb from a living animal for food (apparently a common practice in the ancient Near East).

This body of law, however theoretical its origins might have been, has become the standard in the Jewish tradition for dealing with non-Jewish individuals and societies. By extension, it is the only cogent standard for dealing with the question of international society. This is important at a point in history when we Jews now have a state of our own, Israel, and when we are equal and active participants in states that have international interests and involvements.

Without a universally accepted literary source as the permanent promulgation of these laws, one comparable in function to the Bible and the Talmud for the Jews and their laws, the question arises as to how the gentiles are supposed to know what God requires of them. Three answers have been provided by Jewish thinkers. The first answer points to common normative experience (akin to the later meaning of *ius gentium* in Roman jurisprudence), namely the very generality of the Noahide laws suggests that they denote some international normative commonalities.[15] The second answer points to a political institution, namely that the Jews are to teach and, if they have the power, even enforce these laws among the gentiles they reach (akin to the original meaning of *ius gentium* in Roman jurisprudence).[16] The last answer points to human reason, namely these are norms that humans as rational-social beings should affirm and practice as minimal conditions for their allegiance to any society worthy of it.

This last answer is the most attractive, especially when arguing for the validity of these norms to and for the present world.[17] Surely, the notion of any common normative tradition among all the nations is less and less valid as the world becomes more and more pluralistic and multicultural. And the notion of instruction, let alone the enforcement of morality basically validated by political power, should make anyone committed to contemporary democracy in the world very nervous, especially considering our overall experience with the tyrannies and totalitarianisms in this soon-to-be-concluded twentieth century.

For legal positivists like Terry Nardin, law is justified, not by the command of someone with political power, but by its own internal coherence. As is the case with other legal positivists, like H.L.A. Hart, this criterion of internal coherence is offered as sufficient to answer the charge leveled against legal positivism by such critics as Leo Strauss (specifically against Hans Kelsen) that it could ultimately be used to justify any totalitarian regime that was not erratic in its commands.[18] But as Lon Fuller argued, legal incoherence, as one inevitably sees it in the commands of any tyrant, just as inevitably leads to political collapse.[19] In other words, tyranny and a coherent system of law are, ultimately, mutually exclusive. Thus it is the concept of law itself (to borrow the title of Hart's most important book), embedded in normative experience that can be seen as international as well as just national. As such, a world society would have to be primarily a legally constituted order.

There is support for this view of the self-sufficiency of law itself in the usual order of the Noahide laws, where the requirement of adjudication seems to be foundational. The first Noahide law is the requirement that adjudication (*dinim*) be institutionalized in permanent courts of law. This seems to base the authority of the law on the concept of law itself, not on any of the other three alternative foundations just noted above. In this notion, there is precedent, especially in the treatment of the concept of Noahide law as a Jewish expression of the concept of law per se by the Neo-Kantian Jewish philosopher and theologian Hermann Cohen (d. 1918). Cohen saw Noahide law as a prototype for the modern secular state where citizens function as part of a legal order (*Rechtstaat*) irrespective of their religious beliefs or practices. Cohen also saw this concept of the state entailing the concept of a world state.[20] Indeed, he saw a world state as being in essence the realization of the classical Jewish hope for the Messianic Age (a problematic point as we have already seen above).

As for the two religious requirements (the prohibitions of blasphemy and idolatry), Cohen noted that they are both negative and, therefore, not requirements of any positive affirmation of religious belief or practice. Moreover, they can be seen at most as requirements to respect the religious-cultural climate of monotheism in which the concept of law has received its most consistent and powerful encouragement.[21]

However, there is another ordering of the Noahide laws that reflects a different view of their essential meaning. In this ordering, the prohibition of idolatry, not the prescription of adjudication, is the first and thereby foundational law.[22] Just as Hermann Cohen's more secular notion of Noahide law relies on one textual presentation of these commandments, so does the more religious notion of Noahide law, whose foremost advocate was Maimonides, rely on another textual presentation of them. But what is the difference in principle?

This latter version emphasizes the assumption that all law, whether for Jews or for humankind at large, is in essence divine law. All law is thus divine command in one form or another. The prohibition of idolatry is the first manifestation of God's command because it outlaws anyone or anything else from in any way competing with the absolute authority of God and hence confusing the humans who are to give their primal allegiance to God's will alone.[23] For this reason, idolatry consists of either substituting any creature for the Creator, or even giving any creature parity with the Creator. The acknowledgment of that fundamental truth is prior to the moral judgment of what is good and the legal judgment of what is lawful. Its acknowledgment is negative, I think, because one has to know what the word God *does not mean* before one can identify God if and when God reveals himself. Minimally,

God is *not* identifiable with any finite entity in the world. To make any such erroneous identification is idolatry.[24]

If all law is divine law, and if the difference between the Mosaic law for Israel and the Noahide law for humankind is one of degree rather than one of kind, then one cannot speak of any system of law as being conceptually self-sufficient as legal positivism seems to assert. The fact is that the strength of the system of Jewish law for those Jews who have always been faithful to it (often despite tremendous threats or temptations) has not been because of its systematic legality. It has been because we observant Jews believe this is what God requires of us and that we are doomed if we disobey God. Furthermore, the doctrine of Noahide law has taught that Jews cannot claim to be the sole recipients of God's law in the world. Thus Jewish law is quite different from the other two types of "decentralized legal orders" Nardin mentions, common law and international law. To miss this difference is to lose sight of the very evident theological foundations of Jewish law, an error into which secularist interpretations of Jewish law inevitably fall.[25]

Despite this, though, once one does not posit a foundational role to legal positivism, there is much of what its adherents say about it that those of us in the Jewish tradition can find resonance with, and even resonance with its application to the question of international society. For Jewish legal literature, beginning with the Talmud itself, recognizes that the Jewish legal order, as a real legal order operating in the world, does not function alone in the world. Thus there are numerous occasions where legal overlappings and even more essential commonalities are affirmed and built upon. In this area, there has often been a recognition of a secondary role for the realm of the secular. Let me give one good example of this recognition of the secondary function of the secular realm.

In the Mishnah (which is the core text on and around which the discussions of the Talmud are arranged) we read: "All documents deposited in the courts of the gentiles (*arka'ot shel goyyim*) are Jewishly valid (*kesherin*) except for bills of divorcement for women and bills of manumission for slaves."[26] What is the difference between these two types of documents, and why are the latter type seen as requiring a different validation? The answer to these correlated questions that comes closest to legal positivism comes from the most important of the medieval exegetes of both the Bible and the Talmud, Rashi of Troyes. His answer is that when it comes to ordinary documents (*shtarot*) such as commercial documents, any system of law that on its own terms requires integrity in these matters of common concern can be trusted.[27] In other words, one can recognize here a basis for a certain international jurisdiction even without formal political commonality. (It is important to remember that when Rashi wrote this interpretation, Jews were not citizens of Christian France. They were, rather, a tolerated alien community *in* France but not *of* it.) But in the case of bills of divorcement and bills of manumission, we are now dealing with matters of specifically religious significance. Both marriage and divorce are matters of religious covenant, not secular contract; and the manumission of slaves, that is gentile slaves owned by Jews, makes them full Jews with all the religious privileges and responsibilities this status entails.[28]

The ultimate question a Jewish thinker must pose to legal positivism is whether it requires the acceptance of the *philosophical* premises of positivism in order to operate cogently? That is, must one take it to be the primary political-legal order? Or can one take it on a secondary level only? If the latter, then legal positivism has much to say to and hear from the Jewish tradition, because we can both assume that most law is *positive*, that is, it is posited by those having legal authority most evidently derived from the law itself as a system. (This is true about Jewish law as well, because even though its foundation is divine law, most of the specific rulings are made by Rabbis, who are authorized both by a general warrant in the divine law and popular acceptance of their authority.[29])

Natural Law

Unlike legal positivists, advocates of the idea of natural law see law as having a translegal foundation apprehended by human reason. Natural law theory in our day is usually contrasted with legal positivism, although these two points of view about law are not the only two options for jurisprudence, hence they are not the only two options for ordering international society.

Positive law itself does not answer the fundamental question of obedience. In other words, it does not answer the question: Why should I obey what the law commands? If the legal positivist answers that I should obey what the law commands because I will be punished by the legal-political-penal authorities, then it is conceivable that my legal obligation could be in direct opposition to my moral obligation. For such an answer could justify obedience to the commands of the most evil authorities possible. How can I protest if these legal authorities derive their authority from Hitler, and construct a legal order based on that authority as the Nazis indeed did in Germany from 1933 until their military defeat in 1945? It is this fundamental question more than any other that has enabled a revival of natural law theory in the years since 1945 (a *terminus ad quem* in world history and even more so in Jewish history). Only the extreme type of legal positivism that denies the separate existence of morality at all could avoid this question. The old question *quid sit juris?* ("what is the law to be?") is ultimately a moral question presupposed by the law itself.

And if one answers that obedience to the commands of a legal system is useful, what if that legal system commands me to do things that are contrary to my experienced benefit? For example, what if it commands me to pay in taxes the only money I have to save my business from bankruptcy? In other words, the utilitarian version of legal positivism does seem to operate from a moral base in the sense of being translegal and noncoercive. But being based in experienced human selfishness, it is hardly one that can make any unqualified demands, which seems to be a sine qua non for any such system. For these reasons, the challenge to legal positivism must come from morality, and the type of morality that coherently transcends merely procedural questions. For the question "why be legally obedient" cannot be satisfactorily answered by saying, circularly, "because the legal system requires obedient adherents." For those who acknowledge it in the Jewish tradition (as opposed to those who vehemently deny it), natural law theory is constituted in the following way. God is seen as commanding both through nature and in history. God's commands in history are seen as being direct and specific, and these commands are seen as being addressed to the people of Israel singularly in the Torah. *Torah* means both the Bible and the ongoing tradition of the Jewish people, whose chief literary record lies in the Talmud. But God is also seen commanding more generally and less directly through nature, especially human nature as a rational-social permanent structure, coeval with all human existence in the world.[30] This more general revelation is seen as being available to practical reason. Its affirmation seems to me to be most succinctly and cogently expressed in the rabbinic doctrine of Noahide law that we examined in the preceding section of this chapter. The distinction between this general Torah and the more specific and complete one of Israel is that Israel *receives* her Torah by a definite act of historical revelation whereas other humans have to *discover* their Torah from experience of their natural, created limits and by their rational reflection on what this means in terms of human action.

Natural law theory lies at the juncture between the doctrines of creation and revelation. So, even if some of the precepts of natural law are not deduced from creation theology, nonetheless they cannot be seen as intelligible without it. Any theological proponent of the idea of natural law must reject the famous statement of Hugo Grotius, considered to be the founder of modern natural law theory, namely, that one could constitute natural law "even if we say there is no God" (*etiamsi daremus non esse deum*).[31] If Jews are to engage in natural law theory with authenticity, then it is going to have to be considered as a type of divine law. On this point, one could find a surprising amount of agreement between Maimonides, Aquinas, and Calvin.[32] For all of them, all law comes from God, but not all law is specifically revealed to their respective faith communities in history.

SOCIAL CONTRACT

The notion of a social contract, so attractive to Hobbes, Locke, Rousseau, Kant, and most recently John Rawls, poses serious difficulties for any adherent of Judaism. For it seems to be based on the primacy of human will to autonomously constitute local society and even international society.[33]

Just as for legal positivism, law itself is self-sufficient, so for advocates of the social contract it seems to affirm the fundamental self-sufficiency of humans to contract the basic norms that are to govern their lives. Social contract theory has immediate implications for an international society precisely because it is always imagined as if contract is or should be the basis of every form of human association. So, my question to advocates of this position is similar in its logic to my earlier question addressed to the legal positivists: Must one accept contractarianism as primary, or can one be more eclectic and accept some of its points on a secondary basis? If the latter, I can show how there is a contractarian strain in the Jewish tradition, which can be employed with religious integrity by Jews concerned with international society.

Let me return to the example from the Talmud that I used in dealing with legal positivism, namely, the one about the acceptance by Jewish authorities of civil documents that have been validated in non-Jewish courts. The commentator Rashi gave what seemed to me to be an explanation for this rule that is consistent with legal positivism, namely, one can respect a legal system that functions coherently with definite, systemic procedures. However, another reason is given by the Talmud itself: that "the law of the state is also the law for the Jews therein" (*dina de-malkhuta dina*). And Rashi's grandson, the great exegete Rashbam, argued that the non-Jewish state enjoys secular authority because the state (particularly, the king as the head of state) has contracted with all its citizens, giving its protection in return for obedience to its laws (an argument as old as Plato's *Crito*).[34]

Although the Jews were not citizens of the state (the kingdom of France) in which Rashbam lived, as a community they did have a contractual relationship with the state: that it would tolerate their presence in its midst and give that tolerance legal expression. Of course, Jews regard their primary moral and legal obligations as based on their covenant with God. The covenant is not a contract because although it involves mutual consent, it is not based on such consent but, rather, on God's election of the community. The consent of the community is a *con*firmation of what has already been presented by God.[35] Thus any contract they make with the secular state has to be viewed as secondary. It has to be first authorized at the primary level, even though the specifics of the contract need not (most often cannot) be deduced from that primary level. Minimally, these secondary secular contracts must not be inconsistent with what is viewed as the primary and indispensable covenantal reality.[36]

It has been this ability to engage in contracts on the secondary level that has historically enabled Jews to engage in international relations without having to subordinate ourselves ultimately to the rule of anyone but God. In this sense, we have the basis in our tradition for a partial pluralism, which by virtue of its being partial seems to have more realistic value in the international world in which we are increasingly finding ourselves. As the Talmud put it: "One who grasps too much grasps nothing; one who grasps less grasps something."[37]

Cosmopolitanism

Cosmopolitanism, as presented in this volume by Brian Barry, begins with an assumption bequeathed by the religious traditions of the West: the fundamental equality of all humans' souls. In this view, elementary human equality seems to be essential to any international society having true moral claims on its members.

My question here is: Does the Jewish-Christian-Muslim doctrine of the equality of souls before God simply translate into the secularist version of the equality of rational human selves before each other, or is something essential lost in this translation, something that can speak to our present political reality and the ideals that are projected from it? The fundamental question is: *Before whom* are we claimed and do we make our claims in the world? Here is where the great difference between a religious view (in this case, the common religious view of Judaism, Christianity, and Islam) and a secular view is most essentially manifest. There is a fundamental difference between saying that one is primarily claimed by God and claiming of God, and saying that one is primarily claimed by other humans and claiming of them.

In the secular position, the claims made by and to humans are those of rational moral agents. However, what about those who are incapable of making a choice? Such a group would include the irreversibly comatose, the mentally retarded, the senile, the unborn.[38] And what about those whose choices we might not consider to be rational? Such a group would include members of cultures who make their decisions based on such supernatural phenomena as revelations? In other words, the range of persons who can make moral claims is largely dependent on whether or not they are the kind of people those in power can and want to communicate with? The principle of exclusion at work here is often as powerful as the principle of inclusion. The very fact that human freedom in this worldview is inevitably constituted along economic lines of property suggests a criterion governed by those already possessing power in a bourgeois society and culture. How does that augur for the construction of some sort of world society in which mostly nonreligious westerners will no longer be dominant?

It is, therefore, quite different to say that all humans have essentially equal claims on all other humans because both the claimants and those being claimed are claimed by the God in whose image they are all created and whom they can make a claim upon for justice in the world.[39] Thus the first question posed to a human in the first case of human conflict in the Bible is the question God addresses to Cain: "Where is Abel your brother?"[40] And the first claim made upon God by a human is made by a human whose voice is no longer audible to other humans, that of the murdered Abel. "The voice of your brother's blood cries to Me from the ground."[41] That is why the pursuit of mercy and justice in the world is seen as being an act of imitation of the creating-revealing God, "to keep the way of the Lord, to do mercy and justice."[42] Indeed, it is this vision of the way of the Lord that envisions a world society to be brought about in which "they will not do evil or harm in all my holy mountain for the knowledge of the Lord shall cover the earth as the water covers the sea."[43]

Of course, secularists might well object to the introduction of biblical *myth* into a rational discussion of justice in the world. By "myth" I mean an assertion about the human condition that itself is not based on factors readily accessible to ubiquitous human experience, but one that locates itself in the transmission of a particular story. However, is not the position of those who advocate a hypothetical choosing situation (namely, contractarian adherents of cosmopolitanism) also not a matter of ubiquitous human experience (to which most natural law theorists refer)? It would seem to also be the presentation of a story.

It would seem that the value of either a hypothesis or an actual narrative in determining a moral course of action lies in its heuristic strengths. Furthermore, since those who believe a story to be true, even though they cannot demonstrate that truth by any neutral criterion, do have the advantage of seeing the political reality they are attempting to understand and direct to be part of a larger reality rather than what in essence is a fiction. And although every legal system does employ some sort of legal fiction from time to time, it stretches this privilege quite a bit to posit a generally fictitious situation, such as a "state of nature" or an "original position," as actually foundational.

This last point impinges of the philosophical debate over the question of whether thought is prior to language or language to thought.[44] If one follows the view that language is prior to thought, then a paradigmatic story like the biblical account of creation would seem to have normative priority over a mental construct like the social contract. For this story is the historical source for most of our western notions of human equality. "For all souls are Mine."[45] Moreover, it is a story that still shapes the thought of many in the West and beyond. How can it not be included in speculation about a world society?

In conclusion, then, I reiterate a point I made at the beginning of this chapter about the need to include the perspectives of religious traditions in moral and political discourse without any special privileges or liabilities being placed on them at the outset. Only such an even playing field will enable both religious and secular voices to be heard in discussions like this one concerning international society. Indeed, such a society would hardly be *inter*national without simultaneously being *inter*cultural. Thus my initial methodological concern about the conditions for real communication is very much germane to the substantive issues of international society that are the subject of this volume. In a real sense, as the late Marshall McLuhan became famous a generation ago for asserting, *the medium is the message.*

NOTES

1. See Ernst Cassirer, *An Essay on Man* (New Haven: Yale University Press, 1944), 79ff.

2. See his *Whose Justice? Which Rationality?* (Notre Dame: University of Notre Dame Press, 1988), esp. 389ff.

3. See David Novak, *Jewish-Christian Dialogue: A Jewish Justification* (New York: Oxford University Press, 1989), 114ff.

4. See Hermann Cohen, *Religion of Reason Out of the Sources of Judaism*, trans. S. Kaplan (New York: Frederick Ungar, 1972), 249ff.

5. The most interesting effort in this direction was made by the Jewish Marxist philosopher Ernst Bloch (d. 1977), especially in his three-volume *magnum opus*, which he entitled *Das Prinzip der Hoffnung*. Note: "Men can want to be brothers even without believing in the father, but they cannot become brothers without believing in the utterly un-banal contents and dimensions which in religious terms were conceived through the kingdom. What a faith which, in its knowledge, as this knowledge, has destroyed are the illusions of mythical religion. . . . And the religion which is itself believed, i.e., religion as content, is also valid here, though in a highly corrected form, namely as the religion of knowledge of what is germinating, of what is still unfinished in the world." *The Principle of Hope*, vol. 3, trans. N. Plaice, S. Plaice, and P. Knight (Cambridge, MA: MIT Press, 1986), 279f.

6. See David Novak, *The Election of Israel: The Idea of the Chosen People* (Cambridge: Cambridge University Press, 1995), 152ff.

7. See Reinhold Niebuhr, *The Nature and Destiny of Man*, vol. 1 (New York: Scribners, 1941), 186ff.

8. See, for example, *Babylonian Talmud* (hereafter B.): Baba Metsia 59b re Deut. 30:12; also David Novak, *Halakhah in a Theological Dimension* (Chico, CA: Scholars Press, 1985), chs. 1, 2, 9.

9. B. Shabbat 53b.

10. See Louis Ginzberg, *Legends of the Jews*, vol. 1 (Philadelphia: Jewish Publication Society of America, 1909), 179ff.

11. See Targum Jonathan ben Uziel: Gen. 4:8, where this phrase is put into the mouth of Cain, the first human criminal. See also *Vayiqra Rabbah* 28.1 re Ecclesiastes 11:9; B. Baba Batra 78b and Rashbam, s.v. "avad heshbono."

12. The best example of this can be seen in the most comprehensive modern work on Jewish law, which is especially concerned with those aspects of Jewish law that could be normative in a modern, secular, nation-state, viz., Menachem Elon, *Jewish Law: History, Sources, Principles*, 4 vols., trans. B. Auerbach and M. J. Sykes (Philadelphia and Jerusalem: Jewish Publication Society, 1994). See esp. 1:93ff.

13. The rabbinic *loci classici* of this doctrine are *Tosefta*: Avodah Zarah 8.4 and B. Sanhedrin 56a. For the most complete study of this doctrine, see David Novak, *The Image of the Non-Jew in Judaism: An Historical and Constructive Study of the Noahide Laws* (New York and Toronto: Edwin Mellen Press, 1983).

14. See B. Sanhedrin 57b re Gen. 9:6.

15. See A. P. d'Entrèves, *Natural Law: An Historical Survey* (New York: Harper, 1965), 17ff.

16. See David Daube, "The Peregrine Praetor," *Journal of Roman Studies* 41 (1951): 66ff.

17. See David Novak, *Jewish Social Ethics* (New York: Oxford University Press, 1992), intro. and chs. 1–3.

18. See Strauss, *Natural Right and History* (Chicago: University of Chicago Press, 1953), 4, n. 2.

19. See Fuller, *The Morality of Law*, rev. ed. (New Haven: Yale University Press, 1969), 137ff.

20. See *Religion of Reason*, 236ff.

21. Ibid.

22. See Maimonides, *Mishneh Torah*: Melakhim, 9.1.

23. See B. Sanhedrin 56b re Gen. 2:16 (the opinion of R. Isaac).

24. See Maimonides, *Mishneh Torah*: Avodah Zarah, 1.1ff.

25. For the most cogent presentation of this a-theological view of Jewish law, see Haim H. Cohn, *Human Rights in Jewish Law* (New York: KTAV, 1984), intro.

26. *Mishnah*: Gittin 1.5.

27. B. Gittin 9b, s.v. "huts."

28. See B. Gittin 38b.

29. See B. Shabbat 23a and B. Avodah Zarah 36a.

30. See Nahmanides, *Commentary on the Torah*: Gen. 6:2, 13.

31. *De Jure Belli ac Pacis*, prol. 11. See also Anton-Hermann Chroust, "Hugo Grotius and the Scholastic Natural Law Tradition," *New Scholasticism* 17 (1943): 126ff.

32. See Maimonides, *Mishneh Torah*: Melakhim, 8.11; Thomas Aquinas, *Summa Theologiae* 2.1, q. 94, a. 4 ad 1; John Calvin, *Institutes of the Christian Religion*, 2.7.10 and 4.20.16.

33. Cf. Novak, *Jewish-Christian Dialogue*, 148ff. for a critique of the plausibility of any notion of primary autonomy for humans.

34. See B. Baba Batra 54b and Rashbam, s.v. "mi amar;" *Crito*, 50Aff. Also see *supra*, n. 27.

35. See Novak, *The Election of Israel*, 115ff.

36. See B. Kiddushin 19b.

37. See B. Rosh Hashanah 4b; also *Mishnah*: Avot 2.15–16.

38. See David Novak, *Law and Theology in Judaism*, vol. 2 (New York: KTAV, 1976), 108ff.

39. See Gen. 18:25

40. Gen. 4:9.

41. Gen. 4:10.

42. Gen. 18:19.

43. Isaiah 11:9.

44. See Ludwig Wittgenstein, *Philosophical Investigations*, 2nd ed., trans. G.E.M. Anscombe (New York: Macmillan, 1958), 1.18.

45. Ezekiel 18:4.

Christianity and the Prospects for a New Global Order

MAX L. STACKHOUSE

IT IS no accident that the issue of reconstituting international society appears before us today, at a moment when the economic, medical, cultural, and communication structures that play such a critical role in modern society are changing rapidly. Although civil society in the past largely coincided with the boundaries of the state, it is now being reconstructed internationally in ways that strain the capacity of any government to order, guide, or control. In fact, some observers foresee little but chaos since societies are no longer confined within a single legal system and no one seems to be in control.[1] Even if agreement between states plays an increasingly important role in the future, as we expect, it may well be subject to frequent abuse or breakdown, for its moral and spiritual authority is fragile.

This monumental shift toward a global society and, perhaps, global anarchy, has been well under way for more than a century, although many signs of the shift have been obscured by the radical statism of the twentieth century—most notably those of the antimodern national socialisms of the right and the hypermodern proletarian socialisms of the left, each fueled by the notion that there neither is nor could be any ontological, metaphysical, epistemological, or ethical principle to serve as a reliable basis for law across time or space or condition.

These trends were reinforced after the Second World War by the wave of decolonization movements that, while overthrowing exploitative metropolitan regimes, also joined the territorial and ethnic relativism of nationalism to the historicist and class-based relativism of socialist ideologies. These "liberation" movements repudiated the purported universalism of Western religious and philosophical thought, especially insofar as it legitimized constitutional democracy, human rights, and corporate capitalism.[2] Both Christianity and the Enlightenment were viewed as manifestations of Western hegemony, the by-products of material interests that had to be overcome so that competing interests could be acknowledged. That presumption obscured the growth of a wider global interdependence, invited antinomian efforts to debunk all culture-transcending thought, and prompted militant efforts to overthrow existing institutions.

Life, however, cannot be lived under that presumption. Such views can deconstruct, but they cannot reconstruct. They neither generate nor preserve

the tissues of enduring commitment needed to sustain reliable human relations. Indeed, they evoke distrust of the structures of commonality on which
we depend. Yet a new set of global interdependencies, which we are unsure
how to conceive or assess, much less whether to nurture or resist, is appearing
on the horizon.

Many are today unsure what could shape the fabric of a common life that
is increasingly transnational, cross-cultural, multiethnic, and postpolitical.
Though some argue that a common international legal system is already at
hand, more skeptical observers suggest that we have no reliable theory of
justice or other mode of authoritative legitimization on which to ground such
a system. These skeptics suggest that such law as we possess is little more than
a set of tools for those with means to manage the Global Cultural Bazaar, the
Global Shopping Mall, the Global Workplace, and the Global Financial Network.[3] Such economistic images reveal something of the power of corporate
and market forces today; but they do not convey how much the global economy is itself built on widely accepted values that support science, technology,
democracy, human rights, a work ethic, professional standards, or capital investment. Nor do they give us any guidance as to how we ought to respond to
the economic forces at work or the values on which they rest. Economistic
analysis alone cannot account for the shape and character of international law.

It is also questionable whether we can rely on philosophy alone, as many
sought to do in the past, and as many do in this volume. Philosophy today is
preoccupied with deconstructing itself, and its resources for rethinking our
new situation are therefore thin. The chapters in this book are exceptions to
the wider state of the discussion, in which all sorts of postmodernists (and not
a few antimodern or premodernist traditionalists) are eager to tell us that
Western thought is suffering fatal epistemological and moral disease. It is,
they say, impossible, even totalizing and therefore immoral, to speak of anything as being categorical, general, or universal.[4]

Such voices are of little use to the new Russian or South African governments as they seek to write national constitutions.[5] Nor do they help us think
in wider terms, for every effort to alter a political order must proceed on the
assumption that, although things are contingently disorganized, we can know
something about "the right order of things" or the "ultimate ends of life" so
that we can improve the situation. It is true that every attempt to define justice
has to be repeatedly renewed, because we do not know justice fully and because the concept must be continually reexamined in new situations. This
clarification and recasting, however, presumes that the norms of justice are, in
some sense, universally discernible.[6]

The efforts in this volume to identify principles on which a universal normative order could be built draw little from, indeed scarcely mention, any of
these challenges to the enterprise. They turn instead to contemporary heirs of
Classical and Enlightenment modes of analysis, without noting that these
heirs are under suspicion. But we cannot ignore these challenges, for they
may well expose a weakness—namely, that these forms of thought cannot

guarantee their own foundations. They may require theological treatment.[7] At the same time, the editors have invited responses from the three religious traditions that have most deeply stamped the legal patterns of the past, and which are today again affecting the world—Judaism, Islam, and Christianity.

Such an invitation touches on a still inchoate recognition of the devastations brought about by the intentionally antireligious or postreligious ideologies of our century and a longstanding suspicion of religious concerns in international law.[8] Not only have the secular ideologies (sometimes using religion as weapon or cover) behind the Holocaust, the Gulag, and the modern killing fields of Cambodia, Bosnia, and Rwanda brought more vicious destruction than the Crusades or the Holy Wars of old, these secular ideologies are increasingly recognized as incapable of guiding the common life. And this recognition suggests that the engagement of theology with jurisprudence should be renewed, and even that the biblical heritage can make an indispensable contribution to it.

CHRISTIAN RESPONSES

The varieties of theology most promising in this area are those that remain alert to the contributions of cultures and philosophies beyond the sanctuary. Most forms of Christian theology do this. Orthodox, Catholic, Evangelical, Reformed, Liberal, and Ecumenical modes of thought have all attempted to show the pertinence of biblical themes to ethical and social concerns in ways that invite, and in some ways demand, the formation or reformation of just social and political institutions.

Not all Christians approve such efforts. Early in this century, the great social historian of the relationship of Christianity to the sustaining structures of civilization, Ernst Troeltsch, identified three interpretations of the faith that show a great suspicion of the structures of society. Some focus only on the inner self and its experiences of transcendence (so that social questions are ignored or left to those who deal with merely exterior things). Others try to avoid the evils of civil institutions by constructing alternative communities of holy fidelity distinct from the ways of the world (as in monastic orders and communitarian sects). And still others attempt to defeat the evils of the world by militant action (to bring about an entirely new order, against the bulwarks of evil).[9] All left indelible traces in Christian thought, but only the third, as it found expression in the Crusades, the Inquisition, and the Peasant's Revolt, is thought to have discredited Christian political theology.

These interpretations have a point: the customary or enacted laws of society are not the same as the normative laws of God. A higher order, a greater purpose, a wider authority ultimately is the source and norm of all that is truly right and good, and it is this "other" level that puts every legal order as it appears in human history in perspective. Indeed, a gulf always exists between divine perfection and the necessities of governance in a fallen and divided

world. In substantial measure, the whole of Christianity shares these themes
not only with the minority traditions within itself but with its elder brother,
the Jewish tradition, with its stepbrother, Islam, and even with its more distant theistic cousins in India and Africa.

For the most part, however, the main streams of Christianity do not hold
that the church, the tradition, or its sacred texts are entirely opposed to human society and culture. Indeed, Christianity is driven into engagement with
culture since it does not claim that its sources contain all that is necessary to
form the laws of society. Christianity has never had anything quite like the
Torah or *shari'a* (or even an *Arthashastra*) to propose as a constitution for civil
society, however high its regard for them. In its selective adaptation of the
laws of the Pentateuch, in its establishment of the internal laws of the church
through canon law, and in its attempts to influence civil law in Europe and to
found it under the American Puritans, Christian advocates of biblical insights
always drew on ideas that derived from nonbiblical sources. This in turn
evoked what some call a "Christian social philosophy" or "public theology"—
an effort to address common issues, including those of jurisprudence, by employing theological concepts in public discourse. This effort is undertaken in
the conviction that such concepts provide the firmest base for public policy.[10]

Christians gravitate to those forms of thought that honor human freedom,
for Christians believe that humans are made in the image of God. Christians
also hold that this freedom is to be exercised under moral mandates not of our
own construction—the laws and purposes of God. We can claim to know
these mandates only in part, for they are not fully present in human experience or holy scriptures and everywhere have to be interpreted and applied.
We live nonetheless under a kind of cosmic moral constitution that serves as
the basic framework for all concrete efforts to discern and establish justice.
Further, the human soul, the biophysical world, and the events of history bear
traces of this constitution, so that even the most horrendous betrayal and
distortion cannot finally overcome it. Yet, precisely because it is obscured by
various evils, if this morality is neglected or repudiated, bias, oppression, and
dehumanization will corrode any society.

The majority traditions of Christianity have also held that one can be—
indeed, ought to be—a member of at least two societies. We are born into a
"natural society" with its "orders of creation" as members of a family, a civil
polity, an economy, and a cultural-linguistic group. But baptism (and, for
some, confirmation) is required for church membership, and brings with it
the more universal, catholic, or ecumenical principles of justice. Christianity,
in its central traditions, thus demands a separation of Christ and Caesar, *sacer-
dotium* and *imperium*, patriarch and czar, pope and emperor, minister and
magistrate, and thus, church and state. This principle has been periodically
violated in Christian history, but the deeper logic of the faith presses against
such violations and claims that religious membership cannot be the basis for
citizenship, and that participation in a political order is not a basis for religious identity. Each domain has its own laws, and one cannot say that one is

right and good and the other necessarily wrong and evil. One can suggest, however, that the wider structures of civil society—those that define and regulate marriage, ownership, economic exchanges, race relations, and foreign policy—ought to respect the more general principles of justice pointed to by this second membership, and not only the interests or social consensus that exists within a particular familial, racial, national, class, or cultural tradition. Freedom of religion, in particular, is a decisive mark of justice in the human world.

To be sure, Christians are also taught to be "obedient to the rulers who are appointed by God" and who are "not a terror to good conduct, but to bad," as we learn from Paul, a disciple *and* a citizen, and these teachings imply that we can, in some measure, discern which regimes are constituted on a godly basis according to ethical criteria. But, as Peter taught, when and if it comes to a conflict, we are to "obey God and not humans," and it is Christ, not Caesar, who should guide the discernment of the one from the other.

Thus, while Christianity does not have within itself an intrinsic theory of international law, it does have a profound sense of the basis of "the right order of things," the "ultimate end of things," and the "grounding authority of all structures of society" that is, in some measure, knowable, and which therefore ought to influence all aspects of life. Christian theology tells us that a quite personal ubiquity, whom we call God, is the foundation of all knowledge and makes dialogue between the world religions and between believers and unbelievers possible. God provides the basis on which general laws can be discerned, debated, codified, and reformed under changing conditions. Their confidence in this proposition derives from the fact that Christians believe that something reliable about God, who alone is truly universal, has been disclosed in the very creation of the world, in the creation of humanity in the image of God, in biblical history, in the concrete particularities of the life, teachings, death, and resurrection of Jesus Christ, and in the ongoing presence of the Holy Spirit.

Christians do not deny that others can know something of the reality toward which believers point, nor do they assert that only believers have an exclusive grasp of truth. Indeed, when the faithful speak seriously about these matters, they assume that serious, nonbelieving listeners can understand what is being talked about and can teach believers things that they need to know. Nevertheless, Christians hold that the fullest comprehension of the universality that believers and nonbelievers share cannot be stated without a nuanced, differentiated understanding of God, best framed in trinitarian terms.

Most Christians hold that belief cannot be imposed, for that would lead to a lie in the soul, but also that every effort to deal with international or cross-cultural realities that is closed to theological possibilities will be tempted to cultural imperialism, or else remain unable to convince the world that its presuppositions are grounded in what is ultimately real. It will be tempted to imperialism because it has no higher principles than its own by which to guide its interactions with others or to critically evaluate its own historical convic-

tions; and it will be unconvincing to others because it cannot point to a con-
text-transcending reality that is universally present in being, culture, society,
and a sense of the sacred. Moreover, without a monotheism understood in
trinitarian terms, human beings will be tempted to one or another kind of
monism, dualism, or polytheism, none of which can fully account for the rich
complexities of life.

Much of what Christianity has to offer is shared with other traditions, but
at least two other aspects of Christian theology are especially pertinent to the
question of international society: a view that theology is necessary to a sustainable theory of international law, and a view of sin and salvation with regard to the limits of that law.

Theology and International Legal Theory

Christianity teaches that not every human problem can be solved by law; yet
it also teaches that law is necessary to the common life. Christians have, over
the centuries, honored the efforts of great lawgivers to constitute just societies. American Christians, for example, join other Americans in honoring the
images of Hammurabi, Solon, Lycurgus, Justinian, Confucius, Ashoka,
Manu, and Muhammad flanking Moses above the desk where the justices sit
in the United States Supreme Court. Not only does this frieze symbolize that
American law stands under norms beyond those generated out of its own
history and procedures, but these great figures are properly acknowledged as
framers of legal systems that attempted to approximate justice and bring
about peace in complex civilizations.

In addition, it is widely acknowledged that Gregory, Thomas, Calvin,
Pufendorf, Althusius, Grotius, Locke, and the English religious dissidents
developed many aspects of legal theory that made modern constitutionalism
possible, and they did this because they held that, in the final analysis, the
chief lawgiver for the whole world is God.[11] They pointed to transcultural
principles of justice, provided intellectual resources for subjecting powerful
rulers to the rule of law, recognized the necessity of associations outside the
state, provided for councils, courts, and parliaments to correct and extend the
law, and defined the patterns we consider basic to constitutional government.
They echoed the ancient prophets and the early church: the world is governed by a moral order and undergirded by a providential care; life is most
blessed when humans live by these realities. And they anticipated the recognition that if these truths are denied, the denial brings nihilism in all things.

For this reason, Christian theology has historically embraced those philosophers, social theorists, and scholars of jurisprudence—Christian or not—
who attempt to identify and articulate features of human thought and practice
that point toward the universal, ethical, and spiritual realities that make and
keep human life human. Theology must make its case by the power of persua-

sion. And in that truth lie critical points of contact between a Christian theological perspective and the carefully nontheological chapters in this volume.

We can illustrate this point by noting that theology has long recognized two dimensions of persuasion—intellectualist and voluntarist.[12] The former holds that humans can know something about the basic form of justice because God has written the moral law in every heart. Thus, a common reference point, which major strands of the theological tradition call the *justitia originalis*, is accessible, in principle, to all. This provides the basis for constructing international law or assessing any international agreements and practices that exist. The exact content of this moral knowledge is not altogether clear, however, in part because there are two major theories as to how best to understand this common reference point. One is teleological and seeks to identify the good toward which all things tend, including the common good, and to direct all members of the body politic toward that end. The other is deontological and seeks to identify the first principles of right, and to establish the normative guidelines within which the many members of the body politic may then pursue their distinctive ends. The one tradition is more organic, hierarchical, and comprehending; the other is more associational, pluralistic, and confederative.[13]

Advocates of these "natural right" or "natural law" positions enjoy the prospect of convergence through intellectual persuasion, despite sometimes sharp intramural disputes. This is particularly clear in the chapters here by Robert George, writing in the tradition of Aristotle, and Pierre Laberge, writing in the tradition of Kant. It also informs a modified version of the Kantian view represented by the "cosmopolitan" perspective set forth here by Brian Barry, a version that, in its theory of *the good* and its definition of *the right*, recognizes the dignity of all persons around the globe.[14]

Theology shares with these views a key question, posed by Laberge as the question of the "faculty of philosophy" as to what the law of nations *ought* to be, in contrast to the question of the "faculty of law" as to what the law *is*. From the perspective of the "faculty of theology," however, the philosophers face the difficulty of explaining why, if all human beings have a sufficient natural knowledge of the good or the right, a just and universal international law is not immediately at hand. How is it that unjust convention or arbitrary authority comes to dominance again and again, always managing to distort the natural inclinations, the moral law, and the rights of persons? It is, in other words, a suspicion of theology that the intellectualist impulse is not self-sustaining, although it may be a useful and necessary ally to a stronger foundation.[15]

It is for this reason that we must recognize that persuasion may be voluntarist as well as intellectualist. People make choices, select between loyalties, develop interests, form alliances, willfully ride emotions, and are swayed by symbols. Intellectualist claims about the justice of the law are inextricably mixed with desire and interpretation. People invent moral rules and goals and choose legal ideals ("values") that are in fact merely pragmatic adaptations for securing what they desire. They bend ethics, philosophy, and law to fit the preferred conditions of their lives.

For that reason, those who hold either a teleological or deontological view of the nature and character of law will have to show how and why people would want to choose the good or the right taught by the mind or discovered in the heart. Even more, those who do not accept such "realist" positions, but hold to fully voluntarist theories of law, like positivism or contractualism (represented here by Terry Nardin and John Charvet), will have to show why any person or any group would choose to be obedient to the law so derived if they found doing so to be disadvantageous.

There are two basic answers to this question. The first is that it is in the practical interest of all concerned to yield to the rule of law, and that we often call "right" or "good" "values" (thereby choosing to acknowledge the authority of) that which meets our practical interests. Either we do not want to pay the price of punishment by those who make and enforce the law, or we gain more by obeying the law, or we are successful by taking advantage of it. Nardin and Charvet are probably accurate in pointing out the enormous amount of human choice that goes into the making of law in this mode, and correct in pointing to how much of it is going on today. Their views remind us of Louis Henkin's remark that "the process and politics of law-making in our time can be studied (and nearly understood) as the most ambitious, most populous, most extended, most complex law-making effort in international history."[16] But it is not clear that they understand the grounds on which this is taking place, and they seem unaware how easily law-making can support imperialism, colonialism, or hegemony—as their critics, Frederick Whelan and Chris Brown, suggest.

It may be well to consider again Max Weber's often neglected argument that the formation of rational and legal institutions on what look like positivist or contractual grounds is, in fact, an instance of the "routinization of charisma," and that if this charisma were of a different sort, or if it were rationalized by ill-motivated special interests, it would assume more ominous forms.[17] To put the matter another way, it is the parenthetical "nearly" in Henkin's remark that needs attention, for while the lawyer may wish, for certain purposes, simply to focus on the fact that laws exist and that people obey them for practical reasons, the understanding of law (and, even more, of justice) that can be expressed in purely positivist or contractualist terms is limited.

We should note that many of the values that incline people to favor one rather than another understanding of international law derive from religious assumptions.[18] Many have forgotten where these values came from, but if they are absent, or actively resisted, the laws so derived will be subverted or exploited whenever people find it advantageous to do so. Those who have a voluntarist view of human association rooted in practical interests can have no recourse but to accept that prospect.

At this point, theology suggests that it is necessary to recognize the influence of a realm beyond this one, one that shapes the deeper orientations and dispositions of our will by carving the deep channels of social valuation, of which the positive and contracted law are derivative expressions. It may be necessary, as Weber suggests, for even the religiously unmusical interpreter of modern law to acknowledge how deeply religious impulses influence choice. This is voluntarism at another level, on the brink of "the Will of God."

To be sure, such an acknowledgment is not yet fully theological, it is only religious. To become so, this deepest voluntarist insight must be joined to philosophy. This is the wisdom that discovers the level on which theology and jurisprudence are interconnected. It is with this insight that earlier Islam and later Catholicism adopted the natural law traditions of the Greeks, Calvinism retrieved much of the thought of the Stoics, and Modern Protestantism and Judaism embraced the natural-rights traditions of the Enlightenment. In each case, the formation of a cosmopolitan morality lent authority to international law. All the great world religions point toward a transcending reality that connects the best knowledge of the right and the good to the deepest commitments of the will. Some do it better than others, and that is why jurisprudence cannot neglect theological issues.

Those who presume to shape the common life through law must worry about these connections between the moral and the theological. Their codes determine who shall have and who shall forfeit liberty, wealth, standing, or relationship, even who shall live and who shall die. They decide how coercive force shall be used to defend what society, guided by what morality, philosophy, and—ultimately—theology, have identified as right or good or holy. Those who define these criteria define what is to be considered just, and even if they cannot bring themselves to speak of what is godly, their contribution remains limited if they do not see what they do from the standpoint of ultimacy.

What Is Missing from This Picture?

Most contemporary discourse about international law is uninterested in the theological grounds of international law, perhaps out of fear that these grounds cannot have universal application.[19] What an odd argument! In no other area is this position held. Few doubt that German Jews can discover the laws of relativity in physics, Arabic Muslims the logic of mathematics, or Japanese Buddhists the arts of gardening or poetry, or that these discoveries are of universal interest. And all agree that when a particular tradition identifies a deep structure that is pertinent everywhere, the presuppositions that make that discovery possible are to be honored. Other traditions look deep within their own resources to find whether or not some analogous pattern exists. If so, it is to be cultivated; if not, a conversion or borrowing of some sort is often possible. Confronted with the argument that the authority of international law might have theological roots, however, many scholars ride off like Ichabod in all directions.

To be sure, the question of theology is awkward. Few want to convert and fear being forced to do so. Besides, much that is called theology is simply the semirationalized assertion of a privileged perspective containing elements of magic, superstition, and ignorance. Furthermore, a religious perspective may bring violence if it is convinced that the ultimate forces of the universe need defending to the death. But we have long known that religion is high voltage, that it can electrocute as well as energize. That is less reason to neglect it than to pay it careful attention. Certainly twentieth-century attempts to construct societies on postreligious and antitheological grounds have brought disasters of their own.

But if God is the deep foundation of everything, as theology holds, and if we can know this in any significant way, why do we not already have a world order and, indeed, why do our current political and international structures not more nearly approximate a graceful social order? The answer lies in the unavoidably theological concept of sin. The will is joined perfectly to the right and the good only in God, and therefore always imperfectly in humans. Human beings are always inclined to crime and corruption. Thus, they need to have not only a personal relationship to God but a structured social ecology that constrains their worst inclinations. Law helps create that environment. It must wrestle with the problems of crime, control situations that allow corrupt interests to evolve into exploitation or erupt into war, and sustain a decent social order under conditions in which sin, corruption, and violence are never fully banished. Theology must wrestle with the question of what saving powers—in the face of sin—provide the best prospect for repentance, forgiveness, and renewal internally, and for responsible and reformed living externally, and thus construct a public argument about what law must defend.

Force is always necessary for law to be effective, but it is resisted when it is used by an unacknowledged authority. If the regulatory structures in civil society, domestic or international, are held to be without moral and spiritual legitimacy, law is systematically ignored, avoided, or subverted. It is not quite true, as has been claimed, that power corrupts; it is that human sinfulness seeks to accumulate power to exploit the existing corruption and to secure acknowledgment of its authority. In this way, the law itself becomes a source of crime and corruption. We need, then, checks not only on power but on legitimacy. There must be limits to law, in part because law is incapable of generating the moral authority that sustains it.

What generates moral authority and can limit crime, corruption, and the legitimized distortion of law? More than anything else, this depends on the formation of networks of mutuality, sacrifice, affection, and responsibility that create and sustain trust and trustworthiness. Where these networks are absent, law alone cannot hold relationships together. In personal life, we see relationships of friendship and love in, for example, parents who give years of their lives to nurture the next generation. In public life, we see some who are willing to assume responsibility for the general shape of things: philanthropists who donate their wealth to public works; public servants who suffer abuse from opponents yet still carry out their duties; voters who vote against their private interests for the common good; and soldiers who give their lives that others may live.

Above all, we see this in religious communities, where people not only face the difficulties of personal and interpersonal life, forming the networks of trust that are at the core of every civil order, but reflect on the most important questions. The portion of the population that does this, and the portion of our lives wherein we grasp the significance of this, is close to the soul of civilization. The patterns of life and the institutions sustained by these forms of giving and community are the means by which humans flourish and are preserved from their own worst tendencies.

The institutions, especially the churches, that do these things on a world scale are few, feeble, and frail. Most of the theological world is quite realistic about this, yet it has never believed that the world will be saved by governments. A viable civil society, global in scope, supporting a comprehensive vision of justice and developing a moral and spiritual network of trusting relationships may, however, preserve us from some of the imperialism, ethnocentrism, and exploitation to which we are prone in our dealings with one another.

It is not clear that there is moral progress in history apart from this. Souls today are not notably more perfect than in other ages; Christian hearts are not noticeably more pure than in other religions. Among us, love is not more dedicated than among our forebears, beliefs are not more sincerely held than in other faiths, and habits are not obviously more virtuous than in other times or places. But the possibilities of a wider, more comprehensive cross-cultural order of justice, modulated and sustained by a concrete company of those committed to love, coupled with a quest for God's truth, and justice, may signal a real gain. Such an order would at once disperse power (because it recognizes that corruption constantly distorts us all), allow sufficient concentration of power to control crime, protect the human rights of all, evoke a vigorous participation in civil society, and, especially, provide for the freedom of those communities of faith that remind us that we live under a moral order not of our own making and need resources and guidance we cannot ourselves supply.

At present, though the structures of legitimacy, the tissues of an international civil society, and the moral and spiritual fabric of faith are not sufficiently universal to sustain a global order, they are sufficiently on the horizon that theology must join with leaders in other fields to establish the conditions under which these things can be made more actual. It is potentially a "calling" of our time to be engaged, under God's watchful eye, in cross-cultural research and teaching, in developing new forms of global communication, in struggling with the global implications of disease and poverty, and in seeking to improve international institutions, including the many nongovernmental associations that are building the networks of trust between peoples from the inside out.

Today the material foundations of a global civilization are closer to hand than at any time in human history, thanks in substantial measure to the influence of world-transforming religious impulses that in previous ages inspired trade, missions, and the founding of schools and universities. As a result, it is easier to demonstrate the interdependence of different modes of interaction and the need for wider agreement. Above all, the contention of theology that we live in a common universe created by a single, just, and loving God, and both do and should share a common destiny and therefore need a common ethic, is recognized, implicitly if not explicitly, by all those who are concerned about ecology, peace, and human rights. Theology contends that because of God, we can speak of taking responsibility for the world. Without God, we remain an aggregate of peoples, each with our own gods, cultures, and histories but without duties to one another or to the world as a whole.

The problem is this: we do not yet have a worldwide civil society, even if we recognize that something greater than what we now have is beginning to emerge. But the New Jerusalem, the Kingdom of God, is not present, and stands forever beyond history. The best we can do within history is to strive humbly for greater degrees of duty, virtue, and order in the depths of our will and in the delicate arrangements of common life, and to work toward wider networks of federated interdependence, establishing each provision as close as possible to the universal moral order we almost know.

In concert with a necessary theological vision, the quests for a new international order will have to become not only more substantively just and practically enforceable, but more orthodox, more catholic, more ecumenical, more reformed and reforming, and more attentive to the interfaith realities of our world than they are in any chapter in this volume. Nevertheless, the efforts here to clarify the standards, arguments, and guidelines by which we can imagine what that kind of an order might look like are a blessing to humanity and may prove to be *ad majorem gloriam dei*.

NOTES

1. See Paul Kennedy, *Preparing for the Twenty-First Century* (New York: Random House, 1993).

2. See, for example, Frantz Fanon, *The Wretched of the Earth* (New York: Grove Press, 1968).

3. Richard J. Barnet and John Cavanagh, *Global Dreams: Imperial Corporations and the New World Order* (New York: Simon and Schuster, 1994).

4. See, for examples, Jean-François Lyotard, *The Postmodern Condition: A Report on Knowledge* (Minneapolis: University of Minnesota Press, 1984), and Alasdair Mac-

Intyre, *Whose Justice? Which Rationality?* (Notre Dame, IN: University of Notre Dame Press, 1988).

5. See "The Future of Religious Liberty in Russia," *Emory International Law Review* 8, no. 1 (Spring 1994), entire issue, and Charles Ville-Vicencio, *A Theology of Reconstruction: Nation-building and Human Rights* (Cambridge: Cambridge University Press, 1992).

6. Current discussions about how we can reliably know these things can be found in A. W. Musschenga, et al., eds., *Morality, Worldview, and Law: The Idea of a Universal Morality and Its Critics* (Maastricht: Van Gorcum, 1992), and Arthur Dyck, *Rethinking Rights and Responsibilities* (Cleveland: Pilgrim Press, 1994).

7. See Max L. Stackhouse and Stephen Healey, "Religion and Human Rights: A Theological Apologetic," in J. Witte and J. Van der Vyver, eds., *Religious Human Rights*, Vol. 1 (The Hague: Martinus Nijhoff, 1996), 85–516.

8. See Mark W. Janis, ed., *The Influence of Religion on the Development of International Law* (The Hague: Martinus Nijhoff, 1991), especially 137–46.

9. Ernst Troeltsch, *The Social Teachings of the Christian Churches*, trans. O. Wyan (New York: Harper, 1934).

10. See my *Creeds, Society, and Human Rights: A Study in Three Societies* (Grand Rapids: Eerdmans Publishers, 1985).

11. These are variously treated in John Witte, Jr., and Frank S. Alexander, eds., *The Weightier Matters of the Law: Essays on Law and Religion* (Atlanta: Scholars Press, 1988); Harold J. Berman, *Law and Revolution* (Cambridge, MA: Harvard University Press, 1983); Brian Tierney, *The Crisis of Church and State* (Englewood Cliffs, NJ: Free Press, 1964); Jacques Ellul, *The Theological Foundation of Law* (New York: Seabury Press, 1960); James Hastings Nichols, *Democracy and the Churches* (Philadelphia: Westminster Press, 1961); and Georg Jellinek, *The Declaration of the Rights of Man and of Citizens*, reprint ed. (Westport, CT: Hyperion Press, 1979).

12. This is a main theme of Reinhold Niebuhr's monumental treatment of theological anthropology, *The Nature and Destiny of Man*, 2 vols. (New York: Scribner's, 1939–41). The history of theology is reviewed in terms of this distinction by James Luther Adams, *On Being Human Religiously* (Boston: Beacon Press, 1976), ch. 4.

13. The unsurpassed comparative study of these is F. W. Dillistone, *The Structure of the Divine Society* (Philadelphia: Westminster Press, 1951). A Catholic statement that bends toward certain Protestant themes in this same period is collected in Jacques Maritain, *The Social and Political Philosophy of Jacques Maritain* (New York: Charles Scribner's Sons, 1955); a Protestant view that does the reverse is Emil Brunner, *Christianity and Civilization* (New York: Charles Scribner's Sons, 1949).

14. While the Aristotelian view is identified with Roman Catholic and the Kantian with Protestant thought, both touch the cosmopolitan perspective. See Richard Neuhaus and George Weigel, eds., *Being Christian Today* (Washington, DC: Ethics and Public Policy Center, 1992); David Hollenbach, *Claims in Conflict* (New York: Paulist Press, 1982); and my *Creeds, Society, and Human Rights*.

15. See Joshua Mitchell, *Not By Reason Alone: Religion, History and Identity in Early Modern Political Thought* (Chicago: University of Chicago Press, 1993).

16. Louis Henkin, *How Nations Behave: Law and Foreign Policy*, 2nd ed. (New York: Columbia University Press, 1979), 212.

17. Max Weber, *Economy and Society*, 3 vols., trans. by G. Roth and C. Wittich (New York: Bedminster Press, 1968), esp. vol. 2, ch. 8 and vol. 3, ch. 14. Weber's

argument is best grasped in the context of his comments on law in his five volumes of studies of religion.

18. Max L. Stackhouse, D. McCann, et al., eds., *On Moral Business: Classical and Contemporary Sources on Ethics and Economic Life* (Grand Rapids, MI: Eerdmans Publishers, 1995). See also Max L. Stackhouse, *Public Theology and Political Economy* (Lanham, MD: Scholars Press, 1991).

19. In some areas of engaged reconciliation, the increased role of religion is recognized, if not yet the theoretical importance of theological views. See, for instance, Douglas Johnston and Cynthia Sampson, eds., *Religion, the Missing Dimension of Statecraft* (New York: Oxford University Press, 1994).

Islamic Ethics in International Society

SOHAIL H. HASHMI

> [Mahomet] prit de la morale du Christianisme et du Judaisme, ce qui lui
> sembla le plus convenable aux peuples des climats chauds.
>
> —*M. Savary*, Le Coran, *1783*

FOR THE past fourteen centuries, Westerners have not known quite what to think of Islam. Western and Islamic civilizations are inextricably linked in origins, histories, and even, to a large degree, ethical values, and yet the encounter has been far from easy. Medieval Europeans considered Islam, as Albert Hourani has observed, "with a mixture of fear, bewilderment and uneasy recognition of a kind of spiritual kinship."[1] Modern Europeans puzzled over the place of Islam in their emerging "international society." Today, Islam still remains a source of confusion and concern for many in the West. At the end of the twentieth century, many scholars of international politics are returning to an emphasis on civilizations—not individuals or states—as the most significant unit of analysis for studying international relations. Often they conclude that international society will, for the foreseeable future, consist of civilizations that clash rather than cooperate.[2] Islamic civilization emerges in this literature as the most potent remaining threat to building a liberal international order.

My purpose in this chapter is not to enter this debate, at least not directly. Rather, I intend to present, first, the range of ideas that characterize both historical and contemporary Islamic thought on the character and structure of international society, and, second, my own suggestions for a normative Islamic framework for the evolution of international society. My suggestions assume the need for Muslims to disentangle Islamic ethics from medieval Islamic law (*shariʿa*); to understand the Qur'an and the traditions (*sunna*) of the Prophet in their historical context; and to elaborate new principles of shariʿa on issues relating to international society by treating the Qur'an as a complete ethical system.

Two points should be emphasized at the outset of any discussion of Islam in contemporary international politics. First, it is important to appreciate the unity as well as diversity in Islamic ethical and political thought. The unity emerges from a consensus among virtually all Muslim communities on the authenticity of the Qur'anic text as it exists today. Moreover, there is general agreement among all four Sunni schools of jurisprudence as well as the dominant Shi'ite school on the authenticity of the Prophetic sayings and actions (*hadith*) as found in authoritative medieval collections. Although the interpretation of specific traditions has generated controversy among Muslim scholars since the earliest period, their disputes do not challenge the general and consistent moral framework that emerges from the corpus of the hadith literature.

The existence of a consensus among Muslims regarding the authenticity of the "canonical" sources for an Islamic ethical framework does not, however, lessen the significance of the diversity in medieval and modern moral reasoning. As critics of the "clash of civilizations" thesis have pointed out, the greatest danger of such an emphasis on civilizations is to make them into holistic, nonporous units. There is nothing, of course, more porous than the boundaries of civilizations. Islamic civilization is no exception. Indeed, Islamic civilization has historically evinced a strong syncretistic inclination, adapting easily to specific cultural conditions as the Islamic faith spread through Africa, Asia, and Europe. It is utterly meaningless today to speak of an Islamic "tradition" or "civilization" as a monolithic force operating in international politics.

This brings us to the second point: Islamic thought today is in a state of flux. This situation is particularly acute in Islamic political thought, for Muslims have yet to formulate a coherent response to European political ideas that began to spread in Muslim countries in the nineteenth century. Western thought has provoked opinions about the constitution of a legitimate Islamic political order across a wide ideological spectrum. The current "Islamic revival," manifested in diverse forms in virtually all Muslim societies, is part of a two-century-old Muslim response to a world order shaped and ruled by the West. Since no "authoritative" body exists to interpret and codify the "orthodox" Islamic position, this response is likely to be the source of controversy and conflict well into the next century.

ISLAMIC ETHICS: UNIVERSALISTIC OR PARTICULARISTIC?

The Qur'an is the source of Islamic ethics, yet it is not a book on Islamic ethics. Human beings have been left to discern God's purpose for his creation from within the 6236 verses revealed in Arabic to the Prophet Muhammad over the course of twenty-three years. Throughout this period, the Qur'an addresses itself to *all* human beings (39:41); its ethical framework is presented as one of universal applicability, "a message to all the worlds" (81:27). For the Prophet's community, and for all successive Muslim communities, the Qur'an was accepted as a matter of faith to be the basis of Islamic ethics and law, God's final revelation to man.

And yet what of those human beings who choose not to accept the Qur'an as God's revelation or faith in God as the basis of any ethical system? How can a system of religious ethics, though claiming universal relevance, transcend the particularism of faith?

The Qur'an is aware of this concern and implicitly addresses it in a single enigmatic verse:

> When your Lord drew forth from the Children of Adam, from their loins, their descendants, and made them testify concerning themselves [saying] "Am I not your Lord?" they said, "Yes, we do testify" [this], lest you should say on the Day of Judgement: "Of this we were unaware" (7:172).

Despite the human proclivity to stray from God's commandments or to deny them altogether, each human soul is party to a primeval covenant, a covenant linking it with all other created things who acknowledge their Lord. The covenant establishes the reality of a human conscience, an ingrained aware-ness within each human being not only of the existence of God, but also of God's laws, so that when divine justice is ultimately dispensed, no soul can plead innocence through ignorance.

How do human beings discern God's laws? For medieval Muslim scholars, the answer was self-evident: through God's final revelation, the Qur'an, as interpreted and enforced by the traditions of the Prophet. But what if the Qur'an and the sunna are silent or ambiguous on a specific issue? The legal controversy that inevitably arose on this point in turn fueled a broader theo-logical controversy on the question: What makes God's laws "good" or "right"? Although the debate was conducted by a range of writers over two centuries, it centered on the ethical objectivism favored by the Mu'tazilites and the ethical voluntarism argued by the Ash'arites.

The earliest schools of Islamic jurisprudence were established by men ad-vocating *ijtihad al-ra'y* (legal judgment based on reason). The advocates of *ra'y* found support in the ethical objectivism of the Mu'tazilites. Revelation could be supplemented by reason, the Mu'tazilites argued, because truth and falsehood, right and wrong, are objective categories independent of God's will. Revelation supplements reason in confirming the value of certain ac-tions, particularly those involving man's obligations toward God, such as prayer, fasting, etc. Nevertheless, reason unaided by revelation is adequate in confirming the specific dictates of revelation. Although the Qur'an presents alms-giving as good action by virtue of divine command, for example, reason also demonstrates the value of charity in fostering individual virtue and pro-moting social welfare.

The early juristic preference for ra'y was steadily challenged by later schools who espoused *ijtihad al-qiyas* (legal interpretation based on analogy). Instead of being guided by the public welfare and principles of equity, the jurist was to deduce law through strict analogy with cases in the Qur'an and sunna. This shift away from an emphasis on reason in legal interpretation was mirrored by the rise of the Ash'arite school, which fiercely denounced the ethical objectivism of the Mu'tazilites. The Ash'arites held that God's power could not be subject to any objective ethical values; rather, ethical value was derived entirely from God's command. Man discovers right action through God's grace to his creation, through the scriptures, and through the actions of divinely inspired prophets. These sources of divine law are the only arbiters of the moral content of specific actions. "He who does not validly know the law," Abu al-Qasim al-Ansari (d. 1118) wrote, "does not validly know that a bad action is bad."[3]

By the twelfth century, in part for political reasons that had nothing to do with the intellectual merits of either position, the Ash'arite view had emerged as the orthodoxy in Sunni intellectual circles. The triumph of the Ash'arites had profound consequences for the evolution of Islamic conceptions of ethics, philosophy, and law in general, especially with regard to questions concerning international society. The emphasis on revelation placed those most familiar with revelation, the *ulama*, in a privileged position, while increasing political instability coupled with pressures from various Abbasid rulers forced the *ulama* toward greater conservatism in their legal interpretation.[4] In the tenth and eleventh centuries, further development of the law was seriously curtailed with the "closing of the gates of ijtihad." While this event was more mythical than real—for legal interpretation continued—the ethos that gripped Islamic scholarship was deeply resistant to critical inquiry and change. The consequences for Islamic political thought were particularly dire. The fact that the work of an eighth-century jurist, al-Shaybani (d. 804), remains today an essential source on international relations typifies the stagnation of Islamic political thought.

Another consequence of the Ash'arites' victory was emphasis on the particularistic over the universalistic aspects of the Qur'anic revelation. Human beings could gain true knowledge of right and wrong only by strict adherence to God's revealed will, as codified in the shari'a. This emphasis on the law, as George Hourani has observed, "must have undermined the confidence of ordinary Muslims in their ability to make sound ethical judgments."[5] Moreover, it could only have heightened perceptions of the exclusiveness of the Muslim community: if even the ordinary Muslim could not be confident of ethical behavior without strict conformity to shari'a, then how much more astray must the non-Muslim be?

Although the Mu'tazilites ceased to exist as a distinct theological school by the thirteenth century, their arguments continued to figure in later theological disputes. Their emphasis upon reason as a source of knowledge of God's will decisively influenced, in particular, the development of Shi'ite theology and law. In Sunni Islam, echoes of the Mu'tazilite-Ash'arite controversy may be heard in the discourse of the Islamic revival beginning in the mid-nineteenth century. For modernists like Sayyid Ahmad Khan (d. 1898), Muhammad 'Abduh (d. 1905), and Muhammad Iqbal (d. 1938), the rejuvenation of Islamic culture could occur only through a reexamination of the shari'a in light of modern conditions. This reexamination required the disavowal of two cherished principles of Islamic orthodoxy: the literal interpretation of the Qur'an and predeterminism. In reopening the Qur'an to interpretation, the modernists resorted to the instrument of the earliest Muslim jurists, ijtihad al-ra'y, human reason guided by principles of equity and public interest. In opposing predeterminism, they found scriptural support in the Qur'anic verse: "Truly God does not change the state of a people until they change their own state" (13:12). Muslim history went horribly astray, the modernists argued, when Muslims abjured a central principle of Islamic ethics: man's moral responsibility for his own fate.

Among contemporary intellectuals, Fazlur Rahman (d. 1988) has made particularly important contributions in applying a rationalist, modernist approach to Islamic reform. In several essays on Islamic ethics, Rahman argues that the Qur'anic message should be seen not as a series of legal pronouncements, but essentially as a moral code upon which a legal system can be constructed. The "right" legal principles, Rahman suggests, are those that foster the just and equitable social order that the Qur'an consistently promotes, when it is considered as a complete and consistent ethical system. He is, in effect, rejecting Ash'arite voluntarism when he writes: "This is where the Muslim legal tradition, which essentially regarded the Qur'an as a lawbook and not *the religious source* of the law, went so palpably wrong."[6]

Of course, opening the Qur'an to reinterpretation will not lead all Muslims to the same conclusions. Thus it was inevitable that the Islamic revival would be characterized by two competing visions, the second—for lack of a better word—being the fundamentalist. Fundamentalist thinkers such as Sayyid Qutb (d. 1966) and Abu al-A'la Maududi (d. 1979) share the modernists' concern with the malaise afflicting Islamic civilization. They also share the modernists' conviction in ijtihad as a necessary instrument for rethinking Islam. They diverge fundamentally from the modernists, however, on the substantive conclusions to which their ijtihad leads. Their reinterpretation of the Qur'an ends not with a general moral code or an ethical framework; it ends with the confirmation of divine law, albeit a law more in keeping with the "authentic" message of the Qur'an. The duty of the Muslim community (and ideally the Islamic state) is to apply this law, for "the basis of the Islamic message is that one should accept the shari'a without any question and reject all other laws. . . . This is Islam. There is no other meaning of Islam."[7]

Both the modernist and the fundamentalist positions are based upon the claim of Qur'anic authenticity. Both can be derived from the Qur'an. How then are we to resolve the issue of the universality or particularity of Qur'anic ethics? Are Muslims fated to remain forever mired in theological disputes on this point? Perhaps. But before we leave altogether confused the topic of Islamic ethics, we should turn to the Qur'an itself.

A superficial reading of the Qur'an readily indicates why Ash'arite voluntarism and even more literalist schools emerged as the orthodoxy in medieval theology.[8] First, the Qur'an clearly rejects human subjectivism as the basis of

ethical value. The "good" or "right" are not simply what human beings believe them to be. The human intellect is incapable of *always* discerning truth
from error. The Qur'an frequently links right knowledge (*'ilm*) with faith
(*iman*) and contrasts it with following human desires and passions (*hawa*) (see
in particular 35:8, 45:18, 23). Clearly the Qur'anic message is that an individual or communal life not based on faith and submission to God's laws (*islam*)
is one fraught with actual or potential moral turpitude.

But does the Qur'an foreclose the possibility of *any* independent right
moral judgment by human beings? Can there never be a righteous unbeliever
in the Islamic view? The Qur'an never directly addresses this issue, focusing
instead on its central message: the virtues of faith over disbelief. As Hourani
observes, "From its unquestioning simplicity, much of its religious force is
derived."[9] Read straightforwardly, the Qur'an again seems to preclude the
possibility of righteousness without faith, consistently linking the two in the
formulaic phrase: "Those who believe and do good deeds."

At the same time, the Qur'an accepts the fact that there will always be
unbelievers. They are also part of God's unknown plan for humanity. Is the
Muslims' relationship to them to be determined simply on the basis of their
faith or lack thereof, or upon their actual behavior determined by their own
moral understanding? I will explore some of the answers that Muslims have
historically given to these questions in more detail below when considering
the issues of human rights and international diversity. Here suffice it to say
that I agree with the argument developed by George Hourani and implicitly
embraced by the modernists. The Qur'anic text stresses the perils of a moral
system based entirely on natural reason, but nowhere does it preclude the
exercise of reason in the search for moral truths. Indeed, several verses suggest that reason is a correlate to revelation. God's presence and the truth of
his laws are presented as accessible through human contemplation of nature
and nature's laws. Several verses on this theme are prefaced by: "What will
make clear to you (that is, your reason) . . . ?" and again "Have you not considered . . . ?" The rejecter of faith (*kafir*) commits a double act of rebellion,
one against revelation, the other against his own reason.

Since the Qur'an leaves open the possibility of right moral judgment based
upon reason, it must at the same time leave open the possibility that human
beings are capable of moral action without faith. The objection that lack of
faith will *sometimes* lead to wrong moral judgments and hence wrong actions
can easily be dismissed. For not even faith can assure *absolute* knowledge of
the truth or even more freedom from wrong actions. Whether good deeds
alone are sufficient to earn God's grace in the afterlife is a question the Qur'an
never addresses. But surely the Qur'an does envision, *in this life*, the possibility of an international society consisting of good believers and unbelievers as
well as bad believers and unbelievers, each to be "brought back to God."
"Then shall every soul be paid what it earned, and none shall be dealt with
unjustly" (2:281).

CONSTITUTION AND LEGITIMATE AUTHORITY

Medieval Islamic thought on international relations was built on the premise that the Muslims form a distinct and separate community. This belief was derived from unambiguous Qur'anic verses and the practice of the Prophet. It led to the elaboration by medieval jurists of an international law (*siyar*) whose foundation was the bifurcation of the world into two spheres: *dar al-Islam* (the abode of Islam) and *dar al-harb* (the abode of war). Contemporary Islamic thought on international relations, I will argue, has moved away from this medieval bifurcation. Yet contemporary Muslim theorists—modernists as well as fundamentalists—agree that the Muslims are and should form a distinct multinational society within international society. I will begin, therefore, by considering the constitution of the Muslim community and then move on to Muslim views on the constitution of international society generally.

The Muslim Community

Shortly after his arrival in Medina in 622 C.E., the Prophet concluded a series of agreements that historians have preserved collectively as the "Constitution of Medina." These documents comprised, in essence, a "social contract," freely entered by all parties, that outlined the mutual rights and obligations of members of the Muslim community, the role of the Prophet, and the Muslims' relationship with non-Muslim residents of Medina. They established the framework for the first Islamic state and its dealings with outsiders. They also diminished tribalism as the basis for Muslim identity and society and replaced it with the community of the faithful, the Muslim *umma*. From that day, the belief that all Muslims everywhere form a single community has agitated Muslim theorists and activists, with far-reaching political implications.

The Qur'an endows the word *umma* (or its plural, *umam*) with a variety of meanings. The common element that emerges from its use with regard to human beings is that of moral community. Thus, mankind in its primordial state is described as having being "one *umma*" (2:213). It has since lost this unity, having splintered into a multiplicity of communities professing or denying faith in God. The disputes that divide human beings, the Qur'an suggests, arise from human folly, since God Himself is consistent in revealing His true nature to man through a series of prophets, each of them *muslim* (2:132, 128; 21:92). There is no objective basis for ethical diversity, only willful human distortion.

The Muslim umma, by accepting the truth of the Qur'an as revealed to Muhammad, is heir to the primeval contract that God made with all human souls on the day they witnessed, "Truly you are our Lord." All human beings are therefore potentially members of the Muslim umma. And now that the umma has been realized, it is the Muslims' duty, the Qur'an admonishes, to remain a cohesive community witnessing God's truth: "And hold fast, all together, by the rope which God (stretches out for you) and be not divided among yourselves" (3:103). The Qur'anic injunctions are augmented by several Prophetic traditions, including the famous "Farewell Sermon": "Every Muslim is the brother of every Muslim and the Muslims constitute one brotherhood."[10]

Historically, of course, this ethical injunction went unfulfilled almost immediately after the death of the Prophet Muhammad in 632 c.e. The Muslim community was rent by disputes stemming from both politics and dogma, the most serious and enduring of these being the Sunni-Shi'ite split on the issue of legitimate authority. For the Sunni majority, the Muslim umma was viewed as constituting not just a moral or social community, but a body politic as well. Legitimate authority was invested in the single *imam*, who, as the *khalifat rasul Allah* (successor to the Messenger of God), was theoretically the man considered by the community to mirror most closely the qualities of the Prophet. But with the murder of the fourth caliph, 'Ali ibn Abi Talib, in 661 c.e., political power passed to a series of traditional dynasties.

Although historical realities diverged almost at once from the ideals of the united umma and the just imam, Sunni theory was slow to assimilate such changes. Al-Mawardi (d. 1058), the author of one of the most important Sunni treatises on political theory, still explicitly denies the possibility of two imams simultaneously existing, thus foreclosing the possibility of legitimate political divisions in the umma.[11] This theory is taken to an extreme by Ibn Jama'a (d. 1333), who suggests that anyone able to install himself in power, even though he is otherwise not qualified, is the rightful imam and Muslims are bound to obey him. The reason given for obedience to the usurper is, remarkably, so that the unity, and presumably the stability, of the Muslim community would not be disturbed.[12] The one check left upon the imam was the shari'a, whose integrity was to be guarded by the 'ulama. Any ruler who systematically violates or repudiates the shari'a ceases to be imam and it is incumbent upon the Muslim community to find another.

The theory problematically assumes that a usurper is not necessarily a tyrant. Better to tolerate the corruption of one law, that pertaining to legitimate authority, than to risk the overthrow of the law altogether. Though other theorists did not formulate the issue in such stark terms, the practical impact of Sunni theory was to establish an autocracy with little recourse available to the ordinary Muslim except an "appeal to heaven." That Sunni theorists would accept it reflects the extreme political instability that characterized the central Islamic lands throughout the medieval period.

An attempt to merge the ideals of caliphal authority with the realities of kingly power was made by Ibn Khaldun (d. 1406) in the *Muqaddima*. Royal power is subsumed under the authority of the caliph, because his duty is to establish an order that promotes the Muslims' well-being in this world as well as in the next. Ibn Khaldun notes differences of opinion concerning the possibility of more than one imam, but concludes that the welfare of the Muslims may require the presence of many imams ruling distinct and far-removed territories. This view, he acknowledges, is disputed among scholars.[13]

Six hundred years later, disputes over the constitution of the Muslim world and legitimate authority within it continue. Such disputes, have, if anything, become even more vigorous in the twentieth century, as Muslims face the challenge of defining Islamic political life in a world shaped by others, and particularly according to the Western idea of territorial nationalism.

The ongoing discourse on the connections between nationalism, the territorial state, and Islam is exceedingly complex. We may, however, divide Muslim political thought into three categories. The first may be called the "statist" because it fully embraces the legitimacy of the territorial state. Its proponents tend to be secularists, and may be further divided into two groups. One strand of "Islamically sensitive" secularists attempts to appropriate, coopt, or coexist with Islam in mutually supportive but separate spheres. Islam is regarded as a key source of national identity but otherwise devoid of practical political significance. Another strand sees organized Islam as a threat to national integration or modernization and therefore attempts to eliminate Islam from public life. The secularists have yet to disentangle convincingly the link between religion and politics in Islam. Not surprisingly, they remain peripheral to Islamic political discourse.

The second category is that of the "Islamic internationalists." Its advocates are mostly modernists whose aim is to reconcile Islamic ethical ideals with prevailing realities. Their argument favors accepting separate Muslim states as the best way of meeting the needs of the different Muslim peoples. Yet they are quick to assert that their vision of nationalism does not eliminate the existence of international obligations that transcend the interests of individual states. Several modernist thinkers, including Muhammad Iqbal, 'Abd al-Razzaq al-Sanhuri (d. 1971), and Mohammad Talaat al-Ghunaimi, have suggested that the concept of the umma requires at least some degree of transnational cooperation—a "Muslim League of Nations," to borrow Iqbal's characterization.[14] The existence of the Organization of the Islamic Conference (OIC) and a host of other multilateral Islamic institutions is testimony to the influence of these internationalist ideals.

The third category comprises those who may be called the "Islamic cosmopolitans," and who are often drawn from the ranks of fundamentalist thinkers. The latter argue that the division of Muslims into sovereign, territorially delimited states has no legitimacy in Islam because it violates the Qur'an's ethics of Islamic universality and Muslim solidarity, and because it is a vestige of European imperialism intended to maintain the weakness of the Muslim community. Abu al-A'la Maududi, the founder of the most important Islamic party in South Asia, actively campaigned on these grounds against the creation of Pakistan during the 1940s. He was supported in this by a broad spectrum of religious opinion in India. Likewise, Ayatollah Khomeini described the territorial state system as the "product of the deficient human mind."[15] Iran was to be the center for the propagation of the universal Islamic revolution that would sweep away "un-Islamic" regimes everywhere. Maududi and Khomeini eventually reconciled themselves to existing realities: Maududi settled in Pakistan and played a significant role in that country's politics for nearly three decades. Khomeini's later speeches extol the unique virtues of the Iranian nation. But even though Maududi and Khomeini proved willing to accommodate to political conditions, it would be incorrect to assume that they fundamentally altered their conceptions of Islamic political order, or that they ended their lives as Pakistani or Iranian nationalists.

The details of an Islamic international system and the legitimate means to bring it about remain only vaguely defined in the works of both modernists and fundamentalists. There is broad consensus on one point, however: judged according to Islamic ideals, the current state of Islamic international politics is woefully defective. The history of the Organization of the Islamic Conference illustrates the general discontent. In 1969, twenty-four Muslim states voted to establish an international organization to further mutual cooperation on the basis of the "immortal teachings of Islam." Ever since its founding, the OIC has been repeatedly assailed, particularly by the fundamentalists, for failing to act as an instrument of the collective Muslim community, rather than the assortment of fifty states who are today its real constituents. As the first truly universal Muslim organization, the OIC has come to be viewed by many as a "proto-caliphate," the potential embodiment of a distinct Islamic subsystem within the international system. Despite the vociferous attacks upon it in recent years for its dismal performance in the Gulf War and in the conflict in Bosnia, many Muslim activists continue to hope that the OIC may yet evolve into a political manifestation of the united Muslim umma, as the Islamic revolution triumphs in other Muslim states.

Islam in the International Arena

In the Constitution of Medina, Jewish tribes living in the town are declared to be an umma alongside the Muslim umma. Their religious autonomy is specifically guaranteed and they are brought within a "collective security" framework for the defense of Medina. Since the Jews entered the pact as a free and equal contracting party, the constitution may also be seen as the first "international" agreement in Islamic history.

Subsequent treaties between Muslims and non-Muslims continued the precedent established in Medina of acknowledging a broad sphere of autonomy for the "People of the Book": Jews, Christians, Sabeans, and Zoroastrians, essentially all the religious communities believing in a scripture that were known to the Prophet. But subsequent agreements between the Muslims and other scripturaries were not premised on the equality of the contracting parties. Instead, the Muslims were clearly the superior party and the agreement took the form of a concession granted by the Prophet to the religious community.

The Prophet's approach toward non-Muslim communities may be summarized as follows: First, in accordance with revelation, he considered religious affiliation to be the basis of political organization. Second, recipients of earlier revelations were acknowledged by the Islamic state to be autonomous religious communities, to be governed in their communal affairs according to their own laws. But, third, in their relations with Muslims and other non-Muslims living within the Islamic state, the scriptuaries were to be governed by Islamic law. In return, the Islamic state was to assure their security and autonomy; they were to be *ahl al-dhimma* (protected people). These broad principles of the Prophet's practice continued to be applied by the first four caliphs as the Islamic empire experienced explosive growth.

Some two to three centuries later, jurists rationalized these historical events as the Islamic ideal, making it the basis of Islamic international law. As we observed earlier, their foremost concern was to ensure the application and preservation of the shari'a. Without divine law, society exists on the brink of anarchy in this world and perdition in the next. This understanding of the religious law led inevitably to the division of the world into two spheres: dar al-Islam, where the enforcement of shari'a regulated and harmonized relations among its constituent elements, and dar al-harb, where the absence of shari'a was presumed to foster lawlessness and insecurity.

Nevertheless, the theory did acknowledge the existence of a rudimentary "natural law" applying to relations between the two spheres. The idea of an international society was very much a part of Islamic international law, making possible diplomacy and treaties, travel and commerce, and rules of war. One of the most important aspects of siyar was the guarantee of free passage or security (*aman*) which any Muslim could give to a visitor from the dar al-harb. The converse of this provision was the obligation of Muslims traveling or residing in the dar al-harb to obey local laws, unless, of course, those laws contravened essential aspects of Islamic worship.

Natural law for the jurists was, however, clearly an insufficient basis for ordering international society. An emphasis on God's command as the ultimate source of legal validity led to a view of the dar al-Islam/dar al-harb relationship as one of active ideological contestation. The jurists' concern was to universalize application of the shari'a, their ultimate goal being to propagate the Islamic faith. If a non-Muslim government permitted the peaceful preaching of Islam within its domain, no ground for war emerged. Only if such preaching were foreclosed could the imam initiate war aimed at absorbing that domain territory into the dar al-Islam.

Jurists of the Shafi'i school interposed, between dar al-Islam and dar al-harb, a third category, *dar al-sulh* (or *dar al-'ahd*), the "abode of truce," comprising non-Muslim communities with which the Islamic state had treaty relations. According to al-Shafi'i, the truce could be contracted by the imam if necessity or the welfare of the Muslims required it. But the Shafi'i theory only suspended, not eliminated, the "contest." According to a precedent established by the Prophet's agreement with the pagan tribes of Mecca, the truce could not exceed ten years.

Muslim state practice never fully conformed to the theory, of course. As the dar al-Islam itself became factionalized, various Muslim rulers found support in the dar al-harb for their political ambitions. Yet the general outlines of the theory were never challenged or reformulated. The lingering influence of the medieval theory can be seen in nineteenth-century disputes among Indian 'ulama on whether British India was or was not part of dar al-Islam.

What is the status of the medieval theory today? If formal Muslim accession to the prevailing international legal regime were to determine the answer, then the medieval theory would have to be considered totally obsolete. All the Muslim-majority states are members of the United Nations. In fact, all (except the charter members) petitioned for membership within the first two years of independence. Moreover, the overwhelming majority of these states are signatories to the principal international treaties codifying international law and governing economic relations, environmental policy, and human rights. Nor does the evidence for the obsolescence of medieval theory end here. All the principles guiding relations among members of the OIC that are listed in its charter are derived from the UN Charter. These include the principles of sovereignty and equality of states, noninterference in domestic affairs, and prohibition of the use or the threat of force. Where, then, is the putative "Islamic revolt"?

The answer is not to be found in the militancy of radical Islam, which, despite its prominence in the international media, represents only a small part of Muslim opinion. Rather, it is to be found at the level of political discourse, which constrains policy options and pressures state elites to "Islamicize" their political programs. Today, every Muslim leader must make concessions to Islamic values. At the international level, such pressures were apparent when the OIC voted in 1980 to create an International Islamic Law Commission "to devise ways and means to secure representation in order to put forward the Islamic point of view before the International Court of Justice and such other institutions of the United Nations when a question requiring the projection of Islamic views arises therein."[16] Seventeen years later, this body has yet to convene, largely because the government elites who voted to form it realize that its findings may pose a challenge not only to the Western-originated international system, but to themselves as well.

I would suggest that although Muslim states have accommodated to the prevailing international norms, these norms have yet to be assimilated into Islamic political thought. These states have formally committed themselves to the principles of international law, but there has yet to occur a theoretical incorporation of these principles into a coherent, modern elaboration of Islamic international law. With or without the deliberations of the (still nonexistent) International Islamic Law Commission, Islamic discourse on international relations will remain for some time to come at the normative level, directed at what Islamic law *ought* to say on international issues. The medieval theory will continue to serve as a reference, even as modernists and fundamentalists redefine medieval views on dar al-Islam, dar al-harb, and jihad.

The modernist approach is characterized by the outright rejection of the medieval concepts or by a selective reinterpretation intended to assert the essentially nonbelligerent character of these concepts. Representative of the first approach is Mohammad Talaat al-Ghunaimi, who points out that the term *dar al-harb* is not mentioned in the Qur'an and therefore that the medieval categories have no Qur'anic basis. The theory, he concludes, is nothing more than a reflection of the historical circumstances of Abbasid jurists, and is not applicable to modern Islamic political life.[17] Marcel Boisard typifies the second approach, arguing that though the dar al-Islam/dar al-harb distinction is an intrinsic part of Islamic doctrine, it does not imply a permanent state of war between Muslims and non-Muslims. Dar al-harb is only that state where active oppression, corruption, and injustice are found, a state with which dar al-Islam obviously cannot coexist. If these conditions are present in a Muslim state, it "is identified with the 'world of war' even if its leaders claim to be Muslims."[18]

Boisard's reasoning is strikingly similar to that of the contemporary fundamentalists. Because the shari'a is today enforced in only a few Muslim states, the Muslim world cannot properly be said to constitute the dar al-Islam, except in the loose sense of a shared culture or heritage. It is, they argue, better called *dar al-nifaq*, the "abode of hypocrisy." The most radical fundamentalist groups push the argument even further. In the often-quoted manifesto of Sadat's assassins, entitled *Al-Farida al-gha'iba* ("The Lapsed Obligation"), ʿAbd al-Salam Faraj charges unspecified Muslim "rulers of this age" with apostasy because "they were raised at the tables of imperialism."[19]

Faraj's argument is representative of the fundamentalists' view of the international order. Their focus is on Western imperialism, which, they believe, continues in an unceasing war to destroy Islam. Muslim rulers who have allied themselves with the West have, in effect, declared war upon Islam. Though employing the terminology of the medieval doctrine of dar al-Islam and dar al-harb, the fundamentalists have given new content to these expressions. They may be viewed as providing an Islamic version of the broader third-world critique of dependency. When a Muslim revolutionary like Ayatollah Khomeini characterizes international relations as the struggle between the *mustakbaran* (the powerful) versus the *mustadʿafan* (the oppressed), he is employing in an Islamic context the same imagery used by many other third-world leaders. A third-world orientation is clearly evident in Khomeini's foreign policy. The Islamic Republic of Iran did not withdraw from the United Nations or renounce its commitment to the majority of international agreements ratified by the shah's regime. It did, however, promptly remove itself from the American-backed Central Treaty Organization. Like other third-world critics, the fundamentalists challenge not the constitutional order of international society, but rather the injustices of that order.

JUSTICE

Justice may be seen without oversimplification to be the core value of Islamic ethics, for it runs like a binding thread throughout the Qur'an and the Prophetic traditions. The Qur'an's conception of justice is one of universally applicable principles, valid for all human beings, regardless of their status as Muslims: "O you who believe! Stand out firmly for justice, as witnesses to God, even as against yourselves, or your parents, or your kin, and whether it be against rich or poor" (4:135). "O you who believe! Be ever steadfast in your devotion to God, bearing witness to the truth in all equity, and never let hatred of anyone lead you into the sin of deviating from justice. Be just: this is closest to piety" (5:8).

Acting justly to "witness" God's truth is, the Qur'an indicates, an individual as well as collective obligation. The Muslim umma is termed the "median" community (2:143) and also the "best" community (3:110), because it "witnesses" God's command to "enjoin the right and forbid the wrong." Both characterizations should be seen as normative, not descriptive. The Muslim umma is exceptional to other human communities only so long as it fulfills its Qur'anic obligations (47:38).

The personal and collective struggle to realize justice upon earth is the essence of jihad. S. 'Abdullah Schleifer has described jihad as "the instrument of sacralization of the social-political order in Islam,"[20] that is, as the duty to ensure that Muslim society and politics never become too divorced from Islamic ethics. Underlying the frequent use (and misuse) of this term in contemporary Muslim discourse is the widespread feeling that the realities of Muslim collective life have indeed strayed far from Islamic ideals. For the fundamentalists of the 1930s and 1940s, the Islamic movement's goal was social transformation through education and moral reform. For their less patient offspring of the 1980s and 1990s, the goal is revolutionary imposition of shari'a by an Islamic state of their own creation. In short, the object of jihad today—whether defined by modernists or by fundamentalists—is to realize justice within the Muslim umma. One cannot hope to understand the Islamic revival, in its many and varied manifestations, unless one appreciates this fundamental fact.

The range of specific issues that are addressed in Muslim discussion of international justice is, of course, vast. Here I can only comment on three of the most salient: human rights, democracy, and distributive justice.

Human Rights

Is there a conception of human rights in Islam? Debate on this issue has become so acrimonious that it threatens to obscure the real issue: the systematic abuse of human beings by states that explicitly or tacitly define themselves as "Islamic." Much Muslim writing on this topic is hopelessly apologetic, struggling to prove that Islam introduced human rights into the human vo-cabulary roughly a millennium before Western theorists "discovered" or even "appropriated" the idea. Much Western writing, in turn, is highly conten-tious, suggesting that the language of human rights is fundamentally alien to "Islam," which is usually identified solely with Islamic law (the shariʿa). Yet no adequate discussion of human rights in Islam—or any other topic—can begin without distinguishing Qur'anic ethics from its historical interpretation ex-pressed as law.

Medieval jurists clearly recognized a sphere of individual autonomy and privacy to be protected from state intervention or other arbitrary intrusion. They gave moral and legal content to this protected sphere in the form of "duties" rather than "rights." Surmounting the mutual duties of human be-ings and the mutual duties of rulers and ruled were the duties of all people to God. From God's "rights" (*huquq Allah*) stemmed all human "rights," because God has commanded justice for all His creation. A number of Prophetic tra-ditions elucidate this point, insisting that "no one truly believes until he wishes for his brother what he wishes for himself," and that "the whole of a Muslim for another Muslim is inviolable, his life, his property, and his honor."[21]

These traditions establish the mutual rights of Muslims. But what of non-Muslims? This is an area in which the shariʿa, as it has come down to us, is often at odds with modern conceptions of human rights. The discriminatory provisions of the shariʿa, while understandable in their historical context, are not justifiable, I would argue, given a *complete reading of Islamic ethics*. The Qur'anic verses quoted above (4:135 and 5:8) are in themselves entirely ade-quate to establish equity and reciprocity as the defining principles in an Is-lamic approach to universal human rights.

A problem even more important than religious discrimination is gender discrimination. This issue is extremely contentious because gender relations intrude upon so many "sacred" realms, including the regulation of sexuality and reproduction and the structure of family. The shariʿa contains many pro-visions that are incompatible with international statements on the rights of women, including the woman's status as a legal person apart from her male guardian, her rights in inheritance, her rights in marriage, divorce, and cus-tody of children, her right to work, live, and travel without a male guardian. Again, I can only repeat an argument I have made before: the discriminatory provisions of the shariʿa are based upon specific verses that were held by ju-rists to be legal injunctions. These verses are part of a broader *ethical* position that the Qur'an develops regarding gender relations. The primary result of this ethical position is to affirm women's moral *as well as* legal rights. It is historically undeniable that the Qur'an's legal injunctions—despite their dis-criminatory aspects—represent a significant advance from the status of women in pre-Islamic Arabia. So for medieval jurists there was no tension between the specific legal injunctions revealed for Medinan society and the general ethical framework. This is no longer true, however. Modern Muslims must, therefore, return to the full ethical context of the Qur'an in order to derive new legal injunctions regarding the status of modern Muslim women. Once again, the full ethical context leads us to the principles of equity and reciprocity, the logical derivatives of faith in the equality of all persons as creations of God.[22]

Democracy

The abuse of human rights is directly related to the lack of democratic institutions in the vast majority of Muslim countries. It is quite telling that the worst human rights abusers are also those Muslim regimes that openly assert that representative government is inherently incompatible with Islam. It is disheartening that such disingenuousness is accepted uncritically by many in the West who ought to know better.

So is there an Islamic conception of democracy? Medieval political theory, as we have seen, left little scope for popular participation in politics. By virtue of their enforcement of the shari'a, the caliph and his ministers were owed obedience. They were not obliged in any way to consult "the people," and though they were supposed to rule justly, there was no mechanism to remove an unjust ruler short of his death. And though European imperialism disseminated democratic ideals to the Muslim world, it did little to implement them. It did succeed, however, in connecting concepts of participatory government with a foreign, hostile culture in the minds of many Muslim activists. The choice facing Muslim peoples today is therefore a bleak one: authoritarianism, either in the name of secular nationalism or in the name of Islam. The modernist advocacy of democracy has been squeezed virtually out of existence by the two.

Virtually, but not completely: Muslim societies are not immune to the slow but steady spread of democratic aspirations throughout the world, and organizations espousing democracy and human rights have in fact sprung up all over the Muslim world during the past decade. More often than not, demands for democracy are being made in the name of Islam.

The Qur'an provides little guidance regarding the form of government God ordains for man. Muslim advocates of democracy have latched on to one brief reference to the believers as those who "conduct their affairs by mutual consultation (*shura bainahum*)" (42:38). Because the Qur'an is not explicit on this issue, I believe that the soundest argument for representative government is to be found in Islamic ethics. If social justice is best realized within a democratic framework, as I believe human experience has shown, then this is the form of government that Islam requires.

Discussions of democracy in Islam also raise questions about the status of religious minorities. *Dhimmi* status often meant political discrimination against non-Muslims as well as discrimination in personal relations. Though most of the discriminatory practices found in the shari'a can be dealt with in the same way we dealt with human rights issues, the *jizya* (poll tax), which is explicitly mentioned in the Qur'an (9:29), remains a problematic issue within a democratic framework based upon the legal equality of citizens. Although jizya was treated by some medieval writers as a badge of the dhimmis' subordinate status within the Islamic state, that was not its legal rationale. Jizya was levied upon dhimmis in compensation for their exemption from military service in the Muslim forces. If dhimmis joined Muslims in their mutual defense against an outside aggressor, the jizya was not levied.[23] It can therefore be argued that in a modern Islamic state where all citizens bear equal responsibilities of citizenship, the jizya has become redundant.

Distributive Justice

The Muslim world today includes some of the world's most fabulously wealthy states at one end of the spectrum, and some of the most hopelessly impoverished at the other. There are few countries in the middle. Signs of discontent born of poverty and economic stagnation are legion. The Islamic movements gain their most ardent supporters from the ranks of unemployed or underemployed youth in the slums of every major Muslim city. Because the gap between rich and poor continues to grow, distributive justice may well prove the most explosive issue within the Muslim world of the coming century.

In recent years, distributive justice has emerged as an important topic in discussions among Muslim scholars of "Islamic economics." Underlying these discussions is the strong Islamic ethic of providing basic subsistence for the most disadvantaged members of society. This is both an individual obligation of personal piety as well as a state responsibility for social welfare. The ethical principle is formalized as one of the five "pillars of faith" in the form of a tax on surplus wealth (*zakat*), which is to be collected by the state and used to improve the conditions of the poorest members of society.

Unfortunately, discussions of distributive justice so far have remained at a highly theoretical level. They do little but reaffirm the obligations of "Islamic society" without specifying the identity of that society in modern terms.[24] If the society within which redistribution is to take place is the individual Muslim state, then the satisfaction of distributive justice claims will do little to improve the lives of the poorest Muslims. And if society is defined inclusively as the Muslim umma, as many modernists and fundamentalists would insist it should be, then the discussion must move on to consider how, practically speaking, wealth is to be redistributed from the wealthiest to the poorest Muslim countries. The principles guiding this discussion should, I believe, be cosmopolitan ones: the welfare of the individual Muslim, and not the economic condition of the country as a whole, should be paramount. To focus on countries or states will only exacerbate the existing disparities in income within each state.

DIVERSITY

The Qur'an seems to give contradictory guidance on the issue of moral diversity. In the earlier Meccan verses, the question of faith is left to be decided by God in the next world. As for this life, the Meccan attitude is best captured in the closing line of Chapter 109: "To you your religion and to me mine." Muhammad is consoled after his initial failure to convert the pagan Meccans, as well as Jews and Christians, in the following verse: "If it had been your Lord's will, they would have all believed, all who are on earth. Will you then compel mankind against their will to believe?" (10:99).

This attitude of tolerance seems to shift in Medina, where the Qur'an becomes more aggressive and exclusivist in its polemic against not only the pagans but also Jews and Christians. The Qur'an warns Muslims in Medina not to take unbelievers (4:144) and Jews and Christians (5:51) as *awliya'*, a broad term meaning "allies," "associates," or "protectors." Moreover, the Qur'an in Medina sanctions for the first time the use of force against the Muslims' enemies. Later Qur'anic verses, revealed after years of hostility between Muslims and the pagan Meccans, desert Arabs, and the Jewish tribes of Medina, suggest a belligerent, irreconcilable attitude toward non-Muslims:

> But when the forbidden months are past, then fight and slay the pagans wherever you find them, and seize them, beleaguer them, and lie in wait for them in every stratagem [of war] (9:5).
>
> Fight against those who—despite having been given revelation before—do not believe in God nor the last day, and do not consider forbidden that which God and his Messenger have forbidden, and do not follow the religion of truth, until they pay the *jizya* with willing hand, having been subdued (9:29).

For medieval jurists attempting to rationalize the military conquests of the early Muslim caliphs, these two verses were read as providing legal injunctions regulating relations with non-Muslims. The problem, however, was how to reconcile them with the other, more tolerant verses, as well as important Prophetic precedents. To resolve this dilemma, many jurists argued that the earlier tolerant verses (which, according to one jurist, number one hundred and fourteen verses spread over fifty-six chapters!) were abrogated by the two later, more intolerant ones.[25] Unless the non-Muslims willingly paid the jizya, they were to be fought until they could be incorporated as dhimmis within the Islamic state.

On closer inspection, however, the contradictory nature of the Qur'an's attitude toward moral diversity is more apparent than real. Let us examine first the claim that the Qur'an became progressively more exclusivist and intolerant over time. This argument cannot be sustained by even a superficial examination of the chronology of revelation. As Fazlur Rahman has argued, the Qur'an's attitude toward its rejecters was developed during the Meccan period and remained fairly consistent into the Medinan period. The view that pagan Meccans, Jews, and Christians are groups distinct from the Muslims is already beginning to be articulated in the later Meccan period. This view was, of course, elaborated and developed according to the changed social and political conditions of Medina. Yet the argument of some orientalists that the Qur'an begins to emphasize the separate character of the Muslim community only when the Prophet had been rejected by Jews and Christians in Medina is not borne out.[26] And instead of steadily moving toward an attitude of war with other religious communities, the Medinan chapters contain many injunctions on toleration, including the most significant verse on this topic: "Let there be no compulsion in religion; truth stands out clear from error" (2:256).

If we turn to the content of the Qur'anic message itself, we find not changes or "breaks" but a consistent theme being progressively elaborated. The Prophet believed, from the earliest stages of his teaching, that he was bringing, not a new revelation to mankind, but the original guidance given to all the prophets acknowledged by the Jews and Christians, as well as the pagan Arabs, who considered themselves descendants of Abraham and Ishmael. The fault that the Qur'an repeatedly assigns to these people is innovation in religion, resulting ineluctably in sectarian strife. The Jews and Christians bear a particular obligation in this matter, because as self-professed believers in the one God, they are capable of discerning the essential truth of Islam *as well as each other's faith.*

> The Jews say, "The Christians have nothing to stand on," and the Christians say, "The Jews have nothing to stand on," while both recite the same book (2:113).[27]

The Qur'an thus presents Islam as the affirmation and the summation, not the denial, of earlier religions. Muslims have no monopoly on divine grace, either in this or in the next world (2:62; 5:69). The Qur'an invites Jews and Christians to join Muslims in emphasizing the essential similarities in their beliefs (3:64). And if we read in their full context the verses used by medieval jurists as to rationalize discrimination against non-Muslims, we find again the Qur'an's overriding concern with justice:

> God does not forbid you, with regard to those who do not fight you because of your faith, nor drive you out of your homes, from dealing kindly and justly with them, for God loves those who are just (60:8).

But the Qur'an does not stop with the mere toleration of diversity, which is unavoidable, given man's unique capacity for moral choice. Instead, it transforms this inevitable diversity into an opportunity to promote its own moral vision for human life on earth:

> To each among you have we prescribed a law and a way. If God had so willed, he would have made you a single people, but His plan is to test you in what he has given

you: So strive as in a race in all the virtues. The goal of you all is to God; it is he who
will show you the truth of the matters in which you differ (5:48).

CONCLUSION

In the final years of the twentieth century, a time that some have suggested
would be the end of ideology or of history itself, the oldest kind of ideology
has resumed its role in fashioning history. The "return of religion" has left
many people bewildered, frustrated, fearful. Indeed, human beings have amply
demonstrated their capacity to make out of religion a divisive, exclusivist, often
destructive force. This face of religion, whether it calls itself Islamic, Jewish,
Christian, Hindu, or Sikh, is very much in view today all over the world.

For many Westerners observing the turbulence of Muslim politics, Islam
appears adversarial, militant, even inimical to Western values and to the international society they support. Certainly there are many Muslims who share
the belief that the civilizations of Islam and the West are fated to clash. Yet,
as I have tried to show in this chapter, the contemporary Islamic revolt is as
much against internal demons as it is against the "Great Satan." The Muslim
focus today is essentially introspective. Given the widespread perception
among Muslim activists, across a wide ideological spectrum, that Muslim politics do not reflect Islamic ethics, calls for reform are aimed primarily at the
Muslim states themselves and their relations with one another, not at the
international system as a whole. The international system as a whole figures
in Muslim discourse only to the extent that it impinges upon the development
of the ideal Muslim subsystem.

The Islamic challenges to the broader international society concern not its
structure or even its emerging norms of human rights, religious tolerance,
and democracy. For many Muslims today, the notion of an international society founded on these principles is seriously threatened not by cultural pluralism or religious diversity, but by the equivocation shown by Western powers
in enforcing them. International law is called into question by the uneven
application of its principles by the very Western states who advocate it so
ardently. International institutions, most importantly the United Nations, are
suspect as having become absolutely subservient to Western interests. In the
early part of this century, the Islamic revival was fueled in part by men who
had returned from Europe thoroughly disillusioned with the moral crisis of
Western society that took it headlong into two world wars. For many Muslim
critics of international relations today, the twentieth century does indeed begin and end in Sarajevo.

There is another face of religion that social scientists often neglect, but that
is crucial to the work of moral and political philosophers. This is the central
role that religion has always played in defining the essential, timeless, and
shared qualities of human life. Religion has always been the most powerful
force for uniting human beings in moral community, for motivating them

toward constructive and humane behavior, and for emphasizing the universalistic over the particularistic aspects of human existence. Religion can at times make international order difficult, but it can also contribute to the evolution of a truly universal, representative, and just international society. To grasp this potential of religion is the common challenge facing both believers and unbelievers.

NOTES

1. Albert Hourani, *Islam in European Thought* (Cambridge: Cambridge University Press, 1991), 9.

2. Two of the most well-known and influential elaborations of this view are Bernard Lewis, "The Roots of Muslim Rage," *Atlantic Monthly* (September 1990): 47–60; and Samuel P. Huntington, "The Clash of Civilizations," *Foreign Affairs* 72 (Summer 1993): 22–49.

3. Quoted in Richard Frank, "Moral Obligation in Classical Muslim Theology," *Journal of Religious Ethics* 11 (1983): 208.

4. George Hourani, *Reason and Tradition in Islamic Ethics* (Cambridge: Cambridge University Press, 1985), 47.

5. Hourani, *Reason and Tradition*, 47.

6. Fazlur Rahman, *Major Themes of the Qur'an* (Minneapolis: Bibliotheca Islamica, 1980), 47.

7. Sayyid Qutb, *Milestones* (Indianapolis: American Trust Publications, 1993), 30.

8. I am indebted to Hourani's study of this topic in *Reason and Tradition*, 23–48.

9. Hourani, *Reason and Tradition*, 45.

10. Quoted in Muhammad Haykal, *The Life of Muhammad*, trans. Isma'il al-Faruqi (Indianapolis: American Trust Publications, 1976), 487.

11. Abu al-Hasan 'Ali al-Mawardi, *Al-Ahkam al-sultaniyya*, trans. E. Fagnan, *Les statuts gouvernementaux* (Beirut: Editions de patrimonie Arabe et Islamique, 1982), 14.

12. Muhammad ibn Ibrahim ibn Jama'a, *Tahrir al-ahkam fi tadbir ahl al-Islam* (al-Dawha: Dar al-thaqafa, 1988), 56–57.

13. Ibn Khaldun, *The Muqaddimah: An Introduction to History*, trans. Franz Rosenthal (New York: Pantheon, 1958), 1:392–94.

14. Muhammad Iqbal, *Reconstruction of Religious Thought in Islam* (Lahore: Institute of Islamic Culture, 1989), 126.

15. Quoted in Farhang Rajaee, *Islamic Values and World View: Khomeini on Man, the State, and International Politics* (Lanham, MD: University Press of America, 1983), 77.

16. 'Abdallah al-Ahsan, *OIC: The Organization of the Islamic Conference* (Herndon, VA: International Institute of Islamic Thought, 1988), 36.

17. Mohammad Talaat al-Ghunaimi, *The Muslim Conception of International Law and the Western Approach* (The Hague: Martinus Nijhoff, 1968), 104.

18. Marcel Boisard, *Humanism in Islam* (Indianapolis: American Trust Publications, 1988), 154.

19. Quoted in Johannes J. G. Jansen, *The Neglected Duty* (New York: Macmillan, 1986), 169.

20. S. 'Abdullah Schleifer, "Understanding Jihad: Definition and Methodology," *Islamic Quarterly* 27 (1983): 121.

21. Narrated by Muslim, *Sahih Muslim* (Cairo: Dar al-ihya' al-kutub al-'arabiyya, n.d.), vol. 1:67 and vol. 4:1986.

22. The religious equality of men and women is firmly established in the Qur'anic verse 33:35.

23. See Louay M. Safi, "War and Peace in Islam," *American Journal of Islamic Social Sciences* 5 (1988): 39.

24. See, for example, the proceedings of the International Institute of Islamic Economics in Munawar Iqbal, ed., *Distributive Justice and Need Fulfillment in an Islamic Economy* (Islamabad: International Institute of Islamic Economics, 1988).

25. Mohammed Arkoun, *Rethinking Islam* (Boulder, CO: Westview, 1994), 97.

26. Rahman, *Major Themes of the Qur'an*, 163–65.

27. As Fazlur Rahman comments with regard to the meaning of "Book" in this context, it does not mean "any specific revealed book" but is used "as a generic term denoting the totality of divine revelations." Rahman, *Major Themes of the Qur'an*, 164.

PART THREE

Comparative Overview

CHAPTER 14

Justice, Diversity, and Law in International Society

DAVID R. MAPEL

Of the many issues discussed in this book, two emerge as especially important. The first of these concerns the relationship between international institutions and international justice: does international justice depend on the existence of international institutions, or does justice require us to establish
such institutions? Some contributors to this volume take the view that institutions guaranteeing compliance with common rules of international society
are a necessary condition of justice between states. Others argue that justice
requires us to create such institutions.

If we take the view that justice depends upon institutions, particularly political and legal institutions, then we must begin thinking about duties of international justice within the context of contemporary international society,
understood as a society of states. Because of uncertain compliance with the
rules of international society as it is currently constituted, our duties to those
outside our own state must be understood as relatively weak. If, however, we
take the view that particular institutions are required by justice, then strong,
preexisting duties of justice between individuals throughout the world may
require the creation of a new institutions, such as a world federation of republican states or even a centralized world state. In other words, this first issue
concerning the relationship between justice and institutions emerges as an
important one because it determines our basic approach to understanding the
ethical character of international society. Central to resolving it is whether
reciprocal compliance with a common set of rules is a necessary condition of
duties of justice between states (and between individuals across states). In the
opening section of this chapter, I discuss the extent to which different views
of international society converge and diverge on the question of reciprocity.

Which considerations determine whether states can reasonably expect each
other to observe common rules? One answer is that reciprocal observance of
common rules depends on a coincidence of prudential interests. This answer
points to the need for improved mechanisms of international enforcement to
make selfish states comply with the rules and to make unselfish states less
afraid of being disadvantaged by the noncompliance of others. Yet with the
exception of some strands of legal positivism, all the viewpoints represented
in this book hold that better enforcement mechanisms are not enough to
create reliable expectations of international reciprocity. A more fundamental
transformation is required: states must move beyond a coincidence of pru-

dential interests by coming to have similar conceptions of justice or by recognizing the authority of international law. Here we reach the second, more important, issue about international society: what is the relationship between international diversity, especially moral and religious diversity, and international law?

This question is fundamental, for it is not simply selfishness and fear that lead to noncompliance but differences of belief as well. Establishing a stable international society is not simply a matter of overcoming selfishness through morality and religion; it also requires dealing with the consequences of moral and religious disagreement, at least to some extent, by achieving a common legal basis of association. But is there a set of legal principles that all religious and moral communities should endorse as a charter for their common life? Because each community addresses this question from its own perspective, are there any common rules that all members of international society can endorse? What basis for international society is there?

Reciprocity in International Society: Contractarianism and Cosmopolitanism

In this volume, John Charvet presents two arguments against the existence of a universal international society. The first is that there are no "natural" principles of justice, nor any human rights grounded on an objective moral order. All moral and legal obligations are conventional, and as a matter of fact there are no universally accepted moral or legal conventions in international relations. Second, even if principles of natural justice or universal human rights could be discovered, it is unreasonable to expect compliance with such rules in international relations, and there can be no moral or legal obligations unless there is some level of compliance. More precisely, Charvet recognizes that there are in international society some universally accepted conventions and some expectations of compliance, but he maintains that these are minimal. Let us begin with the second issue about the necessity of reciprocal compliance as a condition of moral and legal obligation, and then turn to the deeper issue of the ultimate justification and authority of moral and legal norms.

Following a standard line of thought in the contractarian tradition, Charvet argues that where there are no effective political institutions, there are generally no reliable expectations of reciprocity, and where there is no assurance of reciprocity or compliance, there can be no duties of justice. Because institutions for making and applying international law are in fact relatively weak, Charvet concludes that duties of international justice are minimal. Other contributors, like Brian Barry, suggest that Charvet has it backwards: justice is not primarily a matter of principles governing a preexisting cooperative schemes undertaken for mutual advantage. Fundamental issues of justice arise even before the emergence of particular cooperative schemes like those represented by territorial states. In particular, gross material inequalities between individual persons throughout the world call into question the idea that the basic problem of international society is one of finding principles to govern a society of states. Instead, we should focus on the needs and deserts of present and future individuals across the world and try to arrive at principles for constituting a centralized or confederal world government accordingly.

Is some minimal level of actual or expected reciprocity a necessary condition for the existence of international duties of justice? In trying to answer this question, we must not exaggerate the extent of disagreement. Let us begin by recalling the broad view of justice shared by Charvet and Barry, namely that justice concerns principles for the general regulation of behavior that no one could reasonably reject, given the common aim of establishing principles on the basis of informed, unforced agreement.[1] Here an element of reciprocity seems already to be presupposed in the idea that principles of justice assume a common aim of mutual justification. Nevertheless, we must also act justly toward the unjust, that is, toward those who will not act on principles that can be justified in this way. Far from it being the case that all principles of international justice presuppose reciprocity, then, there are elementary principles of international society, like the laws of war, that presuppose the absence of reciprocity.

With respect to distributive justice, however, all the views represented in this volume appear to take the position that at least some minimal level of actual or expected reciprocity is required. Although Barry, for example, argues that wealthy states have a stringent duty to redistribute resources, he also allows that there are circumstances in which such duties are canceled by noncompliance with more elementary duties. In the case where a ruling elite simply appropriates international aid intended for a country's poor, for example, there is no case for transferring wealth to that country, and indeed, Barry thinks, there may even be a case for military intervention. Charvet's position is similarly complex. He argues that, under current circumstances, states do not have a strong general duty to redistribute resources. But he also understands a political society to be more than an association for mutual advantage. Because it is also an association requiring authoritative norms that override self-interest, it would be misleading to say that his version of contractarianism reduces political society to a mere relationship of exchange. Do these complicating elements mean that Charvet's contractarianism and Barry's cosmopolitanism are actually closer to agreement with respect to the importance of international reciprocity than it might at first appear?

Perhaps we can discern a convergence among cosmopolitan, contractarian, and Kantian views of justice if we understand them all as subscribing to the same underlying idea. As Pierre Laberge explains, just persons (or states) will not consider themselves excused from cooperative arrangements and act as free riders simply because it is to their advantage to do so. Nevertheless, they will consider themselves excused from any cooperative scheme in which other participants cannot be relied upon to do their part, or in which cooperation encourages other kinds of injustice.[2] Cosmopolitans are therefore right to emphasize that international justice cannot be *reduced* to terms of self-interest. At the same time, one can always reasonably reject a principle of justice that, in Laberge's phrase, allows one to become a prey of others. In this weak sense, the expectation of reciprocal compliance is a necessary *condition* of at least some duties toward others. Understood in this way, the contractarian tradition has good reason to emphasize both authoritative norms based on a desire for mutual justification and the assurance that states will not be victimized by adhering to such norms. Both conditions would seem to be presupposed by international duties of distributive justice.

If there is actually some agreement on the importance of reciprocity in international relations, what explains the appearance of sharp disagreement? To some extent, the disagreement is a philosophical one about how best to ground practical judgments, not a disagreement about the judgments themselves. Should we say, for example, that rich states have no duties of distributive justice until they can be assured that recipient states will not divert that aid for internally unjust or externally hostile purposes (a rather Hobbesian formulation of the scope of justice)? Or should we say that rich states normally have duties of distributive justice to poor states, but that those duties are suspended when there are no reliable expectations that recipient states will behave justly (a more Kantian formulation)?[3] We can disagree about the answer to this philosophical question while agreeing about what our duty may be in any particular case, and vice versa.

It is also important to distinguish several other sorts of agreement and disagreement. First, we may disagree about *how much* noncompliance is needed to cancel a particular kind of international norm. We may agree that norms of just war are less defeasible than norms of international distributive justice, for example, yet disagree about how much noncompliance defeats norms of the latter kind. Second, we may disagree about how little cooperation and how much noncompliance *in fact* occurs in international society. Such disagreement doubtless accounts for much of the controversy about duties of international justice. Third, we may disagree about the extent to which the territorial *state* is the best form of political association for resolving various problems of compliance. Are the most severe problems in international society caused by the internal corruption of particular states or by the state system as such? Is organizing the world into territorial states the best means of assigning responsibility for maintaining natural resources and population levels? (This issue is clearly joined in the essays by Barry and Miller.) There may also be disagreement about the degree to which noncompliance affects the obligations of powerful versus those of weak states. From this incomplete list, it is clear that what looks like disagreement about the place of reciprocity in international society is often really a matter of agreement and disagreement across a much wider range of issues.

We may also agree that compliance is an important condition for the existence or application of various international norms while disagreeing about the extent to which noncompliance cancels a particular *kind* of norm. David Miller's distinction between comparative and noncomparative principles of justice helps to clarify this important point. According to Miller, noncomparative principles of justice, such as those underlying human rights, identify duties that are owed to each person regardless of what is happening to others. Miller argues that Barry's idea of protecting individual vital interests or needs is a such a principle, and therefore that it might form the basis of cosmopolitan duties across borders. On this point, Miller sides with Barry and against Charvet in holding that there are in fact some universal human rights and duties prior to social cooperation. But Miller also sides with Charvet and against Barry in rejecting the idea of universal comparative principles of distributive justice that go beyond protecting vital interests and instead aim at establishing some kind fairness or equality in the allocation of nonessential resources between individuals on a global level. Here, Miller agrees with Charvet that such comparative principles of justice can only arise in an ethical community whose members have a sense of general mutuality as well as a strong sense of communal identity. Miller's view is that nations and nation-states often do constitute such ethical communities and that special obligations to fellow nationals should therefore sometimes be regarded as being of equal or greater weight than general duties to humanity. In short, Miller takes a "weak" cosmopolitan position, located between the more extreme alternatives articulated by Charvet and Barry. Noncomparative principles of justice do not depend upon expectations of reciprocity. Again, the norms governing warfare provide a good example: many of the ethical and religious traditions represented in this book see such norms as unilaterally and unconditionally binding. By contrast, comparative principles, like those of international distributive justice, may be much more dependent on the prior existence of reciprocity or mutuality and therefore much more parochial.

The deeper problem, however, is not merely how to achieve compliance with the rules of the international game, but how to secure agreement about what those rules should be. Some of the viewpoints represented in this book, like Charvet's contractarianism, reject altogether the idea of universal duties of international distributive justice. Other viewpoints, like Miller's weak cosmopolitanism, find a place for noncomparative duties of international aid but are skeptical about extending the idea of global principles much further. Still other ethical and religious viewpoints accept the general idea of international distributive justice but seriously disagree about both the character of redistributive principles and the source of their authority. Yet when there is basic disagreement about the nature and scope of international justice itself, is it any wonder that compliance and cooperation are often lacking between communities that subscribe to different principles? To what extent, then, do moral and religious diversity make agreement on fundamental principles of international society unlikely or impossible? And to what extent should constitutive principles of international society limit moral and religious diversity?

INTERNATIONAL DIVERSITY AND KANTIAN REPUBLICANISM

Of all the perspectives represented in this book, Kantianism appears to place the most definite limits on international diversity. According to the Kantians, all states in the world must become republics. To qualify as a republic, a state must exhibit four features: a principle of freedom for all members, legal equality, dependence on a common legislature, and separation of powers. Separation of powers is particularly important, for Kant thinks that it is necessary to guarantee a republican version of the "rule of law." In this version of the rule of law, rules must be public, known, alterable only by some regular procedure, and consistently applied. There must also be procedures for holding authorities accountable. For Kant, the "rule of law" is not synonymous with "law," but with a certain kind of republican legality that includes specific institutional features like dependence on a common legislature and separation of powers. This conception of the rule of law is more substantive than the customary international law idea of the rule of law, as we shall see. At the same time, the Kantian ideal of a "republic" differs from the yet more substantive ideas of the "liberal democratic" and "liberal democratic welfare" state. It does not guarantee more specific forms of political participation and rights of economic welfare, for example.

Having noted these differences, the main question is whether Kantians have good reason for insisting that all states should be republics. By making such a demand, the Kantian ideal of an international federation of republics significantly restricts permissible international diversity. And because the world is not yet prepared to embrace this ideal, the demand seems to invite a more or less overt struggle between republican and nonrepublican states. Of course, such a struggle might be governed by rules of the game accepted by participants for prudential reasons. In other words, it might settle into a fairly stable international "modus vivendi" between republics and other kinds of states. In contrast to the Kantian ideal of a world of republics, customary international law would appear to offer a neutral framework for coexistence, and therefore a better way of limiting the destructive consequences of religious, ethnic, and cultural differences. Customary international law seems preferable to the instability and injustice that might arise from such a contest between republican and nonrepublican states.

For the sake of argument, let us assume that customary international law is less demanding with respect to the domestic arrangements that all members of international society in good standing must adopt. According to Kantians and other liberals, the neutrality that results if we make this assumption is irrelevant to the prospects for international peace. For Kantians claim that, as a matter of contingent fact, republics do not wage war against one another, and that a stable peace is unlikely unless all states become republics.[4] Far from paving the way to perpetual peace, customary international law permits far too much conflict. Even if customary international law is regarded as genuine law (and Kantians have their doubts about this), it is a law that is too ineffective to constitute a desirable ideal of international association, at least by Kantian lights. It is therefore a mistake to think that we must choose between a peaceful international society of customary international law and a modus vivendi between republican and nonrepublican states. Our real choice is between an international society constituted as a many-sided modus vivendi and international society constituted as a simplified modus vivendi between a republican alliance and the rest of the world, which may or may not have formed itself into a competing ideological bloc. In short, our choice is between one kind of modus vivendi or another.[5] The only way to escape this situation once and for all is to establish the universal domain of republican legality.

Republics can, of course, recognize legal obligations to nonrepublics as a matter of prudence or strategy. Kantians disagree, however, about whether such motives for obeying customary international law are morally permissible. Laberge argues that republics should recognize the international legitimacy of nonrepublics as the price that must be paid on the road to a world federation of republican states. But Fernando Tesón denies that they may extend legal recognition to nonrepublican states, and argues that international law should be reformed accordingly.[6] It is wrong to recognize tyrannies even to promote republican legality in the long run, for this would be to treat the oppressed subjects of those tyrannies as a means to our end.

Kantian morality does not forbid using individuals as a means, however. Rather, it forbids using individuals as a "mere" means, and this prohibition should be equated with failing to treat individuals with respect or as "ends in themselves." Thus, we can and often do treat individuals as a means to our ends in a purely *causal* sense while simultaneously treating them as ends in themselves in a *moral* sense. Indeed, we permissibly "use" people in a causal sense all the time. This is not to say that Tesón is ultimately wrong about the incoherence of legally recognizing tyrannies in order to advance the cause of republican legality. It is only to suggest some of the complexities of this issue. A further complexity is that republics may continue to be bound by important universal legal obligations, even though they reject any general accommodation with nonrepublics. They may continue to be unilaterally and unconditionally bound by the laws of war, for example. To describe this "second-best" Kantian ideal of international society as a pure modus vivendi would therefore be to oversimplify it. Nevertheless, it resembles a modus vivendi and may sometimes lack both peace and justice.

It is also important to stress that the dialogue between Kantians and others does not turn entirely on empirical issues, as a pair of examples will illustrate.[7] Let us suppose, contrary to Kantian assertions, that the result of insisting on republican legality will *not* be eventual global peace but rather a permanent modus vivendi, marked by occasional wars and interventions, between republican and nonrepublican states. Suppose also that under the same circumstances perpetual peace—meaning simply the absence of interstate wars—*is* possible on the basis of customary international law. Presumably, at least some Kantians will wish to argue that the first, conflictual, international society is still to be preferred, because justice is more important than peace. Now let us revert to the Kantian view that permanent peace can only be obtained by transforming all states into republics. Presumably, at least some proponents of the rule of law will wish to argue that an international society based on international law is still preferable, even if it involves more conflict, because this sort of society is based on respect for international diversity rather than on the complete hegemony of a particular moral perspective. In short, there is disagreement not only about which set of arrangements will bring about international peace but also about the sort of peace that it is desirable to bring about and its relationship to justice and diversity.[8]

Kantians insist that some kinds of states are unworthy of international legal recognition. A republican federation is the mode of international association that is compatible with the widest range of morally permissible diversity. The rejoinder would be that an international society of republican or liberal states is compatible with the widest range of morally permissible diversity, as defined by republicanism or liberalism. Once more we run up against the central problem of determining the limits of acceptable moral and religious diversity. Each moral and religious perspective attempts to work out how far it is prepared to tolerate moral and religious views that differ from its own. Each perspective therefore establishes a different outer limit of toleration by defining those who cannot be considered members in good standing of international society. Is there any way of escaping the self-referential way in which such limits are determined?

INTERNATIONAL LAW: NATURAL AND RELIGIOUS SOURCES OF AUTHORITY

Most of the contributors to this volume answer the last question by claiming that the limits of international toleration are not established by ethical and religious traditions as such, but by reason, revelation, or both. Of course, the teachings of reason and revelation have been articulated differently in various historical traditions, but these are merely more or less adequate expressions of an underlying, universal truth. Thus, the Kantian perspective as interpreted by Laberge and Tesón, the natural law as presented by Robert George, and to perhaps a lesser extent Brian Barry's cosmopolitanism all purport to offer the most rationally defensible account of universal principles for the constitution of international society.

The religious commentators in this volume also find a set of universal moral principles within their own traditions. As Max Stackhouse emphasizes, the idea of an objective moral constitution in the universe, at least partially accessible to human reason, is central to the Christian perspective. David Novak considers the view that "the Noahide laws" of Jewish tradition are accessible to the gentiles by means of natural reason and that they might serve as constitutive principles for international society. And Sohail Hashmi discusses the medieval Islamic articulation of principles governing relations between believers and nonbelievers, arguing that the Qur'an and the tradition based upon it contains a universal ethical system supporting international principles of human rights, democracy, and distributive justice. All of these understandings, philosophical and religious, of a universal morality exemplify what Richard Friedman calls "the vertical model of natural law," which views natural law "as a set of higher order rules . . . constituting an objective standard of justice that sets a limit to what positive law may rightfully require of those subject to it."[9] According to this model, natural law is an objective moral law, a law beyond human decision or choice, that determines the moral authority of positive law within and between societies.

At the same time, these views exhibit different degrees of confidence about how far philosophical reason can actually guide practical decisions about the structure of international society. Among the contributors to this volume, Barry makes the most serious effort to describe morally justifiable international economic institutions in detail. George's chapter reflects a somewhat different assessment of the relationship between abstract principles of justice and actual political organizations. Beyond suggesting a general principle of international "subsidiarity," his position is that any account of distributive justice adequate to the complexity of international society must comprise a plurality of principles that can be ranked only roughly, and that these principles must leave much to practical judgment. The theological commentators also identify a rather general and abstract set of natural law principles. All three further insist, in David Novak's words, that "even if some of the precepts of natural law are not deduced from creation theology, nonetheless they cannot be seen as intelligible without it."[10] As Stackhouse and Hashmi emphasize, an individual or communal life not based in faith "is one fraught with actual or potential moral turpitude."[11] Yet these commentators also downplay the potential particularism and divisiveness of religious belief, and argue that their traditions support freedom of religion, human rights, and democracy. Indeed, there would seem to be a fair amount of convergence among both philosophical *and* religious perspectives on the desirability of freedom of religion, respect for human rights, and the promotion of democracy in international society.

It therefore appears that we can reach the same guiding principles of international society from very different ethical and religious starting points. As the preceding chapters illustrate, however, it is also possible to generate different principles of international society by interpreting the same ethical or religious point of view in different ways. All of these perspectives admit of some interpretations that enlarge the possibility of international coexistence and others that greatly restrict it. If, for example, we distinguish between those who are prepared to recognize the international legitimacy of states regardless of their internal constitutions and those who are not, then representatives of both positions can be found among interpreters of virtually all of the perspectives considered in this book. There are Kantians and Muslims who recognize the customary rule of nonintervention, for example, and Kantians and Muslims who do not.

For our purposes, the important point is that all these views support international law (to the extent that they do), not because they accept its authority, but because international law happens to be generally supported by an ethical or religious doctrine whose authority they do accept. In other words, these perspectives form an overlapping consensus in support of international law. And this sort of consensus can create a stable basis for international society. But it can also prove unstable, because subscription to international law always remains conditional in character. The consequence of this conditionality goes beyond whether particular communities will in fact recognize an obligation to observe the common rules of international society. Because these ethical and religious views hold that international law exists to facilitate the achievement of extralegal purposes, it can in principle be disregarded whenever it seriously obstructs the pursuit of such purposes. The international law rule of nonintervention provides the most important example: not only Kantians, but natural lawyers, contractarians, cosmopolitans, as well as Christians, Muslims, and Jews would appear to be prepared to violate that rule whenever it seriously conflicts with moral or religious duties they see as more fundamental.

For this reason, Terry Nardin and Richard Friedman suggest in their chapters that none of these views provides a sound basis for international "law," in the strict sense of the term. This is because the authority of any genuine law must function as an "exclusionary" reason for action, to employ a helpful bit of technical vocabulary. If a rule is an authentic rule of law, its authority must exclude or preempt all other reasons for acting, including those of prudential, moral, and religious desirability. Consider the practice of making treaties, for example. Treaties between states designed to secure some common purpose would be impossible without prior legal procedures for making them. To achieve their purpose, the authority of such procedures cannot depend on considerations relating to the consequential desirability or moral rightness of the particular treaties those procedures enable. Moreover, treaties are ineffective, indeed meaningless, without prior recognition of the customary international law principle of *pacta sunt servanda*. This basic principle, too, must apply regardless of the desirability of the specific goals in question. Other equally basic principles of customary international law include those of political sovereignty, legal equality, territorial integrity, nonaggression, and nonintervention. Together with other less fundamental rules, these principles constitute an authoritative practice of customary international law.[12]

If this argument is sound, none of the perspectives we have considered thus far has demonstrated how international society might be constituted as a genuine legal community. Although such a society might still be constituted to be a universal moral or religious community, the absence of any genuine international law counts as a serious objection to all of these perspectives. For this reason, it is important to look at the idea of an international legal society, and its relation to the idea of international law, in greater detail.

INTERNATIONAL SOCIETY AND INTERNATIONAL LAW

Legal positivism presents an analysis of law that purports to show that the authority of international law can and indeed must be divorced from conflicting conceptions of justice. Unlike other views of international society, which require states to be not only *for* coexistence but also *against* slavery, apartheid, colonialism, and autocracy, the positivist view of international society only requires states to acknowledge the authority of international law. This idea of international society is not as conservative as might first appear, for recognition of the authority of a law is perfectly compatible with criticism and reform of that law in terms of its prudential and moral desirability. Nevertheless, positivism maintains that if there is to be law, then there must be a categorical *distinction* drawn between the authority of law and its instrumental or moral desirability. If states want to live together under a rule of law, they must distinguish between the authority of international law and its holiness, goodness, and expedience. If they do not want to live together under a rule of law—or perhaps if they want a different, more instrumental kind of "law"— then they needn't make this sort of distinction.

Why might states wish to be associated in terms of the rule of law? (We shift here from an analytical to a normative question.) One answer, made on behalf of, if not by, legal positivism, is that an international society constructed on that basis is most compatible with international diversity. Those speaking for some of the other perspectives represented in this volume would disagree with this answer, however. In particular, Whelan, Charvet, Brown, and Novak argue that customary international law is an implicitly liberal and secular form of international society that already limits international diversity in significant ways.

According to these contributors, liberal societies should have no special difficulty accepting, as a basis for international association, the customary law principle of mutual respect between free and equal sovereign states. This is because such societies already accept a similar norm of respect between free and equal persons as a legitimizing principle of domestic society. In liberal domestic societies, persons may live largely as they choose, even if their private lives are in many respects illiberal. But the situation is different for some nonliberal political societies, or so it is argued. A radical Islamic or communist state, for example, may pretend to recognize the authority of international law as a strategic move within an international modus vivendi. Yet such a state cannot in principle regard its own religious or political doctrines as an internal or private matter, either for personal life within its own domestic society

or for the internal affairs of other states. If we understand persons as aspiring
to coherence in their private and public lives, we cannot understand them as
having private and public lives that are completely independent of each other.
In the same way, we cannot understand states as involved in completely independent domestic and international regimes.[13] "Public" principles determine
the boundaries of "private" life, both within and between states, and each set
of public principles draws the boundaries of the private sphere in its own
particular way. This reasoning applies as much to customary international law
as to any other set of principles purporting to be authoritative for international society. As Chris Brown remarks, "norms such as nonintervention and
a clear distinction between domestic and international jurisdiction are . . .
part of a comprehensive scheme, and there seems little point in pretending
that this is not so."[14]

Even liberals have difficulty in accepting the authority of customary international law, as we saw in considering Kantian views of international society.
The awkwardness of describing customary international law as a kind of liberal international order merely reinforces the general point, however. To
recognize the authority of customary international law is not only to reject
revolutionary ideologies that drive states to expand across the world. It is also
to reject liberal, cosmopolitan, Kantian, contractarian, and indeed all other
ways of drawing the public/private distinction in international affairs. This
kind of political society is like any other in being compatible with no view of
"public" justice but its own. In this unavoidable way, customary law must
restrict international diversity.

At the same time, under customary international law each state has a right
to order its own domestic affairs as it sees fit. In this respect, customary international law is more tolerant of international diversity than any other conception of international society considered in this volume. The association it
constitutes is also compatible with almost any cooperative enterprise or relationship between states. A federation of republican or communist or religious
states—indeed a single, centralized republican, communist, or religious world
state—might therefore develop within and by means of international law up
to the point where this law is finally legally extinguished in favor of some
other basis of association.

According to rule of law positivism, customary international law also possesses an inherent justice by virtue of its character as law. The following features are said to define this kind of justice and to distinguish law as such from
other forms of social control: the formal equality of subjects; rules that are
promulgated, prospective, clear, stable, and coherent with one another; rules
with which compliance is not impossible; rules that are "noninstrumental,"
that is, concerned with constraints on actions, not with material outcomes;
and rules whose authenticity as law can be ascertained apart from considerations of their moral or consequential desirability. In domestic legal systems,
such marks of authenticity may be given by various "rules of recognition." (In
the case of international law, Nardin argues, customary law is self-validating:

it simply exists and its existence can be recognized as a matter of contingent fact in the practice of states.)

Frederick Whelan and several other contributors argue that this analysis of law is not an example of legal positivism but of natural law theory. In other words, rule of law positivism does not establish which features of a system of social control are part of the concept of law itself, but instead shows which features of a system of social control are part of the concept of a good or just legal system.[15] Richard Friedman suggests another view of the matter, however. According to Friedman, this opposition between legal positivism and natural law collapses once we recover the original problem of natural law theory. That problem was not to find an objective "higher" law to limit the variability of the *content* of positive law. Rather, it was to offer an analysis of positive law that shows why law is the only mode of governance appropriate to human beings, and therefore why criteria of legal personality or legal membership must be understood as natural rather than conventional in character. To put the point in another way, the original problem of natural law theory was to criticize conventional criteria for the *scope* of positive law.

According to this interpretation of the idea of natural law, what is of crucial importance is that no human being is properly excluded from legal membership by such conventional criteria as birth, descent, kinship, gender, or religion. At the very least, all normal, adult human beings should be deemed capable of legal personality, which means that they are to be jointly obligated and protected by authoritative rules, that is, by rules that are not obeyed simply because they serve some desirable purpose but because they have been identified as authentic law. In this kind of association, it is especially important that only public officials are authorized to use force, that all uses of force are in response to some antecedently defined legal wrong, and that the use of force is never justified on extralegal grounds.

This view of law has several implications for international society. It runs directly against the claim made by Charles Beitz and Brian Barry, for example, that "there is no necessary connection between moral cosmopolitanism and institutional cosmopolitanism."[16] Instead, this view requires that all human beings should be governed by positive law. As Friedman puts it, positive law should fill the human world. Whether this law is located in many different states or in a single world state is a secondary matter. But states that permit slavery, as well as other kinds of tyrannies, cannot be regarded as genuine legal communities, because they deny rights of legal personality to some human beings within their boundaries. Nor can such tyrannies be recognized as members of a genuine international legal order simply because they accept principles of peaceful coexistence. They must also recognize all human beings within their boundaries as legal persons. This analysis therefore suggests that customary international law has not fully measured up to the standard of a genuine legal system in the past, for in recognizing the universal legal personality of all states it has not recognized the universal legal personality of all human beings. Fortunately, this situation would seem to be changing as more states within international society adopt the rule of law internally, and as human beings gradually acquire (through the medium of internationally protected human rights) increased standing as legal subjects within international law itself.

It is illuminating to compare this view of international society with Charvet's contractarian understanding of international society. According to Charvet, legal personality *is* entirely a conventional matter. Therefore, from the perspective of those inside a conventionally constituted legal community, those outside the community have no legal rights, except as such rights may be granted by the first community, even if they have achieved a conventionally constituted legal community of their own. In this respect, Charvet's "post-Enlightenment" idea of international relations resembles the ancient idea of international relations criticized by Stoic natural law.[17] It would therefore seem to follow that if a conventionally constituted legal community can gain greater advantage for itself by conquest than by accommodation, then nothing in this view makes it wrong for that community to adopt an imperial policy, perhaps leading to a world state and thus a universal ethical life. According to Friedman and Charvet, this extreme condition is generated by the very idea of a legal world based on particular, conventionalist ideas of legal membership. Relationships between two conventionally constituted communities are released from all genuine legal restraints. In this situation, for example, peace and war do not exist as legal ideas. As Friedman remarks, "the outsider's community cannot be conceived ... as itself a subject of some wider legal relationship without introducing some other criterion besides the prevailing convention and indeed transcending all such particularistic conventions."[18]

Charvet's view is actually more complicated than this, however. As we noted at the beginning of this chapter, his approach identifies two desires that must be present in any society based on a contractarian conception of justice: a desire to live with others on terms of mutual advantage, and a desire to live with others on terms of mutual justification. On the latter basis, imperialism is not permissible, even against outsider states that have no legal standing, because conquest stands in direct conflict with a desire to live on terms with others that no one could reasonably reject. Thus, a world state and a universal ethical life cannot come about by conquest, but only through the development of worldwide conventions of legal personality (for which Charvet urges us to work). Nevertheless, the central point about this idea of international society remains: international society is purely conventional in character. From this perspective, "human" rights are merely conventional rights that have managed to win universal acceptance.

In contrast, the Stoic natural law view presented by Friedman is that legal personality is not entirely a matter of convention. The Stoic ideal is a universal community of all rational individuals, associated on the basis of a common law. Consistent with this view, natural law thinkers might argue that an imperial policy *is* permissible when facing an adversary that does not recognize the universal claims of law (particularly one that undermines even the norm of communication by killing envoys). To put the point another way, this version of natural law seems to take a more permissive view of the just causes of war than does Charvet's contractarianism. Yet such a war must still be fought in a lawful manner, for it is waged against human beings who are capable of being legal subjects. States that possess genuine law can demand, if need be, that their conquered adversaries undergo political reconstruction. At the end of the Second World War, for example, the Allies were justified in imposing a complete reconstruction and transformation of Germany's political culture and institutions in order to replace Nazism with a genuine rule of law. But rule of law states cannot wage a "total" war, that is, a war fought without any restraints. The implication of this view of international law would appear to be that it is permissible to conquer and reconstruct an adversary that shows a total lack of respect for law, but not by whatever means necessary.

In short, this interpretation of the natural law perspective demands that all political communities become rule of law states. In this respect, it resembles the Kantian ideal of international society as a universal federation of republics. Unlike Kantianism, however, this perspective defines law in largely formal terms. What is to be achieved in each community is a set of exclusionary rules that reflect the legal equality of all normal, adult human beings, that forbid the unauthorized use of force against legal subjects, and that provide some criteria for ascertaining the identity of a rule as a law apart from that rule's religious, moral, or prudential desirability.[19] Compared to other criteria of domestic and international legitimacy, this standard may seem relatively weak. States do not have to become full-fledged republics, for example, in order to be regarded as members of international society in good standing. Nevertheless, this view shares an important feature with mainstream moral and religious doctrines in the modern world. Like almost all such doctrines, this version of natural law insists that its duties are universal in scope. This idea of universality seems obvious to us. Indeed, the original problem of natural law may have been obscured precisely because the modern world has so completely accepted the Stoic idea of a universal ethical life, or so Friedman suggests. The Stoic natural law perspective differs from modern views in demanding the universal rule of positive law (properly understood as a system of authoritative rules binding rational human beings), not the universal sway of republicanism, liberal democracy, or some other, more substantive set of political arrangements.

Conclusion

At the end of this chapter, we find ourselves reconsidering a very old idea about the relationship between natural law and the law of nations. Although it may seem surprising to have arrived at this point, it is not hard to recall how we got here. We began by asking whether international society should be understood as a society based on mutual advantage or as a society based on rules that "no one could reasonably reject," or perhaps as one based on a combination of these two ideas. We immediately ran into disagreement, both about the role of mutual advantage in international society and about what might count as a reasonable set of international principles of justice. The latter kind of disagreement is fundamental. Even with a common desire to find reasonable agreement, disagreement about what is reasonable may prove impossible to bridge. One might reply that such radical disagreement is unlikely, and that we should not be deterred by the fact that we can always find communities ready to affirm the most "outlandish" beliefs and practices. But why should we accept moderate disagreement as part of a description of the circumstances of international justice—a description that ideal theory assumes in order to determine what international justice requires—while radical disagreement is only introduced later on, as an unfortunate obstacle that nonideal theory must help us jump over on our way to our destination? This approach makes sense only if we assume that radical moral and religious disagreement in international society is something that we can overcome, at least in principle. But we might challenge this assumption. If we do challenge it, the possibility of a universal international society is called into question. And this prompts us to ask whether an international legal community might be possible in circumstances where a moral or religious community appears impossible. These questions eventually lead back to long-debated issues in philosophical jurisprudence.

Some believe that the authority of all law, including international law, is ultimately religious in character, a view that is explored in the three theological chapters in this volume. Others hold that the authority of all law, including international law, is ultimately grounded in reason and universal morality, a view explored in the chapters on Kant, natural law, and cosmopolitanism. Still others maintain that law should be reconceptualized as a response to our discovery of the absence of all religious, natural, and moral foundations or—more modestly—that law can at least be identified and described without implicit reference to such foundations (the contractarian and legal positivist perspectives, respectively). Nevertheless, each of these perspectives can agree to acknowledge the authority of positive law for its own reasons. Thus a universal international society is possible on the basis of an overlapping consensus about the authority of principles like pacta sunt servanda, diplomatic immunity, political sovereignty, territorial integrity, nonaggression, and nonintervention. A universal international society is also possible on the basis of an overlapping consensus about the universal value of certain political arrangements, such as institutions for securing the rule of law, or even on a common conception of distributive justice.

The possibility of this overlapping consensus hardly settles the problem of constituting international society, however. On the face of it, these various legal and political ideas stand in some tension with one another. For example,

the legal principle of nonintervention stands opposed to the moral requirement that human rights should be respected everywhere. International pluralism runs up against the wish to extend republican principles and the rule of
law everywhere, or the religious imperative to propagate a religious faith.
This tension between morality and international law is implicit throughout
this volume. While each philosophical and theological perspectives we have
considered claims to recognize the necessity and importance of an authoritative international law, each ultimately subordinates positive law to morality or
religion, thereby undercutting the law's independent authority. When a narrow, proselytizing spirit informs ethical or religious doctrine, the stage is set
for a struggle for ideological uniformity that can only cease when the world
is remade according to a single ideal.

In contrast, legal positivism insists on sharply distinguishing positive law,
on the one hand, from morality and religion, on the other. Making such a
distinction would appear to allow greater space for international moral and
religious diversity. Yet customary international law expresses but one idea of
interstate justice among many others, and it limits international diversity in its
own manner. The question therefore arises whether we can understand international law, and law more generally, as the only appropriate way of governing human beings and therefore as establishing certain limits to diversity that
are beyond reasonable disagreement.

These are some of the most important issues to emerge from a comparison
of the various philosophical and religious ideas of international society represented in this book. Of course, it is quite possible to read the book in ways that
evoke other issues and themes. One might place much greater stress on the
themes of justice and interdependence, for example, while paying less attention to questions about international law. Or one might focus just as insis-
tently on law, but pay more attention to controversies about what sort of
international legislative, judicial, and administrative institutions, if any, might
be necessary to the existence of an international legal society. My aim in this
chapter has not been to discourage such alternative readings. Rather, it has
been to try to clarify a few of the more critical points of agreement and disagreement about the moral character of international society that emerge
from a comparison of the perspectives represented in this book. As the reader
will already have discovered, all these perspectives can be interpreted in ways
that support the rule of law, religious freedom, basic human rights, and democracy. This kind of support may prove sufficient to establish a just international order, even if the philosophical and religious justifications for many of
these practices remain permanently at issue.

NOTES

1. For an explanation of the idea of "what we cannot reasonably reject" as part of an
account of moral wrongness, see Thomas M. Scanlon, "Contractualism and Utilitari-

anism," in Amartya Sen and Bernard Williams, eds., *Utilitarianism and Beyond* (Cambridge: Cambridge University Press, 1982).

2. Pierre Laberge, Chapter 5 above.

3. This is not to say that it is easy to interpret Kant and Hobbes on the idea of reciprocity. In this volume, Laberge reads Kant as holding that a lack of reciprocity excuses individuals from (some of) their moral duties. For an interpretation according to which Kant's view of moral duty is less dependent on reciprocity, see Alan Donagan, *The Theory of Morality* (Chicago: University of Chicago Press, 1977), and, with reference to international relations, Thomas Donaldson, "Kant's Global Rationalism," in Terry Nardin and David R. Mapel, eds., *Traditions of International Ethics* (Cambridge: Cambridge University Press, 1992), 136–50. There are similar disagreements about the role of reciprocity in Hobbes's political thought.

4. See Michael W. Doyle, "Kant, Liberal Legacies, and Foreign Affairs," *Philosophy and Public Affairs* 12 (1983): 205–36. Also see Jack S. Levy, "Domestic Politics and War," in Robert Rotberg and Theodore Rabb, eds., *The Origin and Prevention of Major Wars* (Cambridge: Cambridge University Press, 1989), 87.

5. This paragraph oversimplifies matters, since there are intermediate forms of international society between a society based on customary international law and a federation of republican states. Rawls, for example, describes a kind of international society composed of liberal societies and "well-ordered hierarchical societies." See John Rawls, "The Law of Peoples," in Stephen Shute and Susan Hurley, eds., *On Human Rights* (New York: Basic Books, 1993), 41–82. This society is in turn related to tyrannies in a modus vivendi. For discussion of Rawls's ideas, see the chapters by Charvet and Brown, above.

6. In "The Kantian Theory of International Law," *Columbia Law Review* 92 (1992): 53–102, Tesón argues for changes to the UN Charter to disenfranchise dictators, alter the law of treaties, deny diplomatic status and immunities to representatives of illegitimate governments, and transform laws of recognition in order to ostracize tyrannical states, as the UN did in the case of South Africa.

7. In addition, it is important not to confuse philosophical arguments about the idea of a society fully governed by respect for international law with empirical arguments about the complex and ambiguous role of law in international relations today.

8. Unfortunately, both Kantians and proponents of international law often equate the ideas of legality and peace. In discussing the idea of permanent peace, for example, Kant defines the absence of republican legality in the Hobbesian manner as "a state of war," although there may be no actual fighting in such circumstances. In a similar manner, customary international law gives "peace" a particular juridical meaning. It then becomes true by definition that we can achieve peace only by adherence to international law.

9. Richard Friedman, Chapter 4 above, under "An Alternative Approach."

10. David Novak, Chapter 11 above, under "Natural Law."

11. Sohail Hashmi, Chapter 13 above, under "Islamic Ethics: Universalistic or Particularistic?"

12. See Ian Brownlie, *Principles of Public International Law*, 4th ed. (Oxford: Oxford University Press, 1990). The conceptual primacy of customary international law is argued in Terry Nardin, *Law, Morality, and the Relations of States* (Princeton, NJ: Princeton University Press, 1983), part 2.

13. Thus colonialism, for example, has been seen as posing contradictions for liberal democratic states that can only be resolved by repudiating despotism in the colonies or embracing it at home.

14. Chris Brown, Chapter 8 above, under "Contractarianism and International Society."

15. This disagreement raises issues too complex to discuss here. I discuss whether "rule of law positivism" is a genuine form of legal positivism in David R. Mapel, "Purpose and Politics: Can There Be a Non-Instrumental Civil Association?" *The Political Science Reviewer* 21 (1992): 60–80.

16. See Brian Barry, Chapter 9 above, under "The Cosmopolitan Idea," citing Charles R. Beitz, "Cosmopolitan Liberalism and the States System," in Chris Brown, ed., *Political Restructuring in Europe: Ethical Perspectives* (London: Routledge, 1994), 124.

17. In contrast to ancient conventionalism, the modern contractarian view is more self-conscious in its assertion of the conventional character of legal personality.

18. Richard Friedman, Chapter 4 above, under "An Alternative Approach."

19. It is beyond the scope of this chapter to discuss what else might be included in this concept of law. Nevertheless, it is worth noting one way in which the concept is relevant to Rawls's account of an international society composed of liberal and hierarchical states. As Rawls notes, his idea of a hierarchical state is based on Philip Soper's view of law. See Rawls, "The Law of Peoples," n. 22: 224; also Soper, *A Theory of Law* (Cambridge, MA: Harvard University Press, 1984). Soper's view in turn resembles the natural law view described by Friedman, though the two are not identical. This suggests that Rawls's idea of a law of peoples may actually be closer to the natural law idea of international society than one might expect.